INDIAN NATIONALISM AND POLITICAL AWAKENING IN 1920S

INDIAN NATIONALISM AND POLITICAL AWAKENING IN 1920s

Dr. Garima Prakash

KALPAZ PUBLICATIONS
Delhi-110052

Indian Nationalism and Political Awakening in 1920s
(Political Science, History)

Rs. 790

ISBN:81-7835-250-8

Published in 2004 in India by
Kalpaz Publications,
C-30, Satyawati Nagar, Delhi-110052
E-mail : Kalpaz@hotmail.com

Laser Typesetting at : Shree Vaishnavi Creations, Delhi
Printed at : Chawla Offset Press, Delhi

Contents

Preface

The third decade of twentieth century is a landmark in the annals of our history. There had been most significant changes in the domain of political and constitutional developments. The controversial appointment of the constitutional commission in 1927 and the great reaction and resentment which it aroused at an all-India level were the glaring phenomenon. This kind of reaction flared up on account of various historic facts which had deep links with the all-white commission and non-inclusion of any Indian from such a commission were totally belieed expectations in 1920s.

The work has been well weaved into nine chapters which include a comprehensive Chronology and Bibliography. The main contents have thrust on the Introduction, The Controversial appointment, political awakening and protest meetings, the preliminary survey of problems and reaction, slogans of protest and resentment, 'Simon go back', oral evidence : A Glimpse; submission of report and reaction , turning of the tide, and The concluding remarks.

I have collected the material from several academic institutions, viz. National Archives of India, Nehru Memorial Museum and Library, Teen Murti House, New Delhi, Sapru House Library, Indian Council of Historical Research Library, Central Secretariat Library, Lucknow University Library, Sahitya Akademi Library, Delhi University Library, Jawaharlal Nehru University Library and feel much beholden to the members of the staff of these institutions for their support during my researches.

I have also used some relevant material from the writings of eminent authors to fill up gaps in the book. I acknowledge my thanks to these authors.

Dr. Garima Prakash

Acknowledgements

The present work "Indian Nationalism and Political Awakening in 1920s" is outcome of my independent research under the guidance of my supervisor, teacher and friends. At the very outset I should express my heartiest gratitude to Prof. Ramesh Chandra, Vice Chancellor, Bundelkhand University for permitting me to pursue Ph.D. and providing all facilities.

I am gratefully indebted to both my supervisors Dr. Manju Singh, Reader, Bundelkhand University, Jhansi and Dr. Sangh Mittra, Duputy Director (Research), Indian Council of Historical Research, New Delhi for their unstinted inspiration and encouragement in pursuit of this research work.

I am thankful to my teacher Dr. S.M. Patnaik, Reader, Department of Anthropology, Delhi University for his good wishes and academic guidance given from time to time.

I am also grateful to my esteemed teachers, Dr. Jayshree Deshpande, Lady Shri Ram College, New Delhi, Mrs. Madhok, Lady Shri Ram College, New Delhi, Prof Bhattacharya, Head, Department of Anthropology, Delhi University for their valuable suggestions and goodwill.

I deem it to be my paramount duty to express my sincere gratitude to my father, Dr. Ram Prakash, Additional Director, Kanpur who encouraged and enlightened me throughout my research work. I am highly indebted to my mother Mrs. Kadambari who extended an unfailing enthusiasm and monetary assistance that made me complete the course successfully in time. I am thankful to my Nanaji, Shri Gama Ram, for his inspiration and blessings in my research work.

I am grateful to my brothers Gaurav, Kanishka and Kunal and my sisters Lalita, Saumya, Vidushi, Sneha and Medhavi for giving me all the encouragement and moral support which I needed during my research work.

I am thankful to the library staff of Indian Council of Historical Research, New Delhi, National Museum, New Delhi, Teen Murti Library, Delhi, Delhi University Library, Lucknow University for their help and guidance in completing my thesis.

I am indebted to both my father-in-law, Shri Mata Prasad, Chairman, UPSC and mother-in-law, for allowing and helping me in continuing my research work after my marriage.

Last but not the least I am very thankful to my husband Shri Naveen Kumar who encouraged and inspired me in my research work. I feel grateful to all my well-wishers, who invoked their sincere blessings in my academic life and other pursuits.

Dr. Garima Prakash

I

Historical Background

The report of Indian Constitutional Reforms[1] published in 1918 is the result of the historic announcement[2] of Edwin Samuel Montagu,[3] Secretary of State for India on August 20, 1917, in the House of Commons. It was indeed a significant landmark in the process of political development in India. It pronounced that the policy of the British government was to associate Indians in every branch of administration and to lay self-governing institutions with a view to the progressive relation of responsible government in India. The decision of speedy steps in this direction was also taken. Besides, it was promised that there would be a free and informal exchange of opinion between those in authority in England and in India, and ample opportunity would be afforded for public discussion of the proposals to be submitted, in due course, to parliament.[4] Subsequently, the Montagu-Chelmsford[5] scheme was worked out and was embodied in the Act of 1919. The new constitution created, in place of the Viceroy's Legislative Council, a two-chambered legislature—the Legislative Assembly and the Council of States. The former consisted of one hundred and forty-five members, of whom one hundred and four members were elected. It was vested with the extensive powers including the voting of a large portion of the annual budget. The Council of States consisted of sixty members, of whom thirty-four members were elected. It was vested with the same powers like the lower chamber, but the latter alone was competent to vote the financial grants.[6] Besides, single chamber legislative councils were established in the provinces.[7]

Dyarchic System

The process of transfer of responsibility in the sphere of provincial governments, was considered premature by the framers of the constitution. The dyarchic system of government was, therefore, thought to be preferable in the provinces. Under this system, ministers in the provinces who were constitutionally responsible to the legislature, were to hold charge of such subjects as were transferred to the popular control[8]. The Governor and his councillors were empowered to deal with the remaining subjects, popularly called the 'reserved' subjects.[9] Besides, a few members of the Indian Civil Service were attached to each department dealing with the 'transferred' subjects. These covenanted officials could not be removed or disciplined in any way by the provincial ministers, although they were supposed to obey their orders in the matters of administration. They could only be suspended or dismissed by the orders of the Secretary of State and remained responsible only to the Governor-General of India.[10] In May 1921, Sir Alexander Frederick Whyte,[11] President of Legislative Assembly, remarked, 'The political problem presented by the conjunction of an irremovable executive and a large constitutionally irresponsible majority would be ripe for treatment long before ten years are over. Although power was transferred to popular control in respect of certain specified subjects, and the Governor was directed to act upon the advice of his ministers, he could refuse to accept such advice, whenever he noticed that there was sufficient cause to cause dissent form their opinon. Indeed, the decision of the Governor, with regard to the cases of doubt, as to whether any particular subject belonged to the reserved or the transferred departments, was considered to be final.[12] He could overrule them and act on his own responsibility, when the consequences to their wishes were likely to prove serious; when the safety and tranquility of the province was threatened; and when the interests of minority communities, communal or racial or of the members of the public service were affected.[13]

Obviously, the success of this novel experiment rested on the central figure of the provincial Governor who was required to act as the 'guide, friend and philospher' of the new untried ministers. He was to advise, warn and encourage them, and also to affored them the opportunity of making their own decisions, thus giving them the change of 'learning by making mistakes.' Obviously, the advance towards the goal of provincial autonomy had commenced as, on the whole, the relation between members incharge of reserved departments and individual ministers were apparently good. If anything happened, the latter tended to lean too heavily on their financial colleagues.[14] At the centre, the position was, somewhat different. There was no transfer of power, and the Governor-General-in-Council continued to be responsible to parliament through the Secretary of State-in-Council in respect of all matters. Thus the Act of 1919, was, a limited experiment in the parliamentary system under many safeguards and restrictions. These constitutional changes paved the way for the ultimate establishment of a federation in India.[15]

These constitutional reforms were welcomed by many public men in India. But some of them doubted the wisdom of introducing western methods of government in the country, and, regarded these changes with misgivings. For example, the non-official Europeans were not enamoured of these reforms. But once the Government of India Act became the law, the only alternative left for them was to accept loyally the constitutional position as it was. They declared through their elected representatives in the legislatures that they would cooperate with their Indian colleagues and ensure the successful working of the constitution.[16] The belief that a long period of transition lay ahead was widely held not only by the British officials,[17] but also by the educated people of India. The Conservative-minded Indians and members of the minority groups did not show any interest, for too rapid and a revolutionary change like the displacement of British rule by Indian rule. The Indian princes also did not show any kind of inclination towards the ultimate implications of the announcement of 1917. But for the Congress or at least its more ardent members, the pace set in 1919 seemed intolerably slow. At its annual session of 1918, while the congress admitted that the Montagu-Chelmsford proposals constituted an advance in some directions, the scheme as a whole was declared to be disappointing and unsatisfactory. It asserted that the Indian people were already ripe for full provincial self-government, and dyarchy in the provinces would only be tolerated for six years.[18]

The Rowlatt Act

The Montagu Act was preceded by the Rowlatt Act,[19] and the martial law administration, and these were followed by the Non-cooperation Movement. Gandhi returned to India during the second year of the first global War, He had the conviction and clear realization of India's need for Swaraj. For her deliverance from the British yoke. He had a strong faith in the efficacy of civil disobedience as a peaceful method of attaining it, should other methods fail.[20] In 1920, the Congress rejected the reforms and launched a campaign of boycott throughout the country. Boycott of councils, courts of law and schools and colleges—what was called the triple boycott—the picketing of liquor shops, the establishment of panchayats and of national schools were the main planks of Congress platform.[21] There was also the relinquishment of honorary offices and of titles, and the boycott of all official functions. The temper of the people was roused. Open contempt for law and condemnation of authority were preached in all the regions of India. As a result of it, there were sporadic disturbances in different parts of the country.[22] The government used stringent measures to crush the patriotic fervour and enthusiasm. During the months of December 1921 and January 1922, more than thirty thousand persons were imprisoned.

Though most of the prominent satygrahis were in prison, the leader of the whole struggle, Mahatma Gandhi, was still out, issuing, from day to day, messages and directions, which inspired the people. The government had not touched him so far as it feared the consequences and the possible reaction of the Indian army and the police.[23] In this atmosphere, Congress resolved that Swaraj or self-rule must be attained within one year by means of, 'non-violent non-cooperation.' A new constitution for Congress was adopted in which the first and the most significant article read; 'The object of the Indian National Congress is the attainment of *"Swarajya"* by the people of India by all legitimate and peaceful means.'

The Gandhian Strategy

The Non-cooperation movement did not last long and Gandhi had to alter his strategy. Indeed, the outbreak of violence at Chauri Chaura resulting in the loss of lives of a few policemen, the Moplah outbreak in Malabar and the riots in Bombay on the occasion of the visit of the Prince of Wales had disconcerted Gandhi. He published, My Confession,[24] one of the most extraordinary documents, on February 16, 1922. 'God spoke clearly through Chauri Chaura...when India hopes to mount the throne of liberty through non-violence, mob violence, even in answer to grave provocation is a bade augury...The drastic reversal of the whole of the aggressive programme may be politically unsound and unwise, but there is no doubt, it is religiously sound, and I venture to assure the doubters, that the country will have gained by my humiliation and confession of error...Civil disobedience is a preparation for mute suffering...Let the opponent glory in our so-called defeat. It is better to be charged with cowardice than to sin against God...My fasting is both a penance and a punishment for myself for those who are guilty and repentant to hand themselves voluntarily to the Government for punishment and make a clean confession, for they have injured the very cause they intended to serve.'

Nehru stated in his Autobiography, 'Suddenly, early in February 1922, the whole scene shifted, and we in prison learnt, to our amazement and consternation, that Gandhiji had stopped the aggressive aspects of our struggle, that he had suspended civil resistance. We read that this was because of what had happened near the village of Chauri Chaura where a mob of villagers had retaliated on some policemen by setting fire to the police station and burning half a dozen or so policemen in it.

'We were angry when we learnt of this stoppage of our struggle at a time when we seemed to be consolidating our position and advancing on all fronts. But our disappointment and anger in prison could do little good to any one, and civil resistance stopped and non-cooperation wilted away...The younger people were naturally even more agitated. Our mounting hopes tumbled to the ground, and this mental reaction was to be expected'.[25]

After a few weeks, Gandhi was arrested and imprisoned. The Congress leadership was resentful at what it considered an unnecessary surrender, but as Jawaharlal Nehru was later to recognize, there was political astuteness behind Gandhi's decisions of principle.

Functioning of Reformed Constitution

The reformed constitution came into operation on February 9, 1921, when the central legislature was formally inaugurated by the Viceroy.[26] During his speech he declared that it had been constant aim of the British government to extend to India the benefits and privileges of her own institutions.[27] He made it clear that in the interval, required in connection, with the accomplishment of this tasks, certain powers of supervision and of intervention, if needed, were to be retained, and substantial steps towards redeeming the pledges of the government were to be taken at the earliest moment possible.[28]

The appeals and assurance of the Viceroy and the Duke did not cut much ice. The country was so muchiceagog with the feelings of unrest and restlessness that every person who was an elected member of any legislative council was questioned, disliked and distrusted, while the few, who accepted office as ministers or members of executive councils, came in for special approbrium.[29] The introduction of the new constitution was preceded by a Royal Proclamation and an amnesty to political prisoners. These measures, however, had no healing effect on the patriotic sentiments of the people of India as the memory of the martial law atrocities was still fresh in their minds. In September 1921, when the reforms had been in operation hardly for nine months, further changes were demanded by some members of the Legislative Assembly. At this juncture, William Vincent, speaking on behalf of the government, stated whether after such a short experience of the working of the new constitution, it was reasonable to think from a fixed date in the near future.[30] He argued that the Indian legislature had shown promise of success in the past and that the British Parliament was not likely to lend its ear to the proposals which had been put forward. But, ultimately, by way of compromise, the Legislative Assembly recommended to the Governor-General-in-Council that he should convey to the Secretary of State its views that the progress made by India on the path of responsible government warranted a re-examination and revision of the constitution at an earlier date than 1929.

At this point of time, it became difficult for, Montagu to conceal his chagrin and sense of disappointment over the way the political events were taking shape in India. He stated that the British government granted the people of India a brand new constitution and before the ink on it was dry, they were demanding another. He expressed his unwillingness to be a party to any change unless it could be shown either that the constitution had proved unworkable or that those who were working it, had given proof of their unfitness for further responsibility.[31] Lord Peel, the Secretary of State, took initiative in sending a despatch to the Government of India, in November 1, 1922 in which he held that the demand of the Legislative Assembly was premature. He opined that the possibilities of progress under the existing constitution had not been exhausted and the merits and capabilities of the electorate had not been adequately put to test in the short period during which the reforms were working.

It was evident that the new Legislative Assembly, in its personnel, policies and programmes, was very much different from the old one. The Swaraj Party which had boycotted the first Legislative Assembly, succeeded this time in capturing nearly half the seats allotted to the elected members. They were forty-five in number and thus constituted the biggest single party, compact and well disciplined, and the liberal element was considerably reduced. Some of the 'Independents,' after forming themselves into an organized group, eventually joined the Swarajists. The new Nationalist Party possessed a clear majority over all other political combinations.[32] In the electoral fights for the Provincial councils, it secured a majority in the Central Provinces. In the Bengal Council, it proved to be the strongest individual group, though it did not command a majority as such.[33] Soon the Swarajists made their position clear in their manifesto and announced that they proposed to present an ultimatum to the government demanding the right for the people of India to control their own destiny. If they were refused, they would carry on a policy of uniform, continuous and consistent obstruction, with a view to making the functioning of the government through the Legislative Assembly and the councils, impossible.[34] On January 30, 1924, the second Legislative Assembly, under the Reforms Act, met for the swearing-in of members. The Viceroy addressed the joint opening session of the two chambers the next day. He reminded the members that, 'in their new responsibilities, they will find the fullest opportunity for the display of the highest patriotism and for the noblest mark for the service of India', and assured the audience that the attendance at the polls and the close contest between candidates, during the elections, demonstrated the increasing interest which the system claimed for the electorate and the country at large.[35] He had the conviction that the representative institutions were being built up on a firm basis. To those who felt that the Home Government was going back from the policy embodied in the Government of India Act, he made it clear that the policy of reforms was introduced with the approval of all political parties in England and all stood committed to it as the fundamental policy in relation to India. He further emphasised that with the change of Prime Ministers and of government in England, from time to time, none of them had wavered regarding the Policy of Reforms in India and that it was the policy of the British nation and not of any party.

He stated, I am well aware that words are often used in the heat of political conflict which perhaps convey more than is really intended...I cannot foretell the future; I do not know what it holds; but I cannot conceal from you that the political situation in India in its constitutional aspects causes me some anxiety for the future of the Reforms...No change in the Constitution can be effected by legitimate and peaceful methods save with the assent of the British Parliament, that is, the British people. The British Parliament has already set up the machinery now in operation for some time past...As a devoted friend of India, I am convinced that action based on reason and justice will alone prevail with the British people and will prove the only safe road to the ultimate goals to be attained. I feel sure that you will keep steadfastly in mind in the course of the deliberations of this Session that the eyes of all friends of Reform will be fixed upon the harvest which the Legislature will sow and reap."[36]

It is significant to note that like first session of the new Legislative Assembly was marked by a display of strong opposition and criticism of the Government of India. The Swarajists under the leadership of Pandit Motilal Nehru modified the old demand for a Royal Commission and said what India did not wish to have such a Commission to enquire into her fitness for further reforms, as, in their opinion, India was as fit as England. He made it quite clear that summoning of a Round Table Conference in order to draw up the Indian constitution should be submitted to a newly elected Legislature whose recommendations should be adopted by the British parliament without any material modifications. India, he argued, should be treated as other Dominions were treated in the matter. He was sure that any Royal Commission appointed to extend existing reforms by instalments would meet with resistance. After an animated debate, a resolution was adopted by a majority which called for a Round Table Conference and to prepare a scheme for the establishment of full responsible government. The government, however, would not naturally accept that position. It was not prepared to go beyond what Lord Peel, had indicated two years ago, of exhausting the possibilities of expansion under the statute.[37]

Financial Demands

This was followed by the successive rejection of four of the principal financial demands put forward by the Finance member, and later by the rejection of the Finance Bill itself.[38] The next step was to refuse the introduction of an amended Finance Bill 'recommended' by the Viceroy, in pursuance of the provisions of the Government of India Act, as containing only proposals for raising the revenue essential for carrying on the government. The policy thus pursued had no reference to the merits of the measure involved and the reasons for the rejections, put forward by the leader of the Swarajists, was that the reforms were a failure, and the India's wrongs were unredressed.[39] Meanwhile the pressure of public opinion led to the appointment of the Reforms Enquiry Committee in 1924, presided over by Sir Alexander Muddiman.[40] Other members of this Committee were well-known persons like Muhammad Shafi, Maharaja of Burdwan, Arthur Froom, Henry Moncrieff, M.A. Jinnah and R.P. Paranjpye. This Committee was 'to enquire into the difficulties arising from or defects inherent in the working of the Government of India Act and the Rules there under...and to investigate the feasibility and desirability of securing remedies for such difficulties or defects, consistent with the structure, policy and purpose of the Act.' The Committee first assembled in August 4, 1924 and held its meetings from August to December 1924. It had verbal and written evidence from past and present Indian ministers and Executive Councillors from all the provinces. All these persons were of proven ability and were imbued with the knowledge of working of the councils.

The Report of the Committee was published in 1925. Four of the Indian members presented a separate minority report. Most of the Indian witnesses, who appeared before the Committee, attacked the constitution, as having been found, after trial, to be unworkable. The principal allegations, made against the constitution, and the manner in which it worked, were the failure to encourage joint deliberation between reserved and transferred sides of the provincial government; absence of joint responsibility of ministers; failure on the part of the permanent officials to cooperate with the ministers; vesting of control of the Finance Department in a member of the reserved side of the government and failure of the constitution to vest real authority in the ministers owing to the control of the Government of India and the Secretary of State. The minority report thus declared clearly in detail on the working of the constitution, its inherent defects and practical difficulties in administration. It submitted that the system of dyarchy had failed in the two provinces, viz. Bengal and C.P. and concluded that the constitution should be over-hauled. The report recommended that a Royal Commission, with free terms of reference and larger scope of enquiry, should be appointed to consider whether the constitution should be put on a permanent basis with provisions for automatic progress in the future so as to secure stability in the government, and willing cooperation of the people.[41]

Views of Birkenhead

On July 7, 1925, Lord Birkenhead made a significant statement in the House of Lords in connection with his meeting conference with Lord Reading on the question of further constitutional reforms. He praised to Act of 1919 as an extremely bold experiment. He denied that the new constitution had failed; on the other hand, it had never been given a chance. The door, said the Secretary of State, 'was never closed. It is on the contrary open today, but the condition is clear and precise. There will, there can be no consideration, until we see everywhere among the responsible leaders of Indian thoughts evidence of a sincere and genuine desire to cooperate with us in making the best of the existing constitution.'[42]

Speech of Lord Reading

Lord Reading opened the autumn session of the Central Legislature on August 20, 1925, and delivered an important speech lasting an hour.[43] He set forth before the Legislative Assembly the future policy of the government as regards the reforms. He assured the audience that he was charged with the duty of helping to establish the reformed constitution, and of assisting the country along the road of advance mapped out in the declaration of August 1917.[44] He made it clear that the inquiry contemplated by the Act would be genuine and impartial and nothing would be prejudged. He was sure that it was an inappropriate moment to hold the statutory inquiry, but, as the Secretary of State made it clear in his speech, there was no special sanctity attached to the year 1929. He further opined that the re-examination of the constitution might take place at any time, not later than 1929, when the British government were persuaded that there had been genuine cooperation of the responsible Indian political leaders in working the existing constitution, and when sufficient experience of these new and still largely untried conditions had been gathered to form the basis of a considered judgment. He admitted that, 'the aspirations of Indian politicians, as I understand them are directed towards the establishment of responsible self-government within the Empire as the ultimate goal...whatever may be proposed, will be the subject of most careful examination by the Government of India, and eventually by the Commission, before it is submitted to the British parliament.'[45] In the earlier session of the same year, Alexander Philips,[46] an eminent civil servant, had spoken on similar lines. He made it clear that the commission, when appointed, would not come simply to register that had already been formulated.

The year 1926 witnessed fresh general elections for the Legislative Assembly. Forty-eight per cent voters went to the polls. One of the significant events in the life-time of the third Assembly was the action taken by the government on the report, presented by the Skeen Committee. In fact, in 1918, for the first time, Indians had been made eligible for King's Commission in the Indian army, when ten vacancies were annually reserved for them at Sandhurst. The persons selected were offered opportunities of service in the cavalry and infantry arms. The position was reconsidered by the Indian Sandhurst Committee, presided over by General Andrew Skeen.[47] It presented an unanimous report in November 1926 and recommended that the number of vacancies alloted to Indians in the past, at Sandhurst, be doubled, and that a military college[48] on the lines of Sandhurst be established in India.

During this time featured largely in the House of Commons when questions of importance regarding Indian affairs were asked by Labour members and answered by Lord Wintertion. George Lansbury, a Labour Member of Parliament, said, 'In 1929, a Commission has to be appointed. Somehow we have to make the people of India believe that we really mean that they shall have self-government, that we really do mean that there shall be a Dominion in the sense that Australia is a Dominion within the British Commonwealth of nations.[49] S.Saklatvala stated, 'Between slavery and freedom there is no middle course and a transition from slavery to freedom can never be attained by gradual measures. As long as you continue slavery, it must continue with the full strength in the bond; the bond must be strong to hold down the people. When you make up your mind that there shall be no slavery, the bond must break and it must break completely.

In the reforms granted to India, there is no measure of freedom, and I take the view quite candidly that there can be no measure of freedom. There is no such thing as gradual reform...why does Great Britain presume that of all the savage peoples in the world who cannot manage their affairs, she must be the controller of the people of India ? Why do you not take into your charge the people of Persia, the people of China, the people of Egypt, Turkey, and everywhere else, in the same manner and fashion as you take charge of the people of India.'[50]

Silent Revolution

Thus, it is evident that during the past decade, a great and silent revolution has taken place in the character of relationship between Britain and India. During seven years of the Montagu-Chelmsford reforms, the political leaders of India were in opposition to influence the men who had been working them for the Government of India. They had become politically matured to fight for their rights and privileges. Even Lord Irwin's warning that Parliament would not, in any way, be moved by the policy of coersion, pursued by the Congress, and the future policy of the country lay in a policy of cooperation and in the working of the reforms,[51] did not prove effective. But before the close of the year, on November 8, 1927, Stanely Baldwin,[52] the Prime Minister of England, made an historic announcement regarding the appointment of a Royal Commission[53] under the chairmanship of John Simon.[54] This announcement was two years before the time laid down in the official Statute.

References

1. For complete reference see, *The Report on Indian Constitutional Reforms,* Calcutta, 1918.
2. Parliamentary Debates, House of Commons, August 1917 (Home-Public, National Archives of India) File 112, 1928; An eminent Congress leader like Mrs. Annie Besant condemned the reform proposals as 'ungenerous for England to offer and unworthy for India to accept.'
3. Rt. Hon Edwin. Samuel Montagu, Secretary of State for India, 1917-22. The Secretary of State for India was the Adviser of the Crown and he had the plenary powers of superintendence, direction and control over the Government of India and its revenues and over all officers appointed under the Act of 1919. *See* Rutherford, V.H., *Modern India—Its Problems and their Solution,* pp. 62-63.
4. *See* Report on Indian Constitutional Reforms, p.1.
5. Viscount Chelmsford, served in Indian army during First World War; and was the Viceroy of India, 1916-21, and also First Lord of Admiralty, 1924.

6. Woolacott, J.E., *India on Trial,* p. 154.
7. The list of subjects transferred to popular control included Local-Self-Government, Medical Administration, Education, other than European and Anglo-Indian Education, Agriculture, Fisheries, Cooperative Societies, Excise, Industry and Religious Endowments.
8. It included Land Revenue Administration, Famine Relief, Administration of Justice, Police and Prisons.
9. Reynolds, Reginald, *The White Sahibs in India,* p. 188.
10. He was the first President of the Indian Legislative Assembly, 1921-25 and the Political Adviser to the National Governments of China, 1929-32.
11. Singh, G.N., *Landmarks in Indian Constitution and National Development,* Vol. I, p. 278.
12. Gwyer, Maurice and Appadorai, A., *Speeches and Documents on the Indian Constitution (1921-47)*, Vol. I, p.XXX.
13. Griffiths, P.J., *The British Impact on India,* pp. 319-20.
14. Munshi, K.M., *Indian, Constitutional Documents,* Vol. I, p.10.
15. See the Observation made by E. S. Montagu in August 1921.
16. *Congress in Evolution—Being a Collection of Congress Resolution, 1885-1934,* compiled by D. Chakrabarty and C. Bhattacharyya, pp. 20-22.
17. Horne, E.A., *The Political System of British India,* p.173.
18. Gandhi, M.K., *Young India (1919-22),* part IV, pp. 333 ff.
19. Chintamani, C.Y., *Indian Politics Since the Mutiny,* p. 136.
20. Nehru, Jawaharlal, *An Autobiography,* pp. 80-81.
21. *See The Collected Works of Mahatma Gandhi,* Vol. XXIII, pp. 415-21. The text was originally published in *Young India,* dated 16th February, 1922.
22. Nehru, Jawaharlal, *op.cit.,* pp. 81-82.
23. *Young India,* 16 Feb, 1922.
24. See Nehru's views in his Autobiography, *op.cit.*
25. *Ibid.*
26. Legislative Assembly Debates, Vol. I part, I, p.12.
27. Legislative Assembly Debates, Vol. II, 1921, pp. 1247-54.
28. Woolacott, J.E., *op.cit.,* p. 159.
29. Mitra, H.N., *The Indian Annual Register,* Vol. II, 1923, pp. 223-32.
30. *Ibid,* pp. 229-30.
31. The Swaraj Party issued a manifesto from Allahabad 14 October, 1923 over the signature of Pandit Motilal Nehru, General Secretary. *See,* H.N. Mitra, *op.cit.,* Vol. I, 1924, pp. 57-62.

32. *Ibid.*
33. Legislative Assembly Debates, Vol. IV, 1924, part I, pp. 3-14.
34. *Ibid.*
35. Legislative Assembly Debates, 1924, Vol. IV, part I, pp. 3-14.
36. Mitra, H.N., *op.cit.,* Vol. I, 1925, pp. 37-62.
37. *Ibid.*
38. *Ibid.*
39. Iyer, C.S., Ranga, *India in Crucible,* pp. 46-47
40. *See* Parliamentary Debates, House of Lords, July, 1925.
41. Legislative Assembly Debates, 1925, Vol. VI, part I, pp. 1-15.
42. *Ibid.*
43. *Ibid.*
44. He was the President of the Council of States 1920-24, and Home Member of Executive Council of Governor-General and leader of the Assembly, 1924-27.
45. The Skeen Committee was headed by General Andrew Skeen (1873-1935) who was the C-in-C of armed forces in India in 1929.
46. The Indian Military Academy was established at Dehradun in 1932.
47. Parliamentary Debates, House of Commons. May-June, 1927. Vol. 207, pp. 611-13.
48. Shapurji Saklatvala was a prominent Indian member in the House of Commons. *See* his speech in Parliamentary Debates, House of Commons, *op.cit.,* 1387-88.
49. Address at the opening session of the third Legislative Assembly, *Speeches of Lord Irwin,* Vol. I, pp. 207-13.
    The Viceroy said "Those who are anxious to see constitutional advance must either coerce Parliament or convince it...When Parliament invites India to co-operate in the working of the reformed constitution it does not invite any Indian party, as it was authortatively stated the other day, to lay aside for the time being its demand for Swaraj; it does not desire that any party or individual should forego the freest and fullest right of criticism and constitutional opposition to any action that Government may takes; but it dos invite Indian political parties to show whether or not the ultimate structure, which Parliament is seeking to erect, is one suitable to Indian conditions and Indian needs.'
50. He was the Prime Minister of England from 1923-24, 1924-29 and 1935-37. He said in the House of Commons on November 7, 1929 'None can say when responsible Government will be established; none can say what shape it will take...Nobody knows what Dominion Status will be when India has responsible Government, whether that date be near or distant.'

See Parliamentary Debates, House of Commons, Vol. 210, 1927, pp. 19-21, 1927.

51. *Ibid.*

52. Hardly fifty years of age at the time of his appointment, he was a celebrated constitutional lawyer in England. He was Solicitor-General from 1910 to 1913 in the Liberal cabinet and Attorney-General with a seat in the cabinet from 1913 to 1915.

2

The Controversial Appointment

During the year 1927, Montagu-Chelmsford reforms had been in operation for the last only eight years and the statutory period, had not yet expired.[1] But much pressure, agitation and criticism, mounting from numerous patriotic Indian elements, decided to anticipate the new Statutory Commission's appointment.[2] It was, indeed, the fear of the probable adverse results of the general elections in 1929, in Great Britain, which prompted the ruling party, headed by Stanley Baldwin, to think of accelerating the appointment of such a Commission before the scheduled time. Birkenhead wrote to Irwin, the Viceroy of India. 'We must not run the slightest risk of the delay in selection so much that an election might either interrupt our plans or even come soon enough to make it not wholly unreasonable to attempt some monkeying tricks without selection. It is, of course, obvious that the mere ante-dating of the Commission, would deprive us of nothing valuable. We can play with the time as we want.'[3] Obviously, it was the belief in the high echelons of British politicians that the coming elections would return the Labour Party to power. The Conservatives, therefore, wished to gain a political advantage and it became difficult for them to afford to 'run the slightest risk that the nomination of the Commission should be in the hands of our successors.' Therefore, 'the Secretary of State felt that the acceleration of the Commission was our one card left and that it was a pity to play it until we were certain, it would take a trick.'[4] Besides, it was the belief amongst the Conservatives that a Labour government would be more helpful, sympathetic and considerate in acceding to the political demands of Indian leaders, and that it might also go a step further in granting them such concessions as would be compatible with the vested interests of Britain in India. They, therefore, thought that it would be a safe and prudent measure to appoint the Statutory commission forthwith and thus forestall the Labour government.[5]

It is evident that the Swaraj party[6] was unhappy at the working of the reforms of 1919 and it expressed much dissatisfaction in this regard. It had been pressing hard, for more autonomy in the provinces and responsibility at the centre. The objective, therefore, of the Conservative government was to utilise the appointment of the Commission as a bargain-counter and to disintegrate the Swaraj party.[7] Yet another reason which the Viceroy advanced for the appointment of the Commission was the communal tension prevailing in several regions of India. He opined, 'It seems not impossible that the uncertainty of what constitutional change may be imminent may have been consciously or unconsciously actuated by the desire to strengthen, as they supposed, their relative position in anticipation of the Statutory Commission. Wherever such activities might first begin, the result is to create vicious circle in which all communities are likely to feel themselves constrained to extend their measures of self-defence.[8]

The views of Lord Halifax showed much interest over the changing political trends both in England and India. According to Halifax, 'The legal minds of Birkenhead and Reading were outraged that any one should speak about Dominion Status.'[9] In his private letter,[10] which he wrote to Reading on December 10, 1925, he mentioned that in suggesting the acceleration of the Commission, 'I always had it plainly in mind that we could not afford to run the slightest risk that the nomination of 1928 Commission should be in the hands of our successors. You can readily imagine what kind of a Commission in its personnel would have been appointed by Colonel Wedgwood,[11] and his friends... I have, therefore, throughout been of the clear opinion that it would be necessary for us, as a matter of elementary prudence, to appoint a Commission not later than the summer of 1927. I should, therefore, like to receive your advice if at any moment you discern an opportunity for making this a useful bargain-counter or for further disintegrating the Swarajist Party...I am sure that having regard to political contingencies in this country, we must keep the nomination of the personnel of the Commission in our own hands. In this matter, we cannot run the slightest risk. My present view, therefore, is, and I believe that the Prime Minister share it, that we shall in any event, be playing for safety if we are driven to nominate the Commission in the middle of 1927.[12] If such an acceleration affords you any bargaining value, use it to the full and with the knowledge that you will be supported by the Government.'[13] but, Colonel Wedgwood criticised the hasty appointment of the Statutory Commission: 'I know it is said that things are quiet in India. They are getting along so sweetly now. Why worry ? Wait till next year or the year after 1929, after all, is the date in the Bill. Things are all right now. Why fishing in troubled water ? It is because things are quiet now that I would beg the Government to appoint this Commission at once. There is nothing more contemptible to my mind than to refuse in peaceful times and surrender later to force.'[14]

The personnel of Commission were appointed solely from the British community without any Indian representative, although it was the future constitution of India which was to be the subject of inquiry, discussion and decision. This was obviously a wrong precedent which was bound to give offence to the patriotic sentiments of the people of India. In the past, in every Commission dealing with Indian affairs, Indians were given proportional representation. In the Lee Commission[15] and the Skeen Commission,[16] Indians were well represented and all this led to results without any feeling of resentment.

Sapru on Simon Commission

The exclusion of Indians from the Commission was anticipated by no less a leader than Tej Bahadur Sapru, who had returned from England shortly before its announcement. He was not at all surprised at the action of the British government.[17] When the names of the Commissioners were made public, he said in the course of an interview: 'During my recent visit to England, short as my stay was, there it became abundantly plain to me that the mind of Government had already been made up that India could not hope for any support for its viewpoint from the Conservatives or Liberals, and that, at any rate, so far as some of the Labour leaders were concerned, they had placed serious limitations upon their liberty of action. I cannot understand why this scheme could not have fitted in with adequate representation of Indians on the personnel of the Commission. The fear of minority reports is as naive as it is disingenuous. Nor can I believe that Government could not find in the whole of the country even three or four Indians who could inspire confidence generally.[18]

'It can only mean a complete want of confidence in the judgment and capacity of Indians to serve on a Commission which is to determine the future Government of their country. The utmost that can be said in favour of this scheme is that they want to associate us with them at some stages only to the extent of representing our views, but they deny to us the right of participation in the responsibility of framing our constitution. I have no doubt that this Commission, even though it be presided over by Simon, will inspire no confidence and will command no public support.'[19]

Warning of Pethick Lawrence

Pethick-Lawrence also warned the Conservative government in a somewhat serious tone. 'India, viewed from the standpoint of population, is the most important part of the British Empire, and with the future of India, in my opinion, is bound up not merely the destiny of that country, but of the British Empire. It is not only those who sit on these Benches who are concerned with and committed to self-government for this great part of our Empire. That is a part of a policy which has been definitely set forward by the Government of this country and in all parts of the House of Commons. All parties are committed to a change in that direction...If either through lack of psychological imagination or of administrative capacity, we botch the business, no excuse will serve us. If in place of creating healthy self-Government in India, we produce in that part of the British Empire a festering sore, it will infect the British Empire and make it very doubtful whether that Empire can exist, except utterly weakened and enervated in the future.'[20] Colonel Wedgwood opined,' '...I should say from my small acquaintance with the Indian people that they are very well capable of considering and reporting on the future government of their own country. I should say that there were men with sufficient capacity, sufficient confidence to take serious resolve and to deliver the goods.'[21]

Indeed the excuse given for not appointing any Indian was that the framers of the Act of 1919 intended to confine its scope to only Members of Parliament. But it was a mere pretext.[22] The terms of the Government of India Act of 1919 did not lay down arbitrarily that a purely Parliamentary Commission should examine the working of the reformed constitution. There was no bar to the appointment of an outsider had the cabinet been inclined to make one. But even if the British government wanted to restrict the membership of the Statutory Commission to only the Members of Parliament, the availability of two prominent Indians in the British government was the relevant answer to this decision of Conservative government. There were two well-known Indian members at the time in British parliament: one was S.P. Sinha and the other was Shapurji Saklatvala. In fact, S.P. Sinha had deep connection with various stages of constitutional reforms in India and his inclusion as a member of the Commission would have been of great consequence.[23] Another name that suggested itself in regard to the Commission was that of the Aga Khan. His Highness would surely not have refused if he had been approached by the British government. C.Y. Chintamani, opined 'The stamp of inferiority was fixed on the brow of Indians merely because they were not God's own Englishmen.'[24] Their exclusion from the Commission left no doubt in their minds, that India lacks a statesman of sufficient calibre to sit in conference with men of experience.

The Race Feeling

In mid-1920s the race feeling was in full swing in the East. To ride rough-shod over Indian sentiments and appoint a Commission consisting of all Englishmen on a subject, politically and constitutionally effecting India, was destined to invite trouble. Birkenhead was warned beforehand against adopting such a procedure. The all-British composition of the Commission was destined to be regarded as racially insulting.[25] When Edward Cadogan, a member of the Commission, questioned Birkenhead as to whether he anticipated any trouble in India from the exclusion of representative Indians from it, he replied that although, inevitably, there would be an outcry in certain quarters, he did not believe that it would endure in any case, and ultimately the Commission should experience no difficulty on that account.[26] The ostensible reason advanced by Birkenhead for this departure from precedent only made matters worse to sensitive minds in India. He stated that there were numerous mutually hostile sections in India that it would not be feasible to choose Indians without offending some of them, and, therefore, it would be better to leave them out altogether, and let British representatives decide these important matters for them. According to Lord Halifax, one of the dangers that the Secretary of State foresaw from a mixed Commission was that an unreal 'alliance', might be created between the Indian and the Labour representatives.[27] Obviously, Birkenhead and the Viceroy were in agreement on the point that there was no need of appointing Indians on the Commission as the advantages of having Indians were outweighed by the disadvantages. But they, however, knew that a mixed Commission, consisting of the British and Indians would command the largest degree of confidence in India, and that a Commission without Indians would command no such confidence.[28] Defending the composition of the Commission, Earl Winterton, Under-Secretary of State for India, said in House of Commons, 'No Indian or European who knows India could for one moment suppose that two Indian gentlemen, of whatever position or intellectual attainments, could possibly represent all the various political, religious, racial and economic factors who go to make up British India.'[29]

Non-inclusion of Indians

Thus the arguments against inclusion of Indians were insuperable. It was argued by the British government that if only two or three Indian members were taken, it would not, in any sense, be considered as the representative body of true Indian opinon. It felt difficult to include members from multifarious interests as such a Commission, it was feared, would become a body of very considerable size in which the prospects of an agreed report would be a difficult proposition. Moreover, Birkenhead had never desired that the Commission should recommend a great measure of advancemnt, for which he believed that India was entirely unprepared.[30] He wrote to Irwin on March 23, 1927. 'I am well aware of the arguments in favour of the exclusion of natives, and my mind is absolutely open upon this, and indeed upon every other point; but you must remember that the arguments against the exclusion are a priori very strong. It will be said that the determination of this constitution, with all that it may mean for India, cannot be settled with the least appearance of authority by a Commission which contains no Indian member.[31]

'If the Commission was to be a comparatively small body and at the same time to include Indians, the Indians would not be more than two or three in number, and these would have to be selected in some manner that would ensure that they were reasonably representative of all the cross-currents of Indian views, a condition that was plainly unattainable.'[32]

Views of C.F. Andrews

C. F. Andrew who was[33] instrumental in sponsoring the patriotic sentiments of Indians in their struggle for Swaraj, criticised Birkenhead's statements and called it a decision akin to that of 'a conqueror imposing his sway upon a conquered and subject people.' He condemned it as an undemocratic action as it was like 'a racial superior acting with arrogance towards a racial inferior.'[34] Justifying the non-inclusion of Indians in the Commission, Baldwin, in one of his most significant speeches on Indian policy, delivered at the annual Lord Mayor's banquet, said, 'In including in the Commission not merely no Indian but no Englishman who have been associated hither to with the Government or commerce of India, our sole desire, paradoxical as it may seem, was to give the real, responsible and instructed opinion among Indians the best chance of playing an effective and constructive part in devising a solution.'[35]

There was another important instance which caused anger, resentment and criticism of the people of India. The fact that the Labour Party of England had agreed[36] to serve on the Commission of this character gave to enlightened public opinion in India a grave shock indeed. Birkenhead's attitude and his line of thinking were considered unfavourable towards India, and it could hardly be appreciated if the Labour Party would accord its open sanction, and support his policy and measures. Major Graham Pole, a prominent members of the Labour Party who paid a short visit to India, in a statement[37] to the Associated Press, summed up the situation of India *vis-a-vis* his party and stated that the attitude of the Labour Party was misunderstood in India. It was simply informed that the Conservative government had decided two points; first, that no Indian should be members of the Commission: and second, that no member of Parliament should be on the Commission who had already expressed themselves strongly either on one side or the other or who were directly concerned with the services or with business affairs in India. He further clarified that Labour was asked to nominate two representatives who conformed to the requirements laid down by the British government.[38]

Graham Pole stated that during the previous year a Royal Commission was set up to deal with unemployment insurance. The Labour Party, in spite of its objections to its terms of reference, appointed two of its members to serve on the Commission, and by their representations, they considerably modified the final report of that Commission. Assuring the Indians, he stated that in the present

Commission, his party had no axe to grind, and in nominating two of its members, it was actuated solely by a desire to help India and consider her interest sympathetically. He asked Indians to trust the two Labour members as 'straight and honest men' who would loyally stand by and endeavour to give effect to the policy of Labour Party with regard to India as expressed in its resolutions passed at Liverpool and Blackpool conferences.[39]

Saklatvala and Labour Party

The action of the Labour Party was criticised by Saklatvala. 'I do not wish to offer criticism as to how the Indians will look upon the action of the Labour Party. I know the effect of it will be disastrous for the working Hindu and the British and the Indian workers who will have to work side by side for the benefit of both. The position India may take is that in this country we have a Labour Party. When that party meets at Blackpool, they have one voice, but when the same party meets at Westminster, they shake hands with them and pat them on the back. That is the position. It is not necessary for the Labour Party to insist upon any artfully got up harmony between the political parties when they are dealing with subject races. That is disastrous to the Labour movement.'[40]

"Let me seriously and earnestly appeal to this House that you have all gone mad, and mad and mad...if you want to take care of human interests, if you want to have any sense of honour, any regard for liberty, for freedom and for democracy, do not appoint this Commission."[41]

Evidently it appears to be true that no one questioned the honesty of the two Labour members, but it was difficult to say how they could give effect to their party's professed policy in regard to India as members of this Commission. If Major Pole had read the Royal warrant appointing the Commission, he must be aware that with one exception, every single power that was vested in the Commission, was to be exercised by the Commissioners as a whole or by any three or more of its members. And as the Labour members were only two out of seven, they could not exercise any of these powers unless they could win at least one other member over to their side. On November 24, 1927, the

Labour Party decided not to withdraw its members from the Statutory Commission. An official statement was issued by the Labour Party, MacDonald, presiding, and the following declaration was submitted on the unanimous recommendations of its executive.[42]

'The Labour Party regrets that the Government before making its original proposals in connection with the Indian Commission did not secure cooperation of representatives of the Indian people. In the opinion of the Labour Party, the Commission appointed to proceed to India, should make it its primary duty from time to time to consult on equal terms with the Commission appointed by the Indian Legislature. The Parliamentary Labour Party is further of opinion that there should be joint meetings of the two Commissions for taking evidence (tho' not to the exclusion of either body taking other evidence by itself) and that after all the evidence has been heard and enquiries have been made, further consultations between the two Commissions should be held. The reports of both Commissions should, in due course, be presented to the joint committee of the two Houses of Parliament. The Labour Party has every confidence that its representatives on the Commission will act in the spirit of this stipulation.'[43] Ramsay MacDonald said in House of Commons, 'I do regret that there has not been more consultation between the Government and representative Indians for the purpose of clearing away difficulties.'[44] It is evident that no serious opposition was encountered in British Parliament to the appointment of the Statutory Commission. All political parties were practically unanimous in their opinion that what the Prime Minister and the Secretary of State had done was the best under the circumstances. The few voices of the members of the opposition like those of Saklatvala and Colonel Wedgwood were lost amidst the general chorus of approval.

Selection of Sir John Simon

The selection of a Chairman for the Statutory Commission was anxiously discussed in Lord Birkenhead's private correspondence with the Viceroy. By July 1927, they had agreed with the Prime Minister that John Simon was by far the ablest man available. He had already served on an important Royal Commission which considered the reorganization of the Universities of Oxford and Cambridge. Birkenhead called him a very adroit, patient and tactful and a successful person imbued with great subtlety, astuteness and quickness.[45] So far so, that on November 24, 1927, in the House of Lords, they paid glowing tributes to John Simon for making immense personal sacrifice and undertaking the difficult task in the spirit of public service.[46] He expressed his opinion to the fact that he regarded the Statutory Commission an an exceptionally intelligent jury going to India with no preconceived prejudices. As events proved, there can be no question that both the cabinet of England and the Government of India had egregiously underestimated the effects which the exclusion of Indians from the Commission was destined to produce.[47] Ramsay MacDonald readily helped the Secretary of State in the choice of two more members from the Labour Party in the persons of Stephen Walsh[48] and Clement Richard Attlee,[49] and on July 21, Lord Birkenhead was in a position to assure the Viceroy that the British cabinet had ratified his selection.

On receipt of information of the Secretary of State, the Viceroy, of course, began to guess in his mind about the probable outcome of the appointment of the Statutory Commission. He was confirmed in his opinion that such a Commission if likely to produce a unanimous report, would have advantages that would outweigh the opposition it would create. He was also quite sure that it would be badly received in India,[50] that its appointment would unite all Hindu opinion in opposition, and that its failure to produce an agreed report would have the most damaging results. If such unanimity could not be achieved, he opined that a mixed Commission, although it would produce more than a report, would be far more favourably received: that it would diminish the probability of uniting all Indian opinion against the Commission, and that its minority report would be less injurious that one proceeding from a Parliamentary Commission.[51]

Almost a month prior to the appointment of Statutory Commission, Irwin directed all the Governors thus: "It is possible that announcement of Statutory Commission may be made on November 8th. If this is so, I shall alter my tour and ask certain leading politicians to come and see me at Delhi two or three days before hand, so that I can prepare the ground for announcement. I am particularly anxious that you should, if possible see your leading men and editors in the same way.'[52]

Reaction of Vicerey

The Viceroy was prepared to announce the appointment of the Statutory Commission. He invited a number of leaders of Indian political life to explain the decision of the British government and the reasons for it.[53] Indeed, he had been spending four or five days, rather unpleasant days, in trying to induce the Indian leaders to be reasonable about the scheme of procedure suggested for the Statutory Commission.[54] In this regard, he informed V.J. Patel, President of the Legislative Assembly of India and Dr. M.A, Ansari, of his programme of meeting Mahatma Gandhi. 'I cannot agree to any statement regarding subject matter of interview, as this would inevitably impair confidential character of meeting." Soon after he sent a telegram to Mahatma Gandhi in which he explained: "I am anxious to have a talk with you on certain important and rather urgent matters, and if it is convenient to you, I should be very glad if you could come and see me in Delhi. The most convenient date for me would be Wednesday, November 2nd, at 11.30. I realize that I am giving you very short notice and that this must inevitably cause you inconvenience, but I hope it will not make it impossible for you to come. Please wire whether you can come on that date."[55]

At this point of time, Mahatma Gandhi had made the long journey from Mangalore in the South of India. Probably, he came with the impression that his presence in Delhi was needed to discuss the present unhappy communal situation in the country. It is stated by one of Gandhi's documents announcing the impending arrival of an official British Commission led by John Simon to report on Indian conditions and make recommednations for political reforms.[56] The real point at issue was the nature of enquiry to be undertaken by the Simon Commission and the best form in which the Indian opinion as expressed by the central legislature could be associated with it during the formative and final legislative stages. Soon thereafter, the Viceroy 'dismissed him with a few curt word,' thus missing an opportunity of discussing the issues that lay between them.[57] Gandhi was disappointed, because he never imagined that the Simon Commission would form the dominant topic of discussion. If he had known this, probably he would have excused himself as his other engagements were very pressing.[58] In any case he was glad he had the opportunity to impress on the Viceroy the economic value of his *charkha*. If newspaper reports could be relied on, the 'Mahatma did not hesitate to take his khaddar box of exhibits with him for the Viceroy, though he did not find in Lord Irwin a ready customer.'

Nature of the Commission

The other Indian leaders like Dr. Ansari, Srinivasa Lyengar and Vithalbhai Patel were called only to be informed by the Viceroy that the nature of the Commission had already been finally decided upon by the British government. Irwin's biographer, Alan Campbell Johnson, describes this episode as 'a deplorable lack of tact in the handling of the Indian leaders,' who did not disguise from the Viceroy fact that the Commission as constituted would be boycotted.

In obedience to the orders of the Secretary of State, the Viceroy made an important announcement on November 8, 1927 in connection with the appointment of the Statutory Commission. [59] He stated that the previous statute enacted by the British parliament, eight years ago, had regulated the conditions under which India might learn, by actual experience, whether or not the western system of representative government was the appropriate means through which she might attain responsible self-government and report upon the progress made in the past, the appointment of a Statutory Commission was thought to be essential at the end of ten years. The Commission was to be presided over by one whose public position was due to his outstanding ability, intelligence and character, and it was hoped that the Commission would bring fresh, unbiased, unaffected and impartial judgement to bear upon an immensely complex constitutional issue.[60]

While appointing the Statutory Commission, it was not feasible, of course, to dictate to the Commission what procedure it should follow during its duration of investigation in India; but it was opined that its task in taking evidence would be greatly facilitated if it were to invite the central legislature to appoint a Joint Select Committee, chosen from its elected and nominated non-official members which would draw upon its views and proposals in writing, and lay them before the Commission for examination in such manner as the latter might decide. The committee might remain for any consultation, which the Commission might desire at subsequent stages of the enquiry. It was also suggested that a similar procedure should be adopted with the provincial legislatures. It was made clear that when the Commission had reported and its report had been examined by the Government of India, it would be the duty of the latter to present proposals to Parliament to adopt them without first giving a full opportunity for Indian opinion of different to contribute its view upon them.

Within a week of the announcement of the appointment of the Commission, John Simon wrote a letter to the President of the Spen Valley Liberal Federation in which he said that the British Parliament had a tremendous responsibility to the people of India. The Commission, he stated, would not go to India with any idea of imposing western ideas or constitutional reforms from without. But, it would also listen, learn and then faithfully report its conclusions with regard to the actual conditions and varying proposals made from with. He further clarified by saying, 'Personally speaking, I enter on any part of this duty intensely desiring to be of what service, I can be to India and Britain, and while I am deeply conscious of my shortcomings, I am going to do my best.'[61]

It was decided that the Statutory Commission should proceed to India early in the next year. The purpose of this preliminary tour was taking evidence as for the members to gain some experience of the working of legislatures, local-government institutions, educational centres and any other public department which mainly concerned, the problem they had been set to unravel and also to 'form in the minds' eye a clear picture of Indian conditions with which they were asked to deal.[62]

Members of Commission

The following persons were appointed as members of the Statutory Commission. Sir John Allsebrook Simon (Chairman), Viscount Burnham, Baron Strathcona, George Richard Lane-Fox, Edward Cecil George Cadogan, Vernon Hartshorn, Clement Richard Attlee, J.W. Bhore and S.F. Steward were appointed secretaries of the Commission.

The official composition of the Statutory Commission was one for the decision of Parliament and His Majesty's government, and its procedure was settled by the Commission itself and did not form the subject of correspondence with the Governor-General-in-Council. On November 24, 1927 the resolution was moved in the House of Commons by Earl Winterton that the cost of the Commission would be borne by the Indian revenue.

The views of impending boycott quickly penetrated to the India Office. Lord Birkenhead prepared himself to face it in a conciliatory manner, and not to expose the Commissioners to more insult that could be avoided. He insisted that the Commissioners should reach no hurried conclusion, but should first make a long and non-committal survey. In a private letter of January 19, 1928 to the Viceroy, he wrote that he had a long talk with John Simon whom he advised 'that on this first visit, and until, the situation clarified, it would give as few people as possible the opportunity of snubling the Commission...You and Simon must be the judges whether or not it is expedient in these direction to try to make a breach in the wall of antagonism, even in the course of the present visit...I gave him another word of advice with which I believe you will equally agree. It was that he and his colleagues should, as far as possible, steel themselves against reaching any conclusion on their first visit. I am sure that the attitude of their minds should be receptive, analytic and non-committal.'

Even the Prime Minister, assured the people of India by his conciliatory remark, 'Let Indians, dismiss from their minds any thought of inferiority. They will be approached as friend and as equals, but the responsibility of Parliament remains, and no procedure which suggests that responsibility can be formally shared with representatives of an other Parliament will really advance the inquiry...We are only giving the framework, and within that framework the Commissioners are left free. They can pursue as many of the lines of procedure in which have been suggested today, as seem to them on consideration, wise and practicable, only providing that such procedure in within the framework and does not prejudice the responsibility and the ultimate reponsibility[63].We regard the scheme as the most effective means of satisfying the proper ambition of such men to take part in the settlement of the constitutional future of India, and I take this opportunity of assuring them that His Majesty's Government earnestly desire that their opinon, and the opinion of every man of good-will, Indian or British who has anything to contribute to the very difficult problem of India's future, shall be accessible to the Commission and shall be given the fullest weight in their conclusions.'[64]

Warrant of Appointment

George R.I. George the fifth, by the Grace of God, of Great Britain, Ireland and the British Dominions beyond the Seas Kind, Defender of the faith, Emperor of India, to

Our Right Trusty and Well-Beloved Counsellor Sir John Allsebrook Simon. Knight Commander of the Royal Victorian Order, Officer of Our Most Excellent Order of the British Empire;

Our Right Trusty and Well-Beloved Cousin Harry Lawson Webster, Viscount Burnham, Knight Grand Cross of Our Most Distinguished Order of Saint Michael and Saint George, Member of the Order of the companions of Honour, upon whom we have conferred the Territorial Decoration;

Our Right Trusty and Well-Beloved Donald Sterling Palmer, Baron Strathcona and Mount Royal;

Our Trusty and Well-Beloved Edward Cecil George Cadogan, Esquire (Commonly called the Honourable Edward Cecil George Cadeogan), Companion of Our Most Honourable order of the Bath;

Our Right Trusty and Well-Beloved Counsellor Stephen Walsh;

Our Right Trusty and Well-Beloved Counsellor George Richard Lane Fox, Honorary Colonel, the Yorkshire Hussars Yeomanry, upon whom we have conferred the Territorial Decoration;

Our Trusty and Well-Beloved Clement Richard Attlee, Esquire, Major, late South Lancashire Regiment;

Greetings !

Whereas we have deemed it expedient that the Commission for which provision is made in Section 84A of the Government of India Act should forthwith be appointed for the purpose of inquiring into the working of the system of government, the growth of education, and the development of representative institutions, in British India, and matters connected therewith, and should report as to whether and to what extent it is desirable to establish the principle of responsible government, or to extend, modify, or restrict the degree of responsible government then existing therein, including the question whether the establishment of Second chambers of the local legislatures is or is not desirable:

Now know Yet that We, reposing great trust and confidence in your knowledge and ability, have on the advice of our Secretary of State for India acting with the concurrence of both Houses of Parliament authorised and appointed, and do by these Presents authorise and appoint you, the said Sir John Allsebrook Simon (Chairman); Harry Lawson Webster, Viscount Burnham; Donald Sterling Palmer, Baron Strathcona and Mount Royal, Edward Cecil George Cadogan; Stephen Walsh; George Richard Lane Fox and Clement Richard Attlee to be Our Commissioners for the purposes aforesaid:

And for the better effecting of the purposes of this Our Commission, We by these Presents give and grant unto you, or any three or more of you, full power at any place in Our

United Kingdom or in India or elsewhere in Our Dominions to call before you such persons as you shall judge likely to afford you any information upon the subject of this Our Commission; and also whether in Our said kingdom, or in India, or elsewhere in our Dominions to call for information in writing; to call for, have access to and examine all such books, documents, registers and records as may afford you the fullest information on the subject, and to

inquire of and concerning the premises by all other lawful ways and means whatsoever, including the appointment by the Commission with the sanction of Our Secretary of State for India, of any person or persons to make subordinate enquiries and to report the result to the Commission:

And we do by these Presents authorise and empower you or any of you to visit and inspect personally such places as you may deem it expedient so to inspect for the more effectual carrying out of the purposes aforesaid:

And we do by these Presents will and ordain that this Our Commission shall continue in full force and virtue, and that you, Our said Commissioners, or any three or more of you, may from time to time proceed in the execution thereof, and of every matter and thing therein contained, although the same be not continued from time to time by adjournment:

And we do further ordain that you, or any three or more of you, have liberty to repot your proceedings under this Our Commission from time to time if you shall judge it expedient so to do:

And our further will and pleasure is that you do, with as little delay as possible, report to Us under your hands and seals, or under the hands and seals of any three or more of you, your opinion upon the matters here in submitted for your consideration:

Given at Our Court at Saint James's the Twenty-sixth day of November, One thousand nine hundred and twenty-seven; in the Eighteenth Year of Our Reign.*

By His Majesty's Command

W. Joynson-Hicks. * (Selected from the Report of the Indian Statutory Commission, Vol. I, pp. xiii-xiv).

References

1. Home-Public, File 603, December 8, 1927.
2. Cadogan, Edward, *The India We Saw,* p. 1.
3. Secretary of State to Irwin, September 23, 1926, *Halifax Papers*; available in Nehru Memorial Library, New Delhi.
4. Irwin to Governor of Bombay, January 26, 1927, *Halifax Papers.*
5. Majumdar, R.C., *History of the Freedom Movement in India,* Vol. III, p. 308.
6. The Swaraj Party was led by Motilal Nehru and C.R. Das in 1920 (year 1928).
7. Setalvad, C.H., *Recollections and Reflections,* p. 341.

   'It was thought, however, that if the Statutory Commission was, as everybody seems to expect, appointed earlier than 1929, the Swarajists would claim this as a concession by Government to their demands and would make it the excuse for abandoning pure obstruction,' Irwin to Governor of Bombay, January 3, 1927, *Halifax Papers.*
8. Liberal, A., *The Commission and After,* pp. 6-7.
9. Halifax, Lord, *Fullness of Days,* p.121. Lord Birkenhead was a pessimist over the future of India; he wrote to Lord Reading on December 4, 1924, "To me it is frankly inconceivable that India will ever be fit for Dominion self-Government."
10. Birkenhead, The Earl of, *Frederick Edwin, Earl of Birkenhead, Last Phase,* pp. 252-53.
11. Colonel Josiah Wedgood was a friend and sympathiser of Indian nationalists. He opined'...We cannot get them (people of India) interested in education or irrigation while they are struggling for political freedom. No people struggling for freedom can think of other things. (Debates, House of Commons, 208, 1927, p. 1655) '...It would be better that this Commission should not go out to India. We are obviously digging a gulf between the peoples of Great Britain and the peoples of India—a gulf in which hope and faith lie buried—where a modern Curtins might say: 'Gladly would I leap into the gulf' (Debates, House of Commons, Vol. 210, 1927, p. 2237). He further said, It is better to have no Statutory Commission at all than a Commission which is not representative, even though there may be some that men might call dangerous. I would like to see such a man as Gandhi on that Commission (Debates, House of Commons,

Vol. 208, 1927, pp. 1658-59).

12. Birkenhead, The Earl of, *op.cit.*, pp. 252-53.
13. *Debates, House of Commons,* Vol. 208, 1927, p. 1656.
14. The members of the Lee Commission were Viscount Lee of Farham (Chairman), Sir Reginald Craddock, B.N. Basu, Sir Cyril Jackson, Sir M. Habibullah, H.K. Kaul, D. Petrie, Professor P. Coupland and N.M. Samarth. Mitra, H.N., *op.cit.*, Vol. II, 1923, p.121.
15. The personnel of the Skeen Committee were: Captain J. N. Banerjee, P. Sethna, Joginder Singh, Sir Abdur Qayum, Pandit Motilal Nehru, M. A. Jinnah, Dewan Bahadur Rama Chandra Rao, Dr. Ziauddin Ahmad, Captain Hira Singh, Captain Gul M. Khan and E. Burden.
16. Liberal, A., *op.cit.*, p. 4.
17. *The Tribune,* December 28, 1927.
18. *Ibid.*
19. *Debates, House of Commons,* Vol. 208, 1927, pp. 1974-75.
20. *Ibid,* p. 1659.
21. Chintamani, C.Y., *Indian Problems Since the Mutiny,* p. 171.
22. Setalvad, C.H., *op.cit.,* p. 342.
23. Chintamani, C.Y., op.cit., p. 171.
24. Andrews, C.F., *India and the Simon Report,* p. 32.
25. Cadogan, Edward, *op.cit.,* pp. 3-4 and Secretary of State to the Viceroy, May 5, June 9, July 6, 1927, *Halifax Papers.*
26. Lord Halifax; *Fullness of Days,* p. 115.
27. Birkenhead, The Earl of; *op.cit.,* pp. 251-52.
28. *Debates, House of Commons,* Vol. 210, 1927, p. 2219.
29. Birkenhead, *The Earl of Halifax,* p. 238; Lord Birkenhead used to say 'Look here, you are only a quarrelling mob, flying at each others' throats. Produce, if you can, the constitution you want. I bet you can not': *See* Motilal Nehru Birth Centenary Souvenir, p. 148.
30. *Ibid,* pp. 238-39.
31. *Ibid,* p. 239.
32. B. 1870; started his career as a lecturer in St. Stephen's College; Delhi; a devoted disciple of Mahatma Gandhi; helped India in many ways; by spending his whole life here ; author of numerous books, on Indian nationalism and freedom struggle. d. 1940.

33. Andrews, C.F., *op.cit.,* pp. 37-38.
34. Liberal, A., *op.cit.,* pp. 27-28.
35. Birkenhead wrote the Viceroy, 'My greatest anxiety at this end was relieved when Ramsay MacDonald consented to appoint two members of the Labour Party. If under the influence of the extremists, he has refused to make an appointment, the situation would indeed have been serious.' Secretary of State to the Viceroy, November 3, 1927, *Halifax Papers.*
36. *Time of India,* January 18, 1928.
37. *Ibid.*
38. *Debates, House of Commons,* Vol. 210, 1927, p. 2278.
39. *Ibid,* pp. 2283-85.
40. *Ibid.*
41. *The Tribune,* 26 November 1927.
42. *Debates, House of Commons,* Vol. 210, 1927, p. 2226.
43. *Ibid.*
44. Birkenhead, Earl of; *Halifax,* pp. 238-39.
45. Telegrams of the Viceroy to all the Governors, October 10, 1927, *Halifax Papers.*
46. The Earl of Halifax; *Fullness of Days,* p. 119 and Irwin to Viscount Halifax, November 6, 1927, *Halifax Papers.* [NMML)
47. See *Times of India,* November 4 and 5, 1927.
48. Irwin wrote to Viscount Halifax: 'It was rather like talking to some who had stepped off one planet on to this for a short visit of a fortnight and whose whole mental outlook was quite other to that which was regulating most of the affairs on the planet to which he had descended," Irwin to Viscount Halifax, November 6, 1927, *Halifax Papers.*
49. *Ibid.*
50. Viceroy to Governor of Punjab, October 20, 1927, *Halifax Papers.*
51. Viceroy of State to the Viceroy, November 7, 1927, *Halifax Papers.*
52. *Ibid.*
53. *Ibid.*
54. Birkenhead, Earl of; *op.cit.,* p. 243.
55. *Ibid.*

56. *Ibid.*
57. *Ibid.*
58. *Ibid.*
59. *Times of India,* November 10, 1927.
60. *Ibid.*
61. Debates, House of Commons, Volume 210, 1927, pp. 2294-95.
62. *Ibid.*

3
Political Awakening and Protest Meetings

The reception to the appointment of Simon Commission announced simultaneously by the British Prime Minister in Parliament[1] and the Viceroy in India[2] on November 8, 1927, was extraordinary in its nature. It evoked protest and criticism in the whole country. The leaders of the extreme left and the extreme right of Indian politics regarded the exclusion of Indians from the Commission as a direct insult to the intelligence of the people of India and joined hands in denouncing its constitution and procedure, and advocating its boycott. Moderates and extremists, Swarajists and no-changers, Congressmen and some of the loyalists—all stood on the same platform for critical remarks against the Commission. Meetings of protest were held in several towns and cities, in order to record their emphatic protest against the Commission. However, with the exception of the European Association, the Anglo-Indian press and a small section of the Muslims, headed by Muhammad Shafi in the Punjab,[3] all shades of opinion merged in a common unanimity. Obviously, interviews, letters and reports of protest meetings advocating complete boycott of the Simon Commission poured in ceaselessly. Prominent leaders like Tej Bahadur Sapru, C.H. Setalvad, Annie Besant and A. Rahim on the one hand, and the Congress President and the Swarajists on the other, openly advised their countrymen to abstain from helping the Commission in any way. From North to South and West to East of India, persons of different calling, belonging to various political parties and holding divergent views and interests—all united to lodge a common protest against the Commission. The 'bonafides' of the Conservative party in instituting the Simon Commission were strongly suspected and questioned and the leaders of different parties took no pains to conceal that the Conservatives in Parliament were adopting rushing tactics in Indian affairs lest they should lose their chance in the next general elections.

Views of Leaders

While a few leaders took some time to pronounce their final views, a number of them gave vent to their impressions of disagreement and resentment in various ways. Dr. M.A. Ansari, President-elect of the Indian National Congress, requested the Viceroy to urge the Secretary of State and the British cabinet to desist from the course of action contemplated by them regarding the Statutory Commission and to advise the convening of a Round Table Conference between the British and Indian representatives to make a decision for the future constitution of India. He was afraid the disagreement between the view of Government of India and the British cabinet on the one hand, and people of India as represented by its various schools of political thought, on the other hand, was so fundamental and so great that they would be considered sufficient for people to stand aside and abstain from any participation in the work of the Commission.[4]

The extreme right, that is the section of the old Liberal or Moderate schools of Indian politicians, led by Tej Bahadur Sapru, who found most of his support amongst the Liberals of the United Provinces, Madras and Bombay, attacked the announcement of the Statutory Commission on the ground of the exclusion of Indians from it and the consequent insult to India's national self-respect. He called this concession a mere eyewash.[5] Addressing a largely-attended general meeting of the Liberal association, he criticised the selection of the personnel as arbitary, unjust and unfair to India and pointed out that except the Chairman, the rest of the members of the Statutory Commission were mediocrites, and the procedure to be followed by it was cumbrous and ingenious.[6] He impressed on his audience that Indians were not being treated fairly, because out of three hundred and fifty millions of Indians, even two or three persons were not found out to be capable and intelligent enough to be appointed as members of the Statutory Commission.[7] He emphatically declared that he had no confidence in Birkenhead or the India Office, and asked his fellow Liberals not to have any such confidence.[8] He also advocated the abolition of the India Office and advised his Liberal friends not to submit to such an indignity, injustice and unfair deal.[9] In the biography of Halifax, Birkenhead confirms that it was a painful moment for the Viceroy of India, when Tej Bahadur Sapru decided to boycott the Simon Commission.[10]

The Working Committee of the Indian National Congress felt much dissatisfied and perturbed over the appointment of the Simon Commission. It hastened to pass the resolution which stated that the British government had constituted a Statutory Commission in defiance of the national will and rejected the national demand for a Round Table Conference to settle a Swaraj constitution for India. It called upon the people of India and appealed to all political parties to abstain from cooperation with the Commission; either by giving evidence or by voting for or serving on any committee connected therewith.[11]

Reaction of Mrs. Annie Besant

A conference of all parties was convened by Mrs. Annie Besant[12] in Madras in order to discuss the situation arising out of appointment of the Statutory Commission.[13] The meeting included prominent Indians like S. Srinivasa Iyengar,[14] T.B. Sapru, A. Rangaswami Iyengar, M. Abdul Hameed Khan, and a number of other members of the Legislative Council.[15] All agreed to a common resolution to boycott the Simon Commission.

The women's associations in India did not lag behind and gave the lead in their own way. The Women's Freedom League wrote to the Prime Minister of England urging the inclusion of at least one woman on the Indian Statutory Commission. An other women's organization known as the Women's Indian Association, Madras, lodged a protest against the personnel of the Simon Commission for three reasons viz. Indians had been entirely excluded from the Commission; no Indian woman was on the Commission, and no British woman had been appointed either.[16]

A large number of delegates and visitors including Moplahs and Malayalee ladies representing all parties of Malabar attended the West Coast Political Conference presided over by Annie Besant. Madhavan Nair was the Chairman of the reception committee. It declared that the appointment of the Statutory Commission was the denial to India of her right to determine her own destiny.[17] Besides, a meeting of the women of Bombay, presided over by Sarojini Naidu, unanimously adopted a resolution requesting leaders of India to sink their internal differences and give a befitting replay to the challenge thrown out to the Indian people by more vigorous struggle for complete Swaraj.[18]

Gandhi's Opposition

Mahatma Gandhi opposed the appointment of the Simon Commission and opined that in this matter he had surrendered his conscience to the President of the Indian National Congress and through him to the Congress. He further stated, If a general, and dignified uncamouflaged boycott was brought about, it would be an effective answer to the extraordinary step taken by the British government.'[19]

Muslim opinion did not range itself immediately either for or against the Statutory Commission. With the exception of M.A. Jinnah, no Muslim politician of any standing denoucned the Commission. Even Jinnah waited till the end of November, 1927, when he publicly expressed his adherence to the boycott.[20] When he received a telegram from G.B. Clarkes and A. Fenner Brockway, two prominent members of the Labour Party, he telegraphed to them saying that the exclusion of Indians from the Statutory Commission was fundamentally wrong, and amendments, proposed, so far as reported, were equally improper. He opined that no self-respecting and accredited representative of India would associate himself with or serve on the Commission, unless invited on absolutely equal terms and with equal rights. He appealed to the members of the Labour Party to demonstrate their sympathy with Indian feelings by action, and, in response to the Indian public opinion, at least to refuse to allow any member of their party to serve on the Commission which excluded Indians and was calculated to humiliate and wound the self-respect of the people of India.[21]

Besides, at a protest gathering, represented by prominent Indians like Dinshaw Petit, Chimanlal Setalvad, Jamnadas Mehta, Pheroz Sethna, M.R. Jayakar, Sarojini Naidu, H.P. Mody and B.G. Horniman, where all of them gave vent to their feelings of resentment against the attitude of the British government towards Indian problems, Jinnah emphatically recorded the resolution that it was not a question of having of how few Indians on the Commission, but it was question of how far Indians were prepared to stand together and how much they would sacrifice for their honour. He felt confident that whatever might be the difference among themselves, the Hindus and Muslims would not accept a proposal which was an affront and insult to India.[22]

Interviewed by a special representative of the *Tribune* in connection with the Viceroy's announcement regarding the Commission, the famous Urdu poet, Muhammad lqbal said that it was a great mistake not to allow Indians to participate in the Royal Commission which was going to decide the future constitution of India. I am ashamed to say that the fault is largely ours and not theirs. If we are really in earnest about the ideal that we have set before us, the only way to convince Parliament of the justice of our claim is that we make ourselves a single self-conscious nation.'[23]

The Council of the Bengal Presidency Muslim League could not afford to keep quiet at this hour of national upsurge and expressed its deep and emphatic indignant protest against the deliberate exclusion of Indians from the Statutory Commission and considered it an insult to the country and a menace to its political future.[24] The Punjab Khilafat Committee met at the House of Dr. Muhammad Alam in this regard and urged a complete boycott of the Commission which the committee thought, had been appointed in 'utter disregard of the national demand.'[25]

Reaction of Justice Party

The non-Brahman or Justice party in Madras, which had a companion in the Bombay non-Brahman organization, was one of the most important and powerful of all the political organisations in India. At first, the attitude of these non-Brahman bodies towards the Simon Commission was doubtful and they were merely theoretical adherents, and some of their leaders, in both Madras and Bombay, declared simply their dissatisfaction with the Commission. But as time passed, their attitude changed slowly, but perceptibly, until by the end of the year, the bulk of the non-Brahman opinion in these two provinces had began to be favourable to the idea of cooperation with the Commission.[26]

The working committee of the All-India Hindu Mahasabha which was initially concerned with the Commission and did not mince words, met at Benaras under the Presidentship of Dr. B.S. Moonje and adopted a resolution urging the boycott of the Statutory Commission.[27] Referring to its appointment, Dr. Moonje said that it was thoroughly disappointing as expected. He opined that the government had taken the fullest advantage of the disunion among Hindus and Muslims, who were breaking each others' heads, and the Congress was divided over minor issues into several groups. He suggested that the leaders of all parties should meet and decide upon a common line of action.[28]

The prominent Muslim leaders of the Punjab assembled at Lahore at the residence of Muhammad Shafi to decide the course of action and the attitude that they should adopt towards the Commission. After two and a half hours of discussion, it was decided that the 'boycott of the Royal Commission was detrimental to the best interest of the country in general and the Muslim community in particular, and called upon the leaders of the Hindu and Muslim communities to take immediate steps towards ending fratricidal conflict which has been the most unhappy feature of the internal Indian situation during the last three or four years."[29] He also advised the Muslims of India not to be misled by ideas of false sentiment, but to follow the dictates of reason and common sense.[30] He reminded them not to talk of boycott of Simon Commission which would be impracticable and would produce bad effects in England. In this regard, he got immediate support from Malik Feroze Khan Noon, Zulfiqar Ali Khan, and other prominent Muslims of Punjab.[31]

An extaordinarily crowded meeting was held outside Mori Gate in Lahore, in connection with the appointment of the Simon Commission, under the auspices of the City Congress Committee. It was reminiscent of the non-cooperation days. Representatives of various communities were seated on the same platform, and much enthusiasm was in evidence. The most prominent leaders were Sardar Kharak Singh, Lala Duni Chand, Pandit K. Santhanam, Malik Barkat Ali, Lala Pindi Dass, Sardar Sardul Singh and Sardar Amar Singh Jhabbal. Indeed, the presence of Mardy Jones, Labour member of British parliament, added to the importance of the occasion. The proceedings opened with a stirring song on national unity. The final resolution was moved by Malik Barkat Ali. Resolved that 'this public meeting of the citizens of Lahore consising of all classes and creeds places on record its sense of great indignation at the complete exclusion as well as at the procedure proposed, and calls upon all communities, at this supreme crisis in the constitutional affairs of the country, to sink all their differences and join in organizing a complete boycott of this Commission.'[32]

Lajpat Roy's Reaction

Lala Lajpat Rai[33] felt very sad over the appointment of the Commission and opined that he was not going to associate with it in any shape or manner not because he believed that India could effectively boycott it, but because it was repugnant to his political sense to do so. He knew from his past experience that ('our advice to the Government has no merit,) our representatives no force and our cooperation no value.' According to him it was waste of time and energy to try to offer cooperation. He suggested for calling a Round Table Conference of a hundred leading Indians of all parties and all communities to take up the question of framing the constitution. A committee of twenty-one members might meet at Delhi or Bombay to start the work of drafting it. The Round Table Conference might be fixed on 15th January, 1928. Any constitution drafted by this conference should be forwarded to the Secretary of State.[34] Even during the debate in the Central Legislative Assembly, Lajpat Rai said that he had no faith in the bonafides of the Government or of the people who had appointed the Commission. Their ignorance of India, Indian history and politics was in his judgement, their greatest disqualifcation to enter upon the task which had been entrusted to them. He also challenged to Commission's ability to settle the Indian problems, which might be tackled by representatives both from England and India in a spirit of conciliation and negotiation.[35]

Sikhs and their Feelings

At this stage, Sardar Ujjal Singh, a prominent member of the Sikh community in the Punjab, gave vent to his feelings on behalf of his community, which was indeed, a minority community in the province. He emphasised "So far as the Sikhs are concerned, I would only say that in such momentous matters, they should act as all minorities ought to and Sikhs are in smallest minority though an important one. Whatever the decision of the Sikh community may be on the merits of the question, any isolated action on its part is unthinkable. The Sikhs in such matter have to follow the lead of sister communities."[36]

Besides Sikhs, the other minority community, viz., the All-India Christian Conference met at Allahabad on December 31, 1927, and passed a few resolution.[37] The Conference urged the holding of a Round Table Conference of representatives of all communities to consider the present situation; drawing up a constitution; conducting propaganda in England; reiterating the advocacy of joint electorates for all legislatures and condemning the non-inclusion of Indians in the Statutory Commission. It advocated for higher and adequate status for Legislative Committees which were proposed to function as an auxiliary to the Commission. Besides it drew the attention of their countrymen to the fact that negative and destructive criticism would be of little use and urged the national leaders to draw up a constructive and practicable constitution and submit it to the Commission for the consideration of parliament.[38]

An idea of the attitude of the non-official Europeans towards the impending constitutional developments was given by C.B. Charters, President, European Association, in the Freemason Hall, Madras. He welcomed the appointment of the purely Parliamentary Commission on the ground that such a Commission would tackle the problem without preconceived ideas, and would not only ask for but would also follow Indian and British advice. He opined that the examination of men versed in western self-governing institutions would give a greater chance of practical solution to such a constitutional problems.[39]

With the passage of time, Indian opinion-nationalist and liberal alike—hardened more and more against the Commission. The Indian press featured commentary and interviews from all over India counselling it boycott. The Hindu was much critical of it and observed that the Statutory Commission on Indian reforms was an insult to India. It stood for the betrayal of the solemn pledges, the repudiation of the fundamental principles of Britain's own constitutional practice, in disregard of those external scruples which should regulate the conduct of states no less than that of individuals. 'Cooperation and more cooperation has been the constant refrain of Britain all these eight years, and at least there we have in concrete form her idea of the kind of cooperation she expects from us—the cooperation of the slave in chairs with the overseer who superintends his agony whip in hand, and not the cooperation that exalts equals and draws the ties of friendship tighter. Let India give the only possible reply to this arrogant gesture of the British Cabinet. They count upon our mutual difference, our personal and communal jealousies and the much-tried faith of our moderates in Britain to keep us apart and make ourselves easy prey to their scheming and make ourselves the laughing-stock of the world. Shall it to be said of use that we sold our birth-right for a pottage and merited the course of unborn generations ?"[40] The *Bande Mataram* hailed the Commission as offering an opportunity to Indians to show to the world that the British government in India was based on might. It called upon Indians to be on their guard against the British tactics of putting one community against the other.[41]

Press and its Reaction

The *Milap*, a vernacular newspaper from Lahore, considered the Viceregal announcement regarding the Statutory Commission to be an attempt to wrap up in a 'Silken glove the Iron claw' presented by His Majesty's government. The paper regarded the Advisory Committees of legislatures as merely 'unpaid clerks,', appointed to lighten the burden of the Commission, with a view to throw dust into the eyes of the world. It pointed out that, in this manner, India would not be in a position to achieve responsible Government till Doom's day.[42]

The Leaders of Allahabad in its leading article observed, "We regard this long-looked for Statutory Commisssion as it is constituted as being both an injury and insult to India. It is a calculated affront to the Indian opinion, to the Indian intelligence as well as to the Indian self-respect. We declared our want of confidence as well as the Indian self-respect in the Commission. It is our considered opinion, our countrymen should have nothing to do with it.[43]

Commenting on the announcement of the Statutory Commission. The *Bombay Chronicle* under caption, '*Boycott it*' said that 'The Viceroy's statement aggravated an insult added to the injury by inviting Indian leaders to Delhi in order to face them with a Fete accompli. The exclusion of Indians from the Commission was considered indefensible, unjust and humiliation, and Lord Irwin by his laboured apologia has only lacerated the wounded heart of India.[44]

The *Amrita Bazar Patrika* commented that the government wanted to take full advantage of the unfortunate situation in India to impose a constitution of its liking, regardless of Indian public opinion. The only remedy it suggested was to resort to a rigid boycott of the Commission.[45]

The *Indian National Herald* stated,"The Viceroy's announcement fulfils the worst expectations. The British Cabinet has risen to the full height of Imperialist arrogance and contemptuously refused to admit Indians to the membership of the Commission in defiance of the obvious intention of the fact of Parliament."[46]

Under the caption "Boycott the New Sham' the *Rangoon Mail* said that there must be no prevarication in the attitude of the country. The Statutory Commission must be boycotted. it argued that Indian nationalism in the council and in the assembly was on its trial and it must reject the select committee proposal.[47]

The *Kesari* wrote that instead of unitedly uttering the word boycott and by appealing to all parties and creeds, all should join hands to raise the banner of self-government, casting aside all considerations of self and communities. It also pleaded for the recommencement of a publicity campaign in England by having a British committee and restoring the weekly organ *India* to help labour leaders in their sympathetic attitude towards Indians. Jawaharlal Nehru's name was suggested as the Indian representative to negotiate with the Labour Party.[48]

The eastern region of India, including Bihar and Orissa, joined the boycott movement. A well-attended special conference of the people of Bihar and Orissa drawn from all communities and parties was held at Dilkusha in Patna to consider the political situation created by the appointment of the Commission. Syed Ali Imam presided. Prominent amongst those who attended the meeting were T.B. Sapru, Dr. Rajendra Prasad, Shalfi Daudi, Dip Narayan Singh, Braj Kishore Prasad, Sri Krishna Singh, Syed Abdul Aziz, and Mahendra Prasad.[49]

Dr. Rajendra Prasad moved the resolution calling upon members of the central and provincial legislatures representing Bihar and Orissa, 'not to give their support in any shape or form to election of the committees proposed to be associated in the work of the Statutory Commission and to see that such Committees are not called into existence.'[50] Syed Ali Imam refused to accept Lord

Birkenhead's statement that the Committees of the Legislature in India would be no more witnesses before the Commission, but their colleagues, and that the status given to the Committee of the central legislature which would have the privilege of sitting with the Joint Parliamentary Committee, was unprecedently generous. He opined that the status of the committee of the legislature was only that of a petitioning body and it was only camouflaging the issue to say that they would be colleagues of those sitting in authority.[51]

Nehru and Labour Party

Jawaharlal Nehru, on his arrival from Colombo, on December 22, 1927, said, 'The Labour Party has definitely adopted a fully imperialist attitude towards India...Messrs MacDonald and Lansbury are overfond and cordial towards India, but in no single instance has this effusiveness been translated into action. And I am quite certain that a future Labour Government, if it comes into power, will be as objectionable to the Indian people like Lord Birkenhead and Company. For my part, I prefer a frank opponent like Lord Birkenhead to gentlemen who talk and do nothing like Messrs MacDonald and Lansbury. They are very fond of giving advice to Indians.'[52]

S.P. Sinha and Motilal Nehru

S.P. Sinha during his journey by the Rawalpindi, when interviewed at Aden on December 25, 1927, expressed the view that India would lose nothing by boycotting the Commission.[53] He suggested that the Commission stood to lose grievously by the atmosphere it was helping to create.[54] According to him, no reforms, however, generous, would have a reasonable chance of success if they were ushered in after a spirit of general ill will and feeling of utter mistrust that was being created.[55]

Motilal Nehru was interviewed by a London correspondent on November 24, 1927. He said that he had told the Chairman of the Labour Party plainly that he had not approved of the proposal to accept the present Commission on condition that the Joint Committee to be appointed in India was given power to examine witnesses and to submit a constitution of its own drafting to the Joint Parliamentary Committee in London. He looked upon this as the thin end of the wedge. He hoped that if Indians agreed to such a proposal, they would have to give away the principle of self-determination which they had been claiming all along. He wished all parties would concentrate on the framing of the constitution which the country needed.[56]

Under instructions from the President and Secretary of Indian National Congress, Motilal Nehru wrote to the members of the Labour Party in the House of Commons outlining the views of the Congress party in the Central Assembly as regard the Commission and expressing surprise at their official cooperation. His correspondence described the Commission as an insult to India which could only widen the breach already existing between the two countries and declared that India's fight for freedom would take a turn which was bound to result in increasing bitterness.[57] He wrote to Lansbury asking him to consider the admissibility of withdrawing Labour members from the Commission and desisting from all efforts at a compromise.[58] He warned that any proposal short of some suitable form of full responsible government would not satisfy the Congress.[59] The statement forwarded by Motilal Nehru to the Labour Party enclosing the cablegram from the President and General Secretary of the Indian National Congress calling for a boycott of the Commission, was taken by that party to mean that Swarajists had no use for any kind of Commission, upon which they were not given a predominating voice.

Dr. Ansari's Reaction

The unity conference had been held and the All-India Congress Committee endorsed its resolution.[60] The Statutory Commission was vehemently criticised at the forty-second session of the Indian National Congress held in Madras in December 1927 under the Presidentship of M.A. Ansari who said: "The manner in which the declared wishes and sentiments of the Indian people have been contemptuously disregarded should serve as an eye-opener even to the most confirmed optimist among us. It is the strongest and the most convincing plea for sinking our differences and closing up of our ranks. Much has been said and written on the Commission, but little as it seems to me which touches the heart of the matter. Keen disappointment and surprise have been expressed at the exclusion of Indians from its personnel. I must confess I do not share any of these feelings.[61] I am neither disappointed nor surprised. This was exactly what I had anticipated. It is not a question whether Indians should participate in its work as members, assessors and advisers. The principle involved is totally different. It is basic and fundamental.[62] No sane or self-respecting Indian can even admit the claim of Great Britain to be the sole judge of measures and time of India's political advance. We alone know our needs and requirements best and ours must be the decisive voice in the determination of our future. It is our inherent and inalienable right. Taking its stand on these principles, the Congress had all long advocated the convening of a Round Table Conference of the representative of India and Great Britain with plenipotentiary powers to decide the bases of the future constitution of India, to be incorporated into an Act of Parliament. It is only on these conditions that Indians can consistently, with national honour and dignity, agree to cooperate. Until Great Britain accepts these terms, the Indian National Congress has no other alternative, but to ask the people of India to treat the Statutory Commission as our Egyptian brothers treated the Milner Mission and leave it severely alone. We can have no part or lot in a Commission which has been appointed in direct defiance of the declared will of the people of India.[63]

'The advent of the Statutory Commission should not divert our attention from the work of framing a constitution for India...A constitution of this nature would remove suspense and doubt from the minds of the different communities regarding their position and status in the political decision of the country. It would rally the different political parties round the Congress and prover of incalculable value in the education of the people in their political rights and privileges, telling them in exact language what they are called upon to fight for. Nor can we underrate its value in strengthening our hands generally in our struggle for the achievement of Swaraj. As soon as the Draft Constitution is ready, the Congress should take steps to call a National convention consisting of representatives of all interests, communities and political parties to consider it and give a final shape.'[64]

Resolution of Congress

As we expected, the Indian National Congress passed the resolution drawn up by the subjects committee declaring a complete boycott of the Statutory Commission practically without a dissentient voice.[65] The Congress called upon the people of India and all Congress organizations in the country to organise public opinion by vigorous propaganda so as to persuade Indians of all shades of political opinion effectively to boycott the Commission.[66] It authorized the working committee to confer with and secure the cooperation wherever possible, of other organisation and parties with a view to make the boycott effective and complete.[67] It called upon non-official members of the Indian legislature and leaders of political parties and communities in any leaders of political parties and communites in India not to give evidence before the Commission and cooperate with it in any manner, public or private, nor attend social functions given to them.[68] It suggested to the non-official members of the legislatures neither to vote for nor to serve on select committees that might be set up in connection with the work of the Commission.[69] Maulana Azad, who also attended the Madras session of the Indian National Congress, thanked God for sending the Simon Commission because it had made Indians realize that they could no longer place trust in the British government, but in themselves, the Hindu in the Muslim and the Muslim in the Hindu.[70]

The resolution on Hindu-Muslim unity was put before the Indian National Congress in two parts, dealing with the political rights, and second, with religious and other rights. Sarojini Naidu moved the resolution. Maulana Azad, seconding the resolution said, that it was a great improvement on the Lucknow Pact and they had attained a great point in as much as Muslims had agreed to accept the principle to joint representation.[71] Besides, Jawaharlal Nehru moved the resolution declaring the goal of Indian people to be complete national independence. These addresses indeed enriched the political literature of the country and made no small contribution to the growth of political consciousness of the nation.

Gandhi on Madras Congress

Interviewed by the *Indian Daily Mail,* Gandhi described the Madras session of the Congress as unique as it laid the foundation of Hindu-Muslim unity. He said, 'This I say, not because of the quality of the resolutions, but because of the manner in which they have been presented and accepted. Pandit Malaviya's happy speech and the still happier response made by the Ali Brothers appeared to me a good augury for the future. I was not privileged to the present, when the scene of Maulana Muhammad Ali, falling in ecstacy at Malaviya's feet and Maulana Shaukat Ali fanning him after he had finished his great speech, took place. But it was described to me by the Congress President. It filled me with great joy and hope. I trust this spirit of cordiality and mutual trust will prove infectious and we shall be able to find such trust amongst the rank and file. Both Mr. Ansari and Mr. Srinivasa Iyengar deserve the gratitude of the nation for this happy event.'[72] In order to form a true estimate of the achievement of the Madras Congress, we have to remember what objects it was expected to achieve. These were in the main three: (a) the restoration of the unity of political parties in India and with it the national character of the Congress itself; (b) a settlement of the Hindu-Muslim problem and (c) the declaration of a boycott of the Simon Commission and the taking of steps for the framing of a Swaraj constitution. The last two of these three objects were, more or less, completely achieved, so far as it was possible for a session of the Congress to achieve them. The resolution on Hindu-Muslim unity was passed not only with a virtual unanimity, but amid scenes of enthusiasm. On the political side, the Muslims reconciled themselves to the substitution of joint for separate electorates, the Hindus, on their side, reconciled themselves to the principle of reservation of seats, the Constitution of Sindh into a separate province, and the grant of reforms to the North-West Frontier Province, to all of which they had always been opposed. The resolution on the Statutory Commission advocated its complete boycott, and laid down the concrete steps that must be taken by the country generally and Congressmen in particular in order to make that boycott effective.

National Liberal Federation

Besides, the meeting of the National Liberal Federation opened at Bombay on December 27, 1927, and was attended by leaders like T.B. Sapru (President), C.Y. Chintamani, Pandit H.N. Kunzru, M.V. Joshi and Sivaswami Iyer. It passed the following resolution: "The National Liberal Federation is strongly of opinion that in official announcement made about the constitution of the Statutory Commission and the functions of the Committee of the Indian Legislatures is unacceptable as it flagrantly denies the right of the Indian people to participate on equal terms in framing the future constitution of the country, and that the Legislatures and Indians throughout the country should have nothing to do with the Commission at any stage or in any form."[73] Thus Sapru's address was seething exposure of the tactics of the British authorities and a vigorous condemnation of their policy. The fervent appeal made by him to all India to give up indulging in party of communal squabbles and mud-throwing at that hour of crisis found a ready response from the people. In such circumstances, there was certainly no room for petty squabbles. The *only regret* of the public was that when like Sapru, Chintamani and a few others whose patriotism and sincerity of purpose had always been above suspicion, should still keep themselves aloof from the Indian National Congress and seek a different platform to give expression to their views.

Reaction of Muslim League

The All-India Muslim League under the Presidentship of Maulvi Muhammed Yakub who was also the Deputy President of Legislative Assembly, met in Calcutta on the

30th December, 1927.[74] It subjects committee unanimously resolved disaffiliating the Punjab League and censuring Mohammed Shafi.[75] It called upon the Muslims of India not to have anything to do with it in any form and at any stage.[76] It may be recalled that similar action was taken ten years ago against the Punjab League in 1917, when Muhammad Shafi happened to be also its President.

The separate communal community representation was originally demanded by the Muslim community on the ground that it was the only means by which their rights as a minority community could be safeguarded. It is indeed a striking commentary upon the nature of that demand that at the moment the provinces, where the system of separate electorates had its strongest supporters, were the Punjab and Bengal, in both of which the Muslims were in a majority in the population. It is interesting to note in this connection that while both Muhammed Yakub, the President of the Muslim League and Ali Imam strongly supported the Principle of joint electorates in their speeches at the league, Mujibur Rehman, the Chairman of the reception committee of the League, as well as Mohammed Shafi, President of the loyalist league at Lahore, held forth on the blessing of separate electorates and expressed their determination not to give them up. This attitude on the part of the Punjab and Bengal Muslims also gave the lie direct to Shafi's ingenious assertion that the separate electorates had nothing to do with the communal tension, as evidenced by the fact that from some years since their introduction in 1910 the two communities had lived in an atmosphere of cooperation and goodwill.[77]

Decision of Khilafat Leaders

The All-India Khilafat Conference assembled under the Presidentship of Maulvi Mahomed Shafi Daudi. Among those present were the Ali Brothers, Yakub Hussain, Abdur Rahman and Maulvi Abdul Bari, S.D. Kitchlew, and Syed Mahmud and other Muslim leaders also sent messages of sympathy. The President pleaded for a boycott of Simon Commission which he characterized as a wanton affront to Indians and emphasised the need for a national constitution.[78]

The subject committee of the Indian Industrial and Commercial Congress met under the Presidentship of the Ibrahim Rahimatulla. A large number of delegates from Bombay, Calcutta, Kanpur and other centres were also present. The most prominent were Dinshaw Petit, Erulkar, Manager of the Scindia Steam Navigation Co., D.P. Khatian and Hirachand Walchand, President of the Indian Merchants Chambers.[79] It passed a resolution boycotting the Statutory Commission and calling upon the constituent bodies likewise to decline to tender evidence before it as a protest against the non-inclusion of Indians on its personnel.[80]

A special session of the C.P. Landlords and Tenants Conference to consider the Statutory Commission was held under the Presidentship of Pandit Govindrao Deshmukh, a prominent zamindar and barrister of Nagpur. The Chairman of the reception committee, Seth Jamnadas, welcomed the delegates and said that it was the duty of land-holders and tenants of the C.P. to declare a boycott of the Statutory Commission. The President, in his speech, described the Constitution of the Statutory Commission and appealed to the audience for the boycott without dissentient voice.[81]

Meeting at Banaras

At the invitation of M.A. Ansari, a conference of the prominent representatives of various political parties was held at Seva Bhavan, Banaras on January 15, 1928. Among those present were Madan Mohan Malaviya, T.B. Sapru, Maulana Azad, J.M. Sen-Gupta, Sachchidanada Sinha, C.Y. Chintamani, Pandit Iqbal Narain Gurtu, Professor K. Telang of the Home Rule League, Dr. B.S. Moonje, J.N. Basu of the Liberal Federation, Calcutta, Kiran Sankar Ray, Secretary, Uttar Pradesh Congress Committee, Babu Gauri Shankar Prasad of the National Liberal Federation, Chaudhri Beharila, representing the depressed classes, Shauaib Qureshi and Pandit Jawaharlal Nehru.[82] It passed the following resolution unanimously.

'This Conference representing various political parties is unanimously of opinion that the Statutory Commission must be left severely alone by the people of India and in pursuance of this resolution, it appealed to the people to observe *hartal* all over India on February 3rd, the day the Simon Commission lands at Bombay and to hold public meetings all over India on that day at 4.30 PM. At this meeting the following resolution was adopted.[83]

'This meeting of the citizens of (here name of place to be mentioned) places on record its condemnation of appointment of Statutory Commission in utter disregard of Indian opinion, and its firm resolve to have nothing to do with that Commission in any form and at any stage of its work. It calls upon all elected members of the Council of State, Legislative Assembly and Legislative Councils and in particular, representatives of this (town, province etc.) to do everything that lies in their power to oppose and prevent formation of a committee of the Legislature in connection with the said Commission.'[84] This meeting also placed on record its opinion that the constitution of India should be framed by Indians and strongly supported the proposals of a special convention to frame such a constitution.[85]

It was indeed the first noticeable thing about an important decision arrived at the conference of various parties at Banaras. Since the secession of the Liberals from the Congress in 1918, a decision of such tremendous importance was reached without any dissentient voice at a meeting representing both wings of the party of self-government.

Resolution of Swarajists

In the C.P. Legislative Council, a resolution by a Swarajist member dealing with 'no confidence' in the Statutory Commission and urging the council not to have anything to do with it, was, after an animated debate, declared carried, no division being claimed by the government.[86] The Swarajist member who had since the commencement of the session stood aloof from the council, entered the chamber after the question time to take part in the debate.[87] Brijlal Biyani, the mover, contended both in the resolution and in his speech that the constitution of the Commission had ignored the national demand for self-determination in the matter of the constitution for India and was an insult to the self-respect of the people; there could be no compromise on the question of boycott as the principle involved was basic.[88]

References

1. Debates, House of Commons, Vol. 210, 1927, pp. 19 ff.
2. Reforms Office, F. 15-17/Miscellaneous 1929.
3. *See* Muhammad Shafi's statement dated November 15, 1927 in this chapter.
4. *Times of India,* November 10, 1927.
5. *Bombay Chronicle,* November 9, and 12, 1927.
6. *Ibid.*
7. *Ibid.*
8. *Ibid.*
9. *Ibid.*
10. Halifax, Birkenhead, Earl of, p. 242.
11. *See* the resolution of the Working Committee of the Indian National Congress in *The Tribune,* November 16, 1927.
12. *See The Tribune* November 15, 1927. Annie Besant announced the intensive programme in South India to inaugurate the propaganda for the boycott of the Statutory Commission. *See Times of India,* November 16, 1627.
13. *Ibid,* November 15, 1927.
14. *Ibid,* November 16, 1927.
15. *Times of India,* December 3, 1927.
16. *Ibid.*
17. *The Tribune,* November 15, 1927 and *Times of India,* November 15, 1927.
18. Home-Public, F. 112, 1928. and *Bombay Chronicle,* November 9, 1927.
19. *The Tribune,* November 16, 1927.
20. *Bombay Chronicle,* November 18 and 19, 1927 and *Times of India,* November 18 and 19, 1927.
21. *The Tribune,* November 11, 1927.
22. *The Tribune,* November 20, 1927.
23. *The Tribune,* November 22, 1927.
24. Coatman, J., *India in 1927-28, p. 58* and *The Tribune,* January 13, 1928.
25. *Times of India,* December 21, 1927.
26. *Ibid.*
27. *The Tribune,* November 15, 1927 and *Times of India,* November 15, 1927.
28. *The Tribune, and Time of India,* November 15, 1927.
29. *Ibid.*

30. *Ibid,* December 6, 1927.
31. Lalaji sent a cable to Colonel Wedgwood: 'No change in the scheme of Commission acceptable unless and equal number of non-official Indians are appointed on equal status.' *See Times of India,* November 22, 1927. Wedgwood, in the course of a letter to Lalaji, counselled courage and called petitioning a dirty game. *See Times of India,* December 15, 1927.
32. *The Tribune,* November 18, 1927.
33. Home-Public, F.112, 1928.
34. *The Tribune,* January 3, 1928.
35. *Ibid.*
36. *The Tribune,* January 3, 1928.
37. *Ibid,* January 12, 1928.
38. *The Hindu,* November 16, 1927.
39. *Ibid.*
40. *The Tribune,* November 18, 1927.
41. *Leader,* November 9, 1927.
42. *Bombay Chronicle,* November 9, 1927.
43. *Amrita Bazar Patrika,* November 9, 1927.
44. *National Herald,* November 9, 1927.
45. *Times of India,* November 12, 1927.
46. *Ibid,* November 17, 1927.
47. *The Tribune,* December 6, 1927.
48. *Bombay Chronicle,* December 6, 1927.
49. *Ibid.*
50. *Times of India,* December 24, 1927.
51. *The Tribune,* December 18, 1927.
52. *Ibid,* December 28, 1927.
53. *Ibid.*
54. *Ibid,* December 17, 1927.
55. Quoted in *Times of India,* November 26, 1927. At this time, George Lansubury in an article in the *Daily Herald,* dealing with the criticism of the Labour Party's decision as regards the Statutory Commission declared that the Labour Party was participating because it believed that it would thus serve the best interest of the masses of India. He further said that the Labour movement asked Indians of the all sects and creeds to meet the commission in a broad and generous spirit. He made it clear that a boycott would not help and pleaded for cooperation on terms of mutual respect and equality. For reference see *Times of India,* November 26, 1927.
56. *The Tribune,* November 22, 1927.
57. *Ibid.*
58. Sitaramayya, P., *History of Indian National Congress,* Vol. II, p. 317.

59. *See* text of 42nd session of Indian National Congress.
60. *Ibid.*
61. *See* Text of 42nd session of Indian National Congress.
62. *Ibid.*
63. *Ibid.*
64. *See* Text of 42nd session of Indian National Congress.
65. *Ibid.*
66. *Ibid.*
67. *Ibid.*
68. *The Tribune,* December 30, 1927.
69. *Ibid.*
70. *The Tribune,* January 1, 1928.
71. Mitra, H.N., *op. cit.,* Vol. II, 1927, pp. 421-35 and *Times of India,* December 29, and December 30, 1927.
72. The meeting was attended by prominent leaders like Annie Besant, Sarojini Naidu, Graham Pole, T.C. Goswami, S.C. Mitter and N.R. Sarkar. See *Times of India,* January 2, and January 3, 1928 and *Bombay Chronicle,* January 2, 1928.
73. *Bombay Chronicle,* January 2, 1928.
74. *Ibid.*
75. *Ibid,,* January 2, 1928.
76. *The Tribune,* December 27, 1927.
77. *The Tribune,* December 31, 1927.
78. *Ibid.*
79. *Ibid.*
80. *Times of India* January 17, 1928.
81. *Ibid,* January 17, 1928.
82. *Ibid.*
83. *Ibid.*
84. *The Tribune,* January 22, 1928.
85. *Ibid.*
86. *Ibid.*
87. *Ibid,* January 24, 1928.
88. Fischer, Louis, *Mahatma Gandhi,* p. 275.

4

Preliminary Survey and Reaction

The Statutory Commission, headed by John Simon, left for India on January 19, 1928 to undertake a preliminary survey of Indian problems.[1] When the S.S. *Rawalpindi* which brought the Commission to Bombay, came alongside the wharf, a posse of demonstrators, led by K.F. Nariman, gathered at the gate with placards inscribed, 'Simon go back,' 'No representation no Commission,' '*Swaraj* is our birth-right,' 'Down with the British Imperialism.'[2] A party of student-demonstrators also assembled near the gate of the Alexandra Docks.[3] They raised slogans against the Commission and the police assaulted them and dispersed them.[4] Interviewed by a representative of the Associated Press, John Simon made the following statement: 'We have made a smooth and pleasant voyage, and my colleagues and I set foot in India deeply impressed with the responsibility of our task, and resolved to devote all our energy and goodwill to its discharge. Constitutionally, progress in India depends on the friendly and sincere cooperation of Indian and British representatives; but it is manifest that there exists at the moment in some quarters widespread misunderstanding of what the Commission sets out to do, and uncertainty as to the methods it proposes to employ. We shall make without delay to remove these misapprehensions and after we reach Delhi and have become better acquainted with the actual situation, we intend to make a statement as to our proposed procedure which should leave no ground for the suspicions which have unfortunately arisen. We mean to take the fullest advantage of the opportunities open to us for consultation with Indian representatives who are willing to meet both during this preliminary visit and when we return for a longer tour in October.'[5]

Greeting with Hartal

The arrival of the Commission was greeted with *hartals* and demonstrations all over India. In Delhi, all business houses, with the exception of restaurants and vegetable shops, were closed. Everything looked quiet, but the vehicular traffic, however, remained undisturbed. In Calcutta, *hartal* was observed, and all Hindu shops were closed and no business was transacted at the share and jute markets. Tramcars and tramway buses owned by Muslims were in operation under police guard. Attempts were, however, made by some boycotters to stop tramcars, but they were not successful. About fifty volunteers were arrested on the charge of obstruction. The *hartal* also affected proceedings of law courts in the city. About thirty per cent of the lawyers attended the High Court. Among the Swarajist barristers, who had cases and yet did not attend the courts, were J.M. Sen Gupta and Subhas Chandra Bose.[6]

In Bombay, in European business quarters, many shops were open. But in the Indian business quarters, business was practically at a stand-still. No business was done in the share, bullion, cotton-seeds and piece goods markets. Excepting a mill here and there, all cotton mill-workers came out in a procession through the northern parts of the town led by Spratt and other labour leaders. They were joined by workers of the G.I.P. Matunga workshop. The B.B. and C.I. workshops were partly working. At Oras Road, a labour meeting was held at which the effigies of Stanley Baldwin, Lord Birkenhead, John Simon and Ramsay MacDonald were burnt. The feelings of resentment were echoed by leaders like Nariman and Mrs. Sarojini Naidu at a meeting of students at the Cowasji Jehangir Hall. A procession of nearly fifty thousand people waving black flags and banners marched through the Hornby Road, where a monster meeting was held. Chimanlal Setalvad presided. Among the prominent speakers were Pheroze Sethna, Manmohandas

Ramji, Bhulabhai Desai, B.G. Horniman, K.F. Nariman, Shaukat Ali and Mrs. Sarojini Naidu. A resolution reiterating the decision to have nothing to do with the Commission in any shape or at any stage, and against the appointment of the legislative committees was unanimously adopted.[7]

Hartal was succesfully observed in Madras on the call of the local leaders. Riotous scenes were, however, enacted before Harisons Caterers, on the Broadway, when the excited crowd stoned the premises, broke glass panes and demanded closure of their business. The Harisons was eventually closed. The tram service was dislocated. The number of persons injured was seventeen, of whom one died in hospital.[8]

In all the fourteen districts of Hindustan Central Provinces, a complete and peaceful *hartal* was observed, not in their headquarters alone, but in all their important centres throughout, and the day ended with huge public meetings in which resolutions prescribed were read and passed.[9] A huge protest meeting, presided over by Duni Chand, was addressed by Dr. Satyapal, Dr. Mohammed Alam, Sardul Singh Caveeshar, M. Zafar Ali Khan, Maulana Abdul Qadir of Kasur, and Amar Singh Jhabbal, President of the Punjab Pradesh Congress Committee. Maulana Abdul Qadir of Kasur moved the following resolution.[10] 'This meeting of the citizens of Lahore places on record its condemnation of the appointment of the Statutory Commission in utter disregard of Indian opinion and its firm resolve to have nothing to do with that Commission in any form or at any stage of its work. It calls upon all elected members of the Council of States, the Legislative Assembly and the Legislative Council and in particular the representatives of this city, to do everything in their power to oppose and prevent formation of a Committee of the Legislature in connection with the said Commission. 'This meeting places on record its opinion that the Constitution of India should be framed by India and strongly supports the proposal of a special convention to frame such a constitution.'

There was complete *hartal* in Peshawar. A joint meeting

of Hindus, Muslims and Sikhs was held in Islamia Club, where Abdul Ghaffar Khan presided. Resolution regarding the boycott of the Statutory Commission and the frontier reforms were unanimously adopted.[11]

The long and anxiously awaited 3rd February had come and gone. The *hartal* was neither an unqualified success everywhere as its organizers had desired, nor a failure as those opposed to it were anxious to make it. At some places, it was more or less a complete success; at some places it was only partial. Any way, it is not necessary to attach any exaggerated importance either to the success that had attended *hartal* in most places or partial success at other places; but there had been no disorder or lawlessness except in Madras. What was essential to the successful inauguration of the boycott movement was not the *hartal*, as a complete and a nation-wide *hartal* would undoubtedly have been a demonstration of national resentment, but the public meetings of protest. In fact, no part of the country was found wanting. In every province, and at all important places, public meetings were held to condemn the appointment of the Commission, to express complete want of confidence in it, and to declare India's solemn and unalterable resolve to have nothing to do with it in any form or at any stage.

John Simon and his colleagues arrived in Delhi on February 4. They were invited to confer with Lord Irwin at the Viceregal Lodge. The conference consisted of the Viceroy; the Commander-in-Chief, William Birdwood; the Finance Member, Basil Blackett; the Home Member, James Crerar; the Commerce Member, George Rainy; and the Indian members of the Viceroy's council: Muhammad Habibullah, S.R. Das and Bhupendra Nath Mitra. The main suggestion briefly stated in this conference was that the material which the Government of India and the Provincial Government has prepared for the Commission, should come before a Joint Free Conference over which John Simon would preside, consisting of the six British Commissioners and a corresponding body of representatives chosen by the Indian legislatures, both central and provincial.[12]

Simon to Viceroy

Meanwhile, John Simon wrote a letter to the Viceroy in which he clarified various points. He stated that the Government of India and the local governments had been engaged in preparing the material which they wished to present before the Commission. Such a material should come before a Joint Free Conference, over which he whould preside, alongwith his colleagues and the corresponding body of representatives chosen by the Indian legislatures. The Houses of the central legislature should be invited to choose from their non-official members, a joint committee which might conveniently be seven in number, and that each local legislative council should be asked to constitute a similar body. In a provincial members; but in order that the Central Joint Committee might not have a partial view of the material put before it, it was thought better, if arrangements could be arrived at in a way which would enable its members or some of them to be present as an additional element at provincial sittings. He wished that the Indian side of the joint conference should include, on appropriate occasions, those who were in a position to speak for the provincial councils, just as the joint committee would speak for the central legislatures. Thus their Indian counterpart should be truly representative in character. Besides each side of the conference would require, from time to time, to meet by itself. The evidence from public and representative bodies and from individuals should be given to the conference as a whole, just as evidence presented by or on behalf of the various governments would.[13]

Function of the Commission

John Simon also mentioned the 'true function' of the Statutory Commission. He stated, that it was in no sense, as instrument either of the Government of India or of the British Government, but it entered on the duty laid upon it by the King-Emperor as a completely independent and unfettered body, composed of Members of Parliament who would approach the Indian legislators as colleagues. It was not an executive or legislative body authorised to pronounce decisions about the future Government of India. It was only authorised to report and make recommendations; and in this report, the Commission desired to include a 'faithful account' of the opinions and aspirations prevalent in India and of the proposals for Constitutional Reform so far as those were placed before the Commission. The Commission would report to the authority by which it had been constituted, just as (if the conference was set up) the joint committee would be entitled to report its conclusions to the central legislature. All these documents would be prepared and presented simultaneously. The document emanating from the joint committee and presented to the central legislature, could be forwarded to and made available for the British Parliament. But if the Indian joint committee would prefer it, the Commission would make its report an annexe to its own document, so that both might be presented to the King-Emperor and made public at the same moment.[14] The Chairman made it quite clear that their present visit was preliminary and the sitting of the Joint Free Conference, if it was set up, would not begin till October, 1928; but they would make public their suggestion at once, not only to clear the air, but to show themselves available for any conference about any matter of procedure which this statement did not adequately cover.[15]

Viceroy's Reply

The Viceroy gave the following brief reply, of course, full of assurance, to this letter: 'I have received your letter of the 6th February outlining the procedure which your Commission proposes to adopt. I can assure you, my government will be glad at all stages to give your Commission every assistance they require in carrying out their proposal."[16]

It may be said that within the limits to which it was confined, John Simon's statement was a material improvement upon everything that had been said so far, whether by the Viceroy in India or by the Secretary of State or other authorities in England. In two important respects, it certainly changed the procedure, laid down for the Commission, for the better. In spite of their stimulated indignation at the statement made by Indian leaders that the committees of legislatures in India would be no better than witnesses before the Commission, the authorities, whether in England or India, had said nothing so far to indicate that they would be anything else or anything better. On the contrary, Lord Birkenhead had clearly stated that the business of the committees of legislatures would be to confront the Commission with their proposals which, after examination, would be either accepted or rejected, presumably by the Commission itself—a statement which, if anything, definitely stamped upon the committees the character of witnesses. John Simon, changed all that. For the first time, India was told that these committees would, as a rule, have the opportunity and be able to scrutinize and elucidate from the Indian point of view, and on free and equal terms, all the evidence that was placed before the Commission, whether by government or by public bodies or by individuals; and that if certain cases, which might be exceptional, the Commission would sit separately to receive testimony, it would not only state the reasons for that procedure to the Indian committee, but would give equal liberty to the. Indian committee itself to sit separately in similar cases when it liked.

Similarly, in the matter of report, it had been stated with great emphasis that the Indian committee would not be permitted to write a separate report, or at any rate to present it to Parliament. But John Simon stated that it would not only be able to write a separate report, but both reports would be simultaneously published. As to the authority, the Indian report was to be presented to the Indian legislature and through it to Parliament or if the committee preferred it, be annexed to the Commission's own report and presented to His Majesty. But it did not in any way alter the position so far as the question of India's cooperating or non-cooperating was concerned. The decision to non-cooperate with the Commission was based not on the ground of the defective procedure laid down for the Commission, but on grounds of fundamental principle, and those grounds remained entirely unaffected by John Simon's statement. India wanted one of two things—either a Round Table

Conference or a Commission so constituted as to be a possible substitute for such a conference. Instead, it had been given an all-British Commission, which expressed its readiness to treat the committees of legislatures in India as bodies of equal authority. It was in John Simon's power to confer that authority on the Indian committees which had been conferred upon him and his colleagues by the King-in-Parliament. In reality, the committees of Indian legislatures would, when appointed, enjoy such powers as they would have, under this statement, by the sufferance of the Commission, while it owed its own powers to the pleasure of the highest official authority. This one fact, if nothing else, would definitely fix upon the Indian committees the stamp and character of inferiority. At best they would have the delegated status of coopted and unequal members. Besides, there remained the important question of self-determination. India which wished to be the master in its own affairs, could not possibly play second fiddle in a matter concerning it more vitally than other to a purely British commission. What it wanted was the power to frame its own constitution, which the British Parliament might have the satisfaction of passing, but which, as in other similar cases, must in the main correspond to India's own will.

Leader's Views

Meanwhile, the leaders of all political parties including Dr. M.A. Ansari, Srinivasa Iyengar, Maulana Azad, Maulana Muhammad Ali, Lala Lajpat Rai, Madan Mohan Malaviya, M.R. Jayakar, N.C. Kelkar, M.A. Jinnah, PurushottamDas, Maulvi Muhammad Yakub and Raja Ghaznafar Ali gave a joint statement.[17] 'We have most carefully considered the line of procedure indicated in the statement of Sir John Simon issued today; but our objection to the Commission as constituted and the scheme as announced are based on principles which remain unaffected by it. In the circumstances, we must adhere to our decision that we cannot have anything to do with the Commission at any stage or in any form.'

Saprus Reaction

Interviewed by a press representative in connection with Simon's statement, Tej Bahadur Sapru said, 'It would make no converts to Sir John Simon's mission out of those who care more for substance than for the form. Sir John Simon has tried to put up a specious case of equal opportunities for the Indian Committees, but it is only specious and plausible. In his mind, the statement and the Commission does not become a Joint Free Conference so as to attract the Swarajists demanding a Round Table Conference. Nor does it alter the character of the Commission so as to make it acceptable to the Liberals. I doubt very much whether even the Responsivists will find in it the realization of their idea of equality. I personally think, that the only course open to us now is to maintain the attitude of dignified aloofness from the Commission and to conserve our energy and time for a constructive scheme of our own, which we should place before the country and round which we should rally the largest amount of public opinion in India. The progressive element in the Assembly and Councils should now consolidate their position to meet the situation effectively. It is to my mind a first class constitutional issue which must be fought out on strictly constitutional lines. I have no doubt, some day or other, notwithstanding the anger which our attitude has provoked in certain quarters, the blunder which has been committed, will be realized. Our critics may similarly charge us with blunder, but we can leave the settlement of the controversy to the future in the full confidence that we have a just and a strong case. I see no reason to alter my opinion or to advise my party to alter their attitude.'

At this point of Time

Meanwhile, the working committee of the Indian National Congress was engaged at Dr. Ansari's residence.[18] A number of members of the Congress party in the Assembly present during the discussion of the Congress resolution in regard to work in councils. After hearing them, the committee drafted certain instructions for the guidance of the councils and Assembly members. These instructions were meant to remove doubts in regard to interpretation of the Congress resolution and to lay down the lines which the Congress party members should follow. The committee passed the following resolution regarding *hartal*. 'The Committee congratulates the country on the successful *hartal* observed and demonstrations and protests made all over India against the Statutory Commission on the day of its arrival. The Committee regrets there were some disturbances in connection with the *hartals* at Madras and Calcutta, and that the police opened fire on the crowd in Madras which resulted in the death of one person and injuries to other.[19]

The Committee notes with regret that these disturbances were due to the conduct of those who were determined to defeat the boycott, and that at several places, those in authority and their supporters brough undue pressure to bear upon the people not to observe the *hartal*.[20] The Committee strongly condemns the orders issued under section 144 Cr. P.C. in Madras prohibiting meetings, demonstrations and propaganda for *hartal* which were served on members of the Boycott Propaganda Committee, as arbitrary and unwarranted and condemns also the action of government in having issued these orders in a vindictive spirit and at the instance of interested parties.'

Reaction of Lala Lajpat Rai

Regarding the appointment of the Statutory Commission. Lajpat Rai stated that he had no faith in the *bona fides* of the government or of the people who had appointed the Commission. He opined that the greatest disqualifications of the Commissioners were their ignorance of India, Indian history and Indian politics. He observed that the problem of India was so vast and complicated that if the 'gods were to descend from the heaven, they cannot master it in such a short time as is at the disposal of the Commission.' He was firm of the conviction that the problem of India was not for Commissions, it must be tackled by representative men, both from England and India in a spirit of conciliation and negotiation. He further stated, 'We know that we are hanging over a precipice and any moment an avalanche might overtake us and bury us. We know all that. But knowing all that, we refuse to accept the crumbs they want to throw to us. We are not dogs. We shall not accept the crumbs. We shall stick to our attitude and go down with honour and self-respect.'[22]

He moved a resolution:

'This Assembly recommends to the Governor-General-in-Council to inform His Majesty's Government that the present constitution and scheme of the Statutory Commission are wholly unacceptable to this House and that this House will, therefore, have nothing to do with the Commission at any stage and in any form. M.A. Jinnah supported the arguments put forward by Lala Lajpat Rai. He levelled trenchant criticism against the British government's stand and policy. 'Please do not mislead us. The whole question before you is this. Do you wish any decent party, any self-respecting man, to work with you, then be frank, be honest and tell us plainly, 'You have not got equal status, you have not got power in the present Constitution of the Commission.'[23]

S. Srinivasa Iyengar said, "If you vote for the Commission and if you vote for the Government, you undoubtedly vote for your own downfall. You vote for your own shame and humiliation...Therefore, Sir, I once more implore every member of the House to look into these things patriotically and to vote for the motion which Lala Lajpat Rai has moved in this House not to cooperate with this Commission at any stage and in any form.'[24] Motilal Nehru said, 'We take our stand upon the broad principle that Parliament and the British public and the British government have no shadow of a right to force a constitution upon us against our own will...But when you talk of giving even a measure of freedom to the subject nation, it is hypocrisy, it is dishonesty, to rely upon laws to which that people were no parties...Now, Sir, Congress stands to-day for complete independence.'[25] It was an indictment which the popular leaders drew against those responsible for the appointment of the Statutory Commission.

View of James Crerar

James Crerar, winding up the debate, said that the Commission was appointed under King's orders; and, when it was appointed that body was master of its own procedure. He, therefore, repelled any criticism that the government of India was responsible for the procedure. He advised M.A. Jinnah to carry his realism further and obtain the best possible results for his clients. He further stated that it was a mistake to suppose that the present enquiry concerned the political parties and the government but it related to the country and the whole population of India.[26] When the motion was put to vote, it was adopted and won by a majority of seven votes, viz. 66 in favour and 59 against the motion.[27]

The historic defeat inflicted on the government by the combined forces of popular parties was more remarkable because fourteen elected Muslim members were against the Statutory Commission, and only twelve voted with the government, thus giving a 'crushing' reply to Lord Birkenhead who had pictured millions of Muslims going on their knees before the Commission. The conclusion followed logically from the premises. India must boycott the Commission, and for that action on its part the responsibility must rest solely with the government.

Soon thereafter, the prominent leaders like Motilal Nehru, S. Iyengar, Pandit Madan Mohan Malaviya, M.A. Jinnah, Lala Lajpat Rai and Purshotamdas appealed to the Legislative Councils of the U.P., Bengal, Bombay, Punjab, Bihar and Assam to follow the example of the Legislative Assembly and of the C.P. and Madras.[28] They also appealed to the leading public men of all parties and to all political organizations in the country to unite together in settling sectional or communal differences, to prepare a draft constitution with the maximum amount of agreement and to adopt it at a convention, and to work for its establishment.[29]

Meanwhile, John Simon and his colleagues were busy drawing up their programme confidentially, for they wished to undertake much of their tour of learning incognito as far as possible.[30]

Halt at Calcutta and Boycott

Their next destination was Calcutta. The Government of India and the India Office had originally decided that the Commission should not visit Bengal on this occasion. But Stanley Jackson strongly urged John Simon to alter this decision, and stated that 'if we failed to visit Calcutta, not only would we alienate our friends, but we should be accused by our enemies of faint-heartedness.'[31] The Viceroy supported the Governor of Bengal's advice.

On its arrival, the Commission was welcomed at Howrah station on *February 20, 1928* by officials and non-officials, including representatives of the Marwari Association, the Indian Association, the Central National Mohammedan Association, the Anglo-Indian and Domiciled European Association and the Bengal Central Royots Association. The platform gates were locked and only those who had tickets were allowed admittance to the platform. Elaborate police arrangements were made both at the platform and outside the station premises. There was no hostile demonstration except a solitary 'go back, Simon.'[32]

The Chairman received press representatives at Government House along with Viscount Burnham and Clement Attlee. In this conference, he reviewed the Commission's activities in Delhi, where they had seen members of both Houses of Central Legislature besides representatives of Muslim, Hindu and Anglo-Indian communities as well as the depressed classes who pointed out various aspects of the problem they wished the Commission to investigate. Discussing the Indian wing of the Commission, he said, 'If we can get our Indian colleagues without too much delay coming into joint conference, then we shall have their help, when we come back in October, and set to work on the basis of the memoranda and examine witnesses. If the Commission had that sort of comradeship, their Indian colleagues present at the Conference would have an opportunity of examining statements and elucidating intricate matters. They would also be able to see that all points of view were placed before the Commission who were as much interested in knowing one's viewpoint as any other.'

As a protest against what was described 'outrage on India's national self-respect' by the appointment of the Simon Commission, the Bengal Provincial Congress Committee organized demonstrations in the form of processions in south and north Calcutta and meetings in public parks. Volunteers with banners saying, 'Go back Simon' and 'Boycott foreign-goods,' paraded the main thoroughfares of the city.[46] In the evening, a well-attended public meeting was held at Shraddhanand Park under the Presidentship of P.C. Ray who urged the people to take to charkha and wear swadeshi clothes. J.M. Sen Gupta, the Mayor of Calcutta, said that a general boycott of foreign goods, particularly of foreign cloth, was an appropriate answer to Lord Birkenhead's speech. Subhash Chandra Bose said that if a Commission, composed of Indians only, similar to the Simon Commission, was sent to England to shape the destiny of the British people, they would have protested as Indians were doing, because the British knew very well, that they were the sole judges in matters concerning their own constitution. He added that they had no weapons, arms or ammunitions, but they had a far greater weapon and it was, that they could make the British people starve by creating an economic blockade. He appealed to the people to enlist at least ten thousand volunteers to carry on the agitation for the attainment of *Swaraj*.[47]

It is quite evident that, the appointment of a purely Parliamentary Commission and its advent so far after the first announcement served only as a 'magic wand' to rouse the nation. All thoughts of the Commission were being gradually replaced by thoughts of freedom, swadeshi, self-reliance and power. The declaration of the boycott of the foreign goods, particularly of British goods, had been hailed in all quarters, so far as it could be judged from the mamoth meetings that were being daily held all over the city to bring home to the people the necessity of an economic boycott. One significant feature of this movement was that the organisers had drawn up a programme of work which had the least chance of a clash with the police. They had arranged to make house to house visits throughout the city, enlist Congress members and introduce *swadeshi* cloth into each and every home. In fact, Subhash Chandra Bose had succeeded in enrolling a large number of volunteers to carry out the work. The movement was rapidly spreading into the country-side and reports of boycott meeting were daily pouring in from the *mufussil.*

Reaction in South

Now the Commission started on its southern tour. At Bezwada, it was accorded a cold reception. The boycott resolutions of the Bezwada municipal council and taluk board were sent by special peons to be conveyed to John Simon at the railway station. On February 23, when it arrived at Guntur by a special train, it was received by some officials and non-officials, headed by the Collector of the district. There was no hostile demonstration at the station. But the town observed *hartal.*[48] After Guntur, Madras, the members of the Commission reached Madras *on February 28.* They drove straight to the Government House, where Lord and Lady Goshen who appeared optimistic with regard to the situation, held a meeting of the executive in the garden, on the day of their arrival, to meet the Commission. Thereafter, a deputation of leading non-party Muslims consisting of retired government officials and representatives of the educational and charitable institutions met the Commission. The members of the Commission were invited by the President of the Madras Legislative Council to witness its proceedings. After the adjournment of the House, they were taken round the Chamber library and committee rooms by the Chief Secretary and were introduced to Justice and Council nationalist parties, including the Raja of Panagal, and A. Patro. John Simon also visited the High Court, Madras, when a full Bench was hearing an income tax case. He was offered a special seat on the bench and afterwards taken round the High Court House by the Registrar and Law officials. Besides, the Commissioners had a busy day visiting a number of educational institutions in the city. Burnham and Lane-Fox visited the Ramakrishna Students

Home, Myalapore, the individual School and the Presidency College. They made enquiries from the Principal as to the proportion of Brahman and non-Brahman students.[49] The Commission, however, could not escape the fury of the local public. The procession carrying black flags and banners paraded from George Town to Triplicane beach, where the meeting was held in the evening. *Dr. Varadarajulu Naidu* and other speakers exhorted the people to keep up the boycott campaign.[50]

The next halt of the Commission way at Tanjore on March 3. Consistent with her tradition as 'Garden of South India', Tanjore wore a picturesque appearance on its arrival. The representative body which welcomed the Commissioners on arrival, included the Chairman of the Tanjore municipal committee, the President of the Tanjore district board, the President of the Tanjore taluk board and responsible citizens from all sections of the population. The attempt to adjourn the meeting of the district board by way of protest against the arrival of the Statutory Commission was defeated, only seven hands being held up in its favour. The municipal council extended its welcome to the Commission without any dissentient voice.

A quiet *hartal* was observed considerable section of Indian business quarters.The Congress volunteers holding national and black flags were seen about in a procession singing national songs, and crying, 'Simon, go back.'[51]

The Simon Commission reached Madura on March 5 and a warm reception was accorded to it by the leading zamindars and citizens of the town, besides a large number of municipal councillors and district board members. The Commission motored to the district board to attend its meeting. It also granted interviews to representative bodies and organizations including Christian deputation which urged the scrapping of separate electorates, but preferred to have seats reserved for the minority communities.

Crowds paraded through the principal thoroughfare, waving flags, shouting, 'Simon, go back.' Approaches to the municipal hall were besieged by a large crowd comprising both friendly and hostile sections, when the Commission visited the municipal meeting. R.S. Naidu, the municipal Chairman, welcomed the Commissioners and expressed his willingness to cooperae with them in their investigations. He claimed partnership for India within the Empire and added that the Indians would be a 'source of help to the Expire.' L.K. Tulsiram, M.L.C., a Swarajist, claiming to represent artisans and labourers, ridiculed the welcome as artifical in which they would not participate. He moved the adjournment of the House and was seconded by Ramnath Iyer. Later on, both left the hall in protest. John Simon, thanking the House, said that he had come from the country where they appreciated the difference of opinion. He appealed for Indian cooperation and goodwill during his findings in India.[52]

Commission Reaches Lahore and Visits to Towns of Punjab

Prior to its arrival at Lahore on 10th.March there a students' meeting in the Bradlaugh Hall in tense atmosphere. Sardar Kharak Singh, a prominent leader of the Punjab, exhorted the audience to stand by the country. There were prolonged shouts of Bandemataram when he said, 'What do I care for section 144', 'Tonight is the night of trial. Let us not be found wanting.' The local Congress committee organised a black flag procession which started from Langamandi led by Karak Singh. The procession was followed by the mounted police. Akalis with black turbans, Congress volunteers from Amritsar and local Congress volunteers—Hindus, and Muslims, formed the vanguard. They were singing national songs and were shouting, 'Simon, go back.' As the demonstrators passed through the bazars, their ranks were further strengthened and when they reached the railway station, they became a 'mass of humanity.'[53] Long before the arrival of the train, the precincts of the railway station and all approaches to it were closely guarded by the police. The platform was closed to the public, and only those who had the invitation cards', were admitted in after a close scrutiny. At the station-platform were present ministers of the Punjab government. Some members of the Punjab Legislative Council and

Municipal Corporation, a number of title-holders, loyalists and dignitaries and those who had been specially invited to make up the show of a cordial reception to the Commission. The D.I.G. Police, of Lahore Range, the Deputy Commissioner, the A.D.M. and many C.I.D. officers were present regulating the traffick and pushing back the surging crowd which had joined the demonstrators and was persistently shouting, 'Simon, go back.' And whenever a car carrying those who were proceeding to the platform to welcome the Commission, passed through the road, loud cries of 'shame, shame' cleft the welkin.[54]

At Lahore, the Commissioners interviewed the members of the Legislative Council in the council chamber. They also received various deputations, including one from the martial races of the Punjab.[55]

A party of the Simon Commission consisting of John Simon, Lord and Lady Strathcona and Colonel Lane-Fox arrived at Lyallpur by a special train on March 15. A demonstration was organised by the boycott committee here. As each car passed by the Club Road the demonstrators with black flags and placards shouted, 'Simon, go back,' and cried, 'Shame on those who passed by that road in cars or *gharies*.' There were many Akalis amongst the demonstrators, each of whom carried a placard, 'Simon, go back. We have self-respect.'[56] 'Lyallpur has to forgotten Martial Law Regime,' 'Manufactured reception is not the index of the peoples' heart, 'Beware lest bureaucracy should swallow you.' At Lyallpur, the members of the Commission visited a number of villages, and also schools. They also attended a meeting of the district board, where John Simon addresed the members. The business of the meeting continued for about an hour and the Simon party watched the proceedings with interest.[57]

Ferozepur, it met the deputations from the district board, municipal board and depressed classes. Attlee and Cadogan paid a visit to Gurdaspur, and Simon, Lane-Fox and Strathcona visited Gujranwala. John Simon, in the course of an interview to press representatives at Lahore, said that the Commission had formed no conclusion as yet in respect of its work. The detailed programme of the Commission's work, and the main work to be done, when it returned in October, was to be settled during the next few days in Delhi at a conference to which each of the nine provinces would send a special representative so that the October programme might be arranged to suit every one's Convenience.[58]

Meanwhile, John Simon, Fox and Cadogan left for Delhi and Lord Burnham, Lord and Lady Strathcona and Major Attlee, accompanied by Arthur Peel, Assistant Secretary and Macpherson, private Secretary to John Simon arrived at Rawalpindi on March 23. They were received at the railway platform by Gurbaksh Singh Bedi, Malik Mohan Singh, President of the Rawalpindi municipal committee, Sardar Mohan Singh, Honorary Magistrate, Seth Adamji, Vice-President of the municipal committee and a number of Hindus, Muslims and Sikhs of the division. Gurbaksh Singh Bedi read an address in Urdu which was translated in English by Bakshi Dalip Singh. Lord Burnham replying to the address thanked all those present on the platform for the generous welcome accorded to them on the occasion of their first visit to Rawalpindi division.

Black Flags at Rawalpindi

But there was resentment in the patriotic section of Indian community which it showed on the arrival of the Commission at Rawalpindi. The local Congress committee arranged a procession with black flags with a view to express public resentment. But the procession was stopped by the police who after dispersing the same with force, arrested about twenty-five persons including the President of the Congress Committee. The police arrested, among others, Sardar Gopal Singh, propaganda Secretary of the P.P.C.C., Lala Kanshi Ram Sethi, President of the Rawalpindi Congress Committee, Lala Ram Nath, Tirath Ram Bali, Lala Jankinath Anand of Seva Samiti and Lala Mangal Sain Marwaha of the municipal committee.[59]

Peshawar Border Areas Visit

Thereafter, the Commission left for Peshawar. To express the anger and resentment against it, a meeting was held in the Isamia Club under the Presidentship of Dr. C.C. Ghosh, President of the Congress Committee. The following resolution was proposed and passed unanimously.

'This meeting of the inhabitants of Peshawar declares that no other country or nation has got the right to decide the fate of India, and, expressing its lack of confidence in the Simon Commission, considers its appointment as an extreme insult to India and does not consider those persons as their representatives who cooperate with it on account of their selfish and slavish mentality.' The resolution was proposed by Ala Bakhsh and seconded by Aligul Khan. Besides, it declared that Swaraj was the birth-right of every Indian; and that the reforms were not more than a sham show. It recorded its strong protest against the unjust and unwise policy of the government in depriving the Frontier Province even of such a 'sham thing,' and demanded the immediate introduction of complete reforms, as were in force in the rest of India, in the Frontier Province. Besides, a procession of the Khilafat volunteers and the public went about the city with black flags as a protest against the Simon Commission.[60]

The members of the Commission also visited Kyber, Kohat and Malakand and met a few delegations of the Maliks, Khans and Chieftains. While Muslims were generally in favour of the introduction of reforms in the North-West Frontier Province, Hindus advocated that the executive should be made as strong as possible.

Meanwhile, John Simon and his two colleagues, Lane Fox and Edward Cadogan, gave up the fetish of the position occupied by them in the warrant of precedence and called on V.J. Patel, and in return they received an invitation to attend the sitting of the Assembly. The worst feature was that the Assembly was at its poorest as John Simon and his two colleagues were in the House at a time when it was the dullest because none of the party leader was present, and the Swaraj party walked out after the election of the committees. Thus, probably, the feeling of John Simon and his colleagues was that they had visited 'India's Parliament,' and could speak authoritatively on its working.

Departure for England

The members of the Commission left for Bombay on March 29 in order to proceed to England. John Simon addressed a letter[61] to Viceroy a day earlier with the intention of clearing two points which arose during his provincial tours, but more for the purpose, it seemed, of 'disabusing' the public mind from some reports circulated by a press agency that the government was thinking of nominating a committee to sit with the Commission.

'It is now seven weeks since the Indian Statutory Commission made public by means of my letter addressed to you on February 6, the outline of the scheme for conducting the enquiry which the Commission will undertake next October, by the method of a Joint Free Conference of which Indian Committees would form one wing while the Commissioner would form the other. In the interval, the scheme proposed has been accepted as a basis for cooperation by the Council of State and by the Legislative Assembly and the U.P. Council have by small majorities adopted resolution on the contrary.

'Other Legislative bodies in India are likely to be considering the matter before the Commission returns, and we think that it would be useful to clear up two points of possible ambiguity which have been brought to our notice in the provinces in the course of our preliminary visit before we leave at the end of this month.

'We have been asked whether a provincial committee, after close of its sittings with us in the province, would have an opportunity of summarising its own views in a report which we might consider before arriving at our own conclusions. Our reply is that if at the end of the sittings of the Joint Conference, it furnishes the report to us in time, we shall be glad to give this report full consideration as one of the documents before us and further that we would in due course include such report in the Appendices which will be printed and presented to Parliament.

'It has been pointed out to us that the necessity of the Commission passing from one province to another in accordance with a pre-arranged time table might result in placing one province at a disadvantage as compared with another. A province which was visited early in our itinerary might suffer because its Committee had conferred with us before certain matters which might emerge at later stage of our tour had become prominent. We think that there is force in this criticism and we shall be glad to arrange after we have been round the provinces and before we finally leave India, to meet representatives from each of provincial committee if they desire it, in order to hear from them their final views or confer with them on outstanding matters which seem to require treatment by this means.'

The Viceroy replied as follows to John Simon: 'I have received your letter of March 28th and have taken note of the proposals you make for dealing with reports of the provincial Committees before the Commission leaves India at the conclusion of the next visit. I will take steps to ensure that these proposals are brought to the notice of the local Governments and their Legislative Councils.[62]

On behalf of the members of the Commission, John Simon gave the following farewell message to India.[63]

'The preliminary visit of the Commission ends today. It was undertaken for the purpose of appreciating on the spot what are the principal problems with which we shall be concerned and for inviting the cooperation of all those who are sincerely working for the future welfare and prosperity of the country.

'We have never at any time under-estimated the diffculties and complexities of the task, but we came to this country hoping that our honest endeavours to serve it would meet with a friendly response.

'We believe that our confidence has been justified by the results already achieved. We have established personal contact with all communities and classes in the various parts of India. We have visited north and south, town and country.

'There is no task in which patience and sympathy

are more necessary and we leave for these few months with renewed confidence in the ultimate success of our mission.'

Besides the members of the Bombay government, there were present at the Gateway of India to see the members of the Commission off, representatives of the Muslim Federation, the Pathas Prabhu community, the non-Brahmans, Anglo-Indians and Europeans. The party was cheered as the launch *Diamon* headed for the mail steamer *Mooltan.*[64]

Thus the Statutory Commission completed the preliminary phase of their allotted task and left the Indian shores. During the short stay *it failed to enlist the cooperation of the 'better mind of India,'* as represented by all the three principal parties in the country. *It could not visit a single place of importance without being greeted by hostile popular demonstrations.* The Commission's claim that it had established personal contact with all communities and classes in various parts of India, did not appear to be authentic when hundreds of thousands of people who greeted it with black flags and millions represented by the *Congress, the Liberal Federation, the Hindu Mahasabha, the All-India Muslim League, the Sikh leaders, the Legislative Assembly, the Provincial Councils of Madras, C.P. and U.P.* the hundreds of crowded public meetings held all over the country, and last but not the least, the entire Indian press with one or two exceptions,—all stood and spoke against it. The plain fact, as *Fenner Brockway* declared in an interview on his return from India, is that, 'the mass of politically awakened opinion in India is behind the boycott of the Simon Commission and that no mistake can be more fatal than to imagine that the deputations that waited on the Commission represented a substantial body of India opinion.'[65]

Simon to Irwin

Your Excellency,

In your speech to the Central Legislature on Thursday you laid renewed emphasis on the 'full discretion as to methods' which has from the beginning been left in the hands of the Indian Statutory Commission; and I myself as Chairman, on landing in India next day, authorised the issue of a statement on behalf of the Commission, that it hoped without delay to announce the line of procedure which it would propose to follow. Evidence accumulates that throughout India there is much uncertainty as to the manner in which we may be expected to exercise our functions, and even considerable misunderstanding as to what we conceive those functions to be; while amidst many messages of welcome and encouragement—we note that speeches are being made and resolutions passed which are based on a complete, though doubtless genuine, misconception of our intentions. It is my plain duty, therefore, as Chairman to set out forthwith the true position as we regard it, and, since on this preliminary visit there is not likely to be any formal sitting of the Commission when the Statement could be made, I venture to address this letter to your Excellency.

We understand that the Government of India and the Local Governments have been engaged for some time past in preparing the material which they might put before the Commission. We have not seen these documents and do not know how far they may consist of matters of fact and how far of matters of opinion, or whether they deal with that events or with suggestions for the future. But whatever they are, instead of dealing with them by ourselves, we wish to propose that they, and the evidence given in explanation or amplification of them, should come before a 'Joint Free Conference,' over which I should preside, consisting of the seven British Commissioners and a corresponding body of representatives chosen by the Indian Legislatures (just as we ourselves have been chosen by the British Parliament).

We put forward the plan of a 'Joint Free Conference' not only because we should welcome the assistance of colleagues from the Indian Legislatures, but because we think it is only right and fair, and in the truest interests of India and Britain alike, that opportunity should be provided for such memoranda and testimony to be scrutinized and, if necessary, elucidated from the Indian side on free and equal terms. we suggests therefore that the two Houses of the Central Legislature should in due course be invited to choose from their non-official members a Joint Committee, which moght conveniently be seven in number, and that each Local Legislative Council should be asked to constitute a similar body. The Indian side of the Conference would consists, when Central subjects were being dealt with, of those first named; in a Province, the Indian wing would primarily consist of the Provincial members, but, in order that the Central Joint Committee may not have a partial view of the material put before it, we should be glad if arrangements could be arrived at which would enable its members, or some of them, to be present as an additional element at provincial sittings.

We have no wish to dictate the composition of the Indian wing of the Conference in more detail; and we should greatly prefer that the precise scheme should be reached by agreement between the different elements in India concerned. Our main object will be met so long as the arrangement is one which sources that the Indian side of the Joint Conference includes, on appropriate occasions, those who are able to speak for the Provincial Councils just as the Joint Committee would speak for the Central Legislature, and so long as the members representing India sitting with us do not amount to an unwidely number. We assume of

course that, just as we ourselves are a body selected from the British parties and both Houses of Parliament, so our Indian counterpart would be, so far as may, truly representative.

Two matters remains to be dealt with the question of evidence other than that above referred to, and the question, of Report. I wish to deal candidly and clearly with both.

Some of us have had considerable experience of the method of Joint Conference as applied both to industrial and political questions, and it is quite clear to us that each side of the Conference will require, from time to time, to meet by itself. We see no reason, however, why evidence from public and representative bodies, and from individuals, should not normally be given to the Conference as a whole, just as evidence presented by or on behalf of the various Governments would be. If a case arises when this general plan cannot be followed, I should make no secret of it, and should ask my colleagues in the Joint Free Conference, when, as I hope, they learn to have faith in my sense of fairness, to accept from me such account of the matter as I can give them on behalf of the Commission, with due regard to the reason why the testimony has been separately received. I imagine that the Indian side may find occasions when they would think it well to act in the same way.

As regards the Report, it is I feel, necessary to restate the true function of the Commission and its place in the general scheme which you announced last November. The Commission is in no sense an instrument either of the Government of India or of the British Government, but enters on the duty laid upon it by the King Emperor as a completely independent and unfettered body composed of Members of Parliament who approach Indian Legislators as colleagues. It is not an executive or legislative body, authorised to pronounce decisions about the future Government of India. Before these decisions can be reached, the full process, of which the present investigation is a first step, must be completed, including the opportunity for the views of the Indian Legislature, amongst other bodies, being presented by delegations in London to the Joint Parliamentary Committee. The present Commission is only authorised to report and make recommendations, and in this Report we desire to include a faithful account of the opinion and aspirations prevalent in India, and of the concrete proposals for constitutional reform so far as these are put before us. The British Commissioners, therefore, are bound to be solely responsible for the statement of the effect upon their own minds of the investigation as a whole. We shall report to the authority by which we have been constituted just as (if the Conference is set up) the Joint Committee would, we presume, be entitled to report its conclusions to the Central Legislature. It is obvious that those documents should be prepared and presented simultaneously. There are well-known constitutional means by which the document emanating from the Joint Committee and presented to the Central Legislature can be forwarded to and made available for the British Parliament. But, if the Indian Joint Committee would prefer it, we would make its Report an annexe to our own document, so that both might be presented to the King Emperor, and made public, at the same moment.

Above all, I would urge that one of the merits of the method of Joint Conference is that, besides securing due recognition of equal status, it provides the opportunity for that free exchange of views and mutual influence which are best calculated to promote the largest measure of agreement that is possible.

Our present visit is preliminary and the sittings of the Joint Free Conference, if it is set up, would not begin till October. But we make public our suggestions at once, not only in order to clear the air, but in order to show ourselves available for any conference about any matters of procedure which this statement does not adequately cover.

The Commission, is, of course, bound to carry through its task in any event and discharge to the full the duty cast upon it, but we are undertaking this duty only after having made it known that the methods of collaboration on honourable and equal terms is open, and that we put it forward in all sincerity and goodwill. We will only add that in making these proposals we are in conflict that we are correctly interpreting the intentions of the British parliament.

The carrying out of our proposals will require, at a later date, that the Council of State, the Legislative Assembly, and the Local Legislative Councils should be moved to elect their representatives who would take part in the Joint Conference, and the Commission will be glad if the Government of India will take such steps as seem appropriate for this purpose in due course.

I have the honour to be,

Your Excellency's Obedient Servant,

(Sd.) John Simon

Selected from the Report of the Indian Statutory Commission, Vol. I, pp. xvii-xix.

References

1. *The Bombay Chronicle*, 21, 1928; Cadogan, Edward, *op.cit.*, p. 18.
2. *Ibid*, February 4, 1928.
3. *Ibid*.
4. *Ibid*.
5. *Times of India*, January 21, 1928.
6. *Ibid*.
7. *Ibid*, February 6, 1928.
8. *Ibid*.
9. *The Tribune*, February 7, 1928: Seth Govind Das was the leading figure in this region.
10. *Ibid*.
11. *Ibid*.
12. Cadogan, Edward, *op.cit.*, p. 27.
13. *Times of India*, February 11, 1928.
14. *Ibid*.
15. *Ibid*.
16. *The Tribune*, February 11, 1928.
17. *Ibid*.
18. *The Tribune*, February 10, 1928.
19. *Bombay Chronicle*, February 13, 1928. Nine members were present, namely, Dr. M.A. Ansari, Maulana Azad, Muhammad Ali, Madan Mohan Malaviya, Srinivasa Iyengar, Sarojini Naidu, Sard'ul Singh, Shuaib Qureshi and Jawaharlal Nehru.
20. *Ibid*.
21. *Ibid*.
22. *Legislative Assembly Debates*, Vol. I, 1928, pp. 382-83.
23. *Legislative Assembly Debates*, Vol. I, 1928, pp. 382-83.and p. 429
24. *Ibid*, p. 411.
25. *Ibid*, pp. 443-44.
26. Legislative Assembly, Vol. 1928, I, pp. 501 ff.
27. *Ibid*, John Simon referring to the no-confidence motion passed by the Legislative Assembly said, 'I regret it as a misfortune that the Legislative Assembly by a narrow majority, should have failed to adopt our proposals which called for collaboration. I do not think a majority of six decides the issue for all-India and for all time. We have plenty of patience, good temper and a great desire to do our best to be helpful. The Commission has its own plans and will carry through its work which will be to the real advantage of India.' Quoted in *The Tribune*, February 22, 1928.
28. *Bombay Chronicle*, February 17, 1928.

29. *Ibid.*
30. *Ibid.*
31. *Ibid.*
32. *Times of India,* February 23, 1928.
33. *Ibid.*
34. *Times of India,* February 27, 28 and March 1, 1928.
35. *Ibid.*
36. *Times of India,* March 5, 1928.
37. *Ibid.*
38. *Ibid.*
39. *Ibid.*
40. *Ibid*
41. *Ibid.*
42. The crowd was led by S. Kharak Singh, Amar Singh, Satya Pal, Zafar Ali Khan, Malik Lal Khan, Lala. Achint Ram, Lal Chand Falaq and Kedar Nath Sehgal.
43. *The Tribune,* March 17, 1928.
44. *Ibid.*
45. *Times of India,* March 24, 1928.
46. *The Tribune,* March 27, 1928.
47. *Times of India,* March 28, 1928.
48. Reforms Office, Miscellaneous, F. No. 8, 1929.
49. *Ibid.*
50. *Ibid.*
51. *The Tribune,* April 3, 1928.
52. *See* Fenner Brockway's statement in *The Tribune,* April 4, 1928.

5
Anti-Simonite Demonstrations

Departure for India

The members of the Commission set out from London for its second visit to India, on Sept. 26, 1928. When it reached Aden, it received a communication from the Viceroy which contained the information about the composition of the Central India Committee[1] from both the Central Legislatures, and its re adiness to sit and work with the Commission.[2] John Simon and other members accompanied by Lady Strathcona and Lady Hartshorn *arrived in* Bombay on October 11, 1928 by *S.S. Majola.*[3] They were received by the elite of the town. John Simon told the representative of the *Times of India,* 'Tell India we return fully conscious of the gravity of our task. We hope that our work will prove to be not only of value to India, but of value to the world.' About 500 anti-Simonite demonstrators had collected outside Ballard Pier gate and shouted, 'Simon, go back' by waving black flags.[4]

The official party reached Poona, on October 12. The prominent persons who received them included the ministers and officials of the Bombay government, members of the provincial legislative council and the members of the provincial committee and the Central Committee.[5] Poona city presented a deserted appearance as complete *hartal* was observed in the town. Black flags were displayed in prominent places. K.F. Nariman, B.G. Kher, N.C. Kelkar, R.P. Paranjpye, M.V. Joshi and N.V. Gadgil led the procession of nearly eight thousand persons who waved black flags with shouts of 'Simon, go back,' 'India does not want you,' when the Commissioners came out of the station. Windows of the cars were open and John Simon and Burnham were seeing the boycott procession with interest and were all along smiling, while Attle did not care to look at the procession and hung down his face.[6]

A huge attended public meeting was held at the Shivaji Mandir. It was addressed by Professor Paranjpye who exhorted the people to observe complete hartal. N.C. Kelkar who presided declared that India ought not to submit to any examination on its fitness for Swaraj and condemned the Commission in vehement critical terms.[7]

Meanwhile, Dr. M.A. Ansari, President of the Indian National Congress, issued the following statement to the press.[8]

'The hour of trial has come. The Simon team reached Poona today. My message to my countrymen is to greet the Commission with the complete and effective boycott that would create an atmosphere to prepare the country for the sanction required to make the constitution prepared by the All-Parties' conference a reality.

'I appeal to my countrymen to give the Statutory Commission the only answer a self-respecting people could give, namely complete boycott.'

Commitees at Work

The members of the Central Committee and the provincial committee met for the first time on October 13. Before the conference began, John Simon had a preliminary discussion with Sankaran Nair and S.N. Bhutto, the Chairman of the central and provincial committee respectively. It was decided that the first four days' sittings were to be set apart for hearing representatives of the Bombay government. It was also decided that C.W.A Turner, Chief Secretary, Bombay government, was to be the first spokesman and his evidence was to be supplemented by opinion from the various departments.[9] The Joint Free Conference opened on October 15 and all the three wings were fully represented. John Simon presided.[10] The conference devoted this public sitting to the lengthy examination of C.W.A. Turner, who, in the course of his evidence, stated that the introduction of communal representation had led to a serious fall in efficiency. He also opined about the working of the local self-government, municipalities, district boards, methods of election to Legislative Assembly and Legislative Council and condition of Anglo-Indians in the province. Other officers interviewed by the committees were Secretary Finance, Inspector-General of Police, Secretary Home, Secretary Revenue, Chief Conservator of Forests and President of the Bombay Chamber of Commerce. Ghulam Hussain Hidayatulla, Minister for Local self-government was also examined and he advocated communal representation in local bodies.[11]

Moreover, a few deputations including a deputation from the Sardars and Inamdars Central Association, Bombay Presidency and a deputation from the All-India Muslim Federation were presented before the Commission. Their main intention was the representation of their communities in the legislatures. The government of Bombay also submitted a memorandum to the Commission. It contained complete picture of the administrative set up of the province. It requested for certain changes in the provincial administration, education, local-self-government, working of representative institutions, legislature and finance department.[12] Besides, Dr. B.R. Ambedkar submitted a memorandum on behalf of the *Bahishkrita Hitkarini Sabha* in which he demanded the safeguards and protection of the interests of the depressed classes as a minority in Bombay presidency by giving them adequate representation and educational facilities and more and more jobs in the public services.[13]

The seven members who represented the Bombay province were S.N. Bhutto (Chairman), Abdul Latif Haji Hajrat, E. Miller, Syed Miran Muhammad Shah, Dr. B.R. Ambedkar, D.R. Patil and G.N. Majumdar.[14] The committee gave its recommendation for the development of the local-self-government and opposed separation of Sindh from Bombay. It favoured representation of depressed classes, representation of labour, separate electorate for Muslims, of Anglo-Indians, Indian Christians, Marathas, land holders and inamdars and Hindus of Sindh. It supported the idea of separation for judicial and executive functions, protection of minorities and changes in the constitution of Central Legislature.[15]

Black Flags in Bombay

No Representation: No commission

Sir John & Co. In Bombay

Demonstrations with Black Flags

Shout, "Simon Go Back"

Constables Posted at Every Few Yards

Newspapermen Assail Commissioners And Ask

Major Attlee If Labourites Are Not Traitors

Bombay, Feb. 3

'S.S. Rawalpindi' which brought members of the Statutory Commission, came alongside the wharf more than an hour later than usual, owing to a strong head-wind. The weather was unusually cloudy and a slight shower fell about an hour before the boat was sighted. In spite of it, a large crowd of demonstrators had already gathered at the gate, armed with black flags and placards, inscribed, 'Simon go back.' No representation, no Commission; Swaraj is our birthright; Down with British Imperiailism.' Police pickets were equally astire and were stationed at the gate and in different parts of the city. There was no sign of demonstration on behalf of anti-boycotters. It is reported that at about 5-30 in the morning, a large party of student-demonstrators were passing the gate of the Alexandra Docks, but on seeing the police, the party at the gate came to a stop immediately. According to the leader of the demonstrators, some of them were assaulted from behind. The students were entirely peaceful and passed the gate after some time. Mr. Nariman who is incharge of the demonstrations has taken up the matter and intends to lodge a complaint. The police version is that the party tried to force their way into the gate and were pushed back. Except for th rush everythings is so far peaceful.

Pressmen Assail Commissioners

As soon as the boat anchored, pressmen swarmed aboard reinforced with a battery of cameras. The first member whom they lighted on was Col. Lane Fox who put them off saying that the Secretary of the Commission had a statement ready on behalf of all the members. Not satisfied with the formal statement which they secured from the Secretary, they tackled other members including Sir John Simon, one after another, but none of them was disposed to be communicative about the work of the Commission; but three of them were plied with volleys of questions on general topics to which they freely and affiably replied.

Spirit of cordiality

Viscount Burnham was especially cordial and expressed great pleasure in meeting India's press representatives. He spoke of the work of the last International Press Conference over which he presided and said he would like the press of the world to come closer together. Conversation passed on the recent amalgamations of newspapers in England. Though he regretted it inevitable in an age when a sage tendency was observable in all industries generally. He had read Indian papers on the subject of the Commission and had noted the strong opposition created. He, however, assured Indians that the Commission came in utmost spirit of cordiality and friendship especially Sir John Simon.

The Misunderstanding

It was explained to the Viscount by pressmen that the opposition in India was not against the members personally but against them as a Statutory body. Quick came the retort, "Equally, we may say we are here as a Statutory body and not as individuals," probably meaning to convey that as individuals, they fully reciprocated the goodwill and friendship of Indian and understood the opposition. He finally expressed the hope that the misunderstanding would be gradually removed.

Labour Position

Major Attlee was the next member to receive the attention of the pressmen who succeeded in conveying to him an idea of the intensity of the feeling aroused in a section of Indian opinion by the support of the Labour Party to the Parliamentary Commission. He was asked, "Was it not going back on the Blackpool Conference resolution favouring self-determination for India and had not the Labour Party proved themselves, "Traitors" ? Major Attlee received the onslaught with good humour, and assured them that the Labour Party had throughout stood by their word. After having run the gauntlet of pressmen and cameras, members of the Commission who were received by Mr. Bhore and a representative from the Bombay Government entered the waiting cars and as one by one the cars moved out of the Ballard Pier, shouts of "Simon, go back" rose from the demonstrators. The members drove to Government House; and after breakfast they will leave for Delhi at 12-30.

Activities in Punjab

Meanwhile, hectic activities were in full swing in Punjab, particularly Lahore, its capital. This was the substance of the eloquent address that Pandit Madan Mohan Malaviya delivered at a mass meeting consisting of thousands of repesentatives of all castes and communities.

'Every day that passes convinces me that we will get *Swaraj* in 1930. But *Swaraj* will not come to us through commissions or conferences, but through our efforts. We should, therefore, be fully determined to sacrifice, if need be, even our lives, for establishment of full self-government in India. Our duty should be to carry on a vigorous campaign of Swaraj, we should spread the message of Swaraj to every nook and corner, to every village and hamlet. We should preach the gospel of Swaraj to all young and old, man or woman.'[16]

The Commission left Poona for Lahore on October 28. The whole city resounded with the cries of 'Simon, go back' even three days before Simon Seven's arrival here. Sensing trouble in the city, the District Magistrate of Lahore issued the following order:

> 'Whereas it appears to be necessary in the interests of good order to regulate the holding of processions within the limits of the Lahore Municipality on October 30, 1928, I hereby direct that the public shall abstain from organizing or joining any procession which has not been permitted by the Senior Superintendent of Police,

Lahore, within the limits of the said Municipality on that day.

'Whereas it is further necessary in the interests of good order to control assembling of crowds in the vicinity of railway station of Lahore junction, on Express and Egerton Road, and the roads adjacent thereto, I hereby direct the public that they shall not assemble within the precincts of the railway station or on the roads abovementioned except at such places as the Superintendent of Police may permit.'[17]

To express their resentment against the Commission, a largely attended meeting of the citizens of Lahore was held in the evening of October 29, 1928 in the municipal gardens outside Mochi Gate, under the Presidentship of Sheikh Siraj-Ud-Din Paracha. A number of prominent leaders from outside Lahore, including Lala Bodh Raj of Multan, Raizada Hans Raj of Jullundur, Syed Ata Ullah Bokhari, Lala Duni Chand of Ambala and others attended. L. Bodh Raj exhorted the people of the Punjab to offer a united front and a resolute will to boycott the Commission. Sardar Kharak Singh talked of the attainment of *Swaraj* and advised the people to work hard for it. He further stated that the appointment of the all-white Commission was the greatest insult that the Tory government of England could offer to India.[18]

On arrival of the Commission at Lahore on October 30, 1928. Enthusiastic scenes were witnessed in the town on this day. A procession led by prominent leaders with several thousand followers carrying black flags with the inscription, 'Simon, Go Back,' started at about 1 P.M. from the municipal gardens towards the railway station. It passed through Circular Road via Lunda Bazar and halted at the Mool Chand Temple Road, a place about two hundred yards from the main gate to the railway platform. There it was confronted with barbed wires with strong wooden posts barricading the way to the railway station. In the first row near the barbed wires stood Lala Lajpat Rai, Maulana Zafar Ali and others. While the procession was perfectly non-violent, some police officials used their *lathis* on the first row of the procession, which included Lala Lajpat Rai. One of them struck him hard in the chest which proved fatal after a few days.[19]

Public Meeting at Lahore

In a public meeting, Lala Lajpat Rai condemned police officer's action and stated the whole incident thus: 'We were absolutely peaceful and gave no provocation to the police to attack us. But quite unprovoked, a police officer began to strike us with *lathis.* He had a knobbed *hunter* in his hand. He gave me two blows and two of his constables gave another two. One of these blows given to me was aimed at my heart, and very near my heart. I received a stroke which has caused a bruise sufficiently long and broad.

'Similiar blows were struck at Raizada Hans Raj whose hand was bleeding profusely even there at the spot. Dr. Satya Pal and Dr. Muhammad Alam received blows on their arms, which are still paining and I can swear that none of these gentlemen did anything, which deserved this cowardly treatment from the police.

"Every blow that was hurled at us this afternoon was a nail in the coffin of the British Expire.I wish to warn the Government that if a violent revolution takes place in this country, the responsibility for bringing it about will fall on such officers as misbehaved themselves today. If the Government and its officers continue to behave; as they did today, I would not wonder if the young men go out of our hands and do whatever they choose with the objects of gaining the freedom of their country."

Referring to the Statutory Commission, Lalaji said: 'If the Government did not wish that the Commission should see all those demonstration, the best thing for them to do was to put bandages over their eyes and to take them to Government House.' Indeed, his unpretentious bearing, his superb logic and unquestioned oratory, imbued his audience with respect and admiration for his dynamic leadership. Among other speakers in this meeting, the prominent were Dr. Muhammad Alam, Dr. Satya Pal, Dr. Gopi Chand Bhargava, Maulana Atta Ullah Shah Bokhari and Dr. Kahn Chand Dev.[20]

Receipt of Telegrams

Lala Lajpat Rai received a large number of telegrams from his numerous friends. Gandhi wrote: 'Hearty Congratulations Wire details, assault and condition of health.' M.R. Jayakar wrote: 'Distressed to hear assault. Hope injury not serious.' Motilal Nehru wrote: 'Returned last night. Just heard of the cowardly assault by official hooligans. Regard it as our first great victory. Blows aimed at you have really hit the bureaucracy hard, and I see it tottering before us. Trust Lahore will march undaunted from victory, and the other places that the Simon Commision visits will follow Lahore's example Hope your injuries are not serious. Please wire condition. Am ready to join you, necessary.'[21]

Writing in *Young India,* Gandhi expressed his views thus. "Nor are we to think that the Punjab incident is to be the last of the barbarities committed during the pendency of the Statutory Commission. The boycott of the Simon Commission is a continuing sore for the Commission and the Government.The moral, therefore, I would have workers to draw from this incident is not to be depressed or taken aback by the assault, but to treat it as part of the game, we have to play to turn the irritation caused by the wanton assault into dynamic energy and husband it and utilize it for future purposes.[22]

Jawaharlal Nehru said, "I am not surprised at what happened at Lahore. It was but to be expected. I am glad, Lahore has done well and I hope Lucknow would do better."[23]

Dr. Annie Besant wrote in New India, 'Violence and bloodshed at Lahore are a forerunner of the coming troubles. Will England lose India as she lost the American colonies? As in the latter case, the best brain and strongest hearts in India will not bear many repetitions of Lahore outrages.'[24]

Raizada Hans Raj met the Governor to appraise him of the whole incident. He gave him a patient hearing and promised full enquiry into the matter. Soon the government announced the appointment of an enquiry by D.J. Boyd, Commissioner of Rawalpindi division who was instructed to record the statement of any witness to make a relevant statement.[25]

Lathi Charge on Lajpat Rai

Cowardly Assaslts on Peaceful Procession. Lalaji Condemns Police Officers' Action

Says, "Every Blow Hurled At Us was A

Nail In The Coffin of

British Empire'

Lahore, Oct. 30,

Mammoth Meeting At Lahore

This morning when we were told that the Government had changed their order about Section 144 so as to meet our wishes with regard to the route of the procession and meeting, we determined to carry out our programme without violating any of the conditions laid down in the new rules and we did so. But when we assembled near the railway station we stopped in front of the barbed wire barricades and made no attempt to cross or rush it. We were absolutely peaceful and gave no provocation to the police to attack us. But quite unprovoked, a police officer began to strike us with *lathis*. He had a knobbed *hunter* in his hand. He gave me tow blows and two of his constables gave me another two. One of these blows given to me was aimed at my heart and vey near my heat. I received a stroke which has caused a bruise sufficiently long and broad.

Processionists were Quite Unarmed

Before taking the procession, we took care to take back all *lathis*. In the whole procession, I did not see more than two or three walking sticks. I am thankful to the young men in the procession who obeyed my orders and sat down and did not retaliate. That itself should have put the police officials on the other side to shame. But nothing daunts arrogance and intoxication born of political power and military strength. Several time, I shouted for the name of the officer who had attacked me, but he had no courtesy or the courage to give me his name.

Still, these are men who boast of courage and tactfulness in times of emergency. Behaviour like this shows their cowardliness. To start assault on an unarmed crowd without that crowd having in the least given them any provocation and without declaring that crowd to be illegal or unlawful, or without giving them any warning, it is the most cowardly thing which can be done by a man, much less by an officer of position. I am on the other hand happy that this Government rules India by means of these officers, because the greater their number, the sooner will be the dawn of the day of emancipation.

Nails in Coffin of British Empire

I want to say from this platform that every blow that was hurled at us this afternoon, was a nail in the coffin of the British Empire. Nobody who has seen that sight is ever likely to forget it. It has sunk deep into our soul. We have to avenge ourselves of this cowardly attack, not by violently attacking theme but by gaining our freedon. I wish to warn the Government that if a violent revolution takes place in this country, the responsibilites for bringing it about will fall on such officers an misbehaved themselves this afternoon. Our creed still stands and we are pledged to struggle for peaceful non-violence. But if the Government and its officers countinue to behave like this, I would not wonder if the young men were to go out of our hands and do whatever they choose with the object of gaining the freedom of their country. I do not know whether I shall be alive to see that day. But whether alive or dead, if that day is forced on them by the Government, my spirit from behind will bless them for their struggle.

If the Government do not wish that the Simon Commission should see all these demostrations, the best thing for them to do is to put bandages over their eyes when they travel from one station to another—when they travel from railway station to Government House—so that they may not see anything.

I am of opinion that the responsibility for the blows that were given to us today by the police officers, is shared by those Indian who have, by flouting the public opinion of the country, expressed their desire to cooperate with the Simon Commission. I think they are abettors of this crime, if not the original perpetrators thereof. And we wish to deal with them too after we have carried on our struggle successfully. I can well understand honest difference of opinion, but I can never forgive those who in spite of difference of opinion go to the enemy's camp by flouting the public opinion of the country.

Last year, when I moved the resolution of boycotting the Simon Commission in the Legislative Assembly, I stated that we are boycotting it not only because it was an insult to us to send a commission purely British, but also because I believed that those who had appointed the Commission were dishonest in appointing this Commission and also because in my judgment no good would at all come out of a Commission of this kind.

I repeat that the object with which the Commission was appointed was to make an exhibtion of our failings before the world.*

Lajpat Rai's Reaction

At this point of time, Lala Lajpat Rai was very unhappy over the attitude of the Punjab government and stated: "We do not accept this enquiry, and I have no intention of appearing before Mr. D.J. Boyd to give any 'relevant evidence.' If any enquiry is to be made, it must be an open enquiry by a Commission consisting of two non-officials and one Judicial officer. The members of police must be subjected to cross-examination if the falsity of their statements is to be exposed."[26] Dr. Muhammed Alam said, "We must boycott such a farcical enquiry."

The Commission interviewed a number of officials and non-officials at Lahore. Amongst them, were the Chief Secretary, Additional Secretary (Reforms), and Secretary, Transfered Departments. Besides it received a number of deputations, deputation from the Cental Labour Board of the Punjab; deputation of the National Reforms Party; deputation of the All-India Muslim League; deputation from the Punjab Zamindars Association; deputation from the Chief Khalsa Diwan; deputation from the Punjab National Unionist Party; deputation from the Martial Races of the

---

* An extract from the speech of Lala Lajpat Rai delivered at Lahore on October 30, 1928. *See The Tribune,* Nov. 2, 1928.

Punjab, and deputation from the Punjab Chiefs' Association. Whereas the officials gave a factual report of the working of the political and non-political organisations of the Punjab as well as the picture of working of the provincial government, the deputationists demanded the representation and more and more facilities in services and other concessions concerning their respective communities.[27]

The official committee for Punjab representing different communities, regions and interests in the province which recorded its views before the Commission, consisted of Sir Sikander Hyat Khan (Chairman), Chaudhri Zafarulla Khan, Chaudhri Chhotu Ram, Dr. G.C. Narang, Raja Narendra Nath, Sardar Ujjal Singh[28] and Owen Roberts.[29] Its report was as follows:

Franchise qualifications should be considerably lowered with a view to the attainment of universal adult sufferage by stages within a reasonably short period, size of constituencies should be appreciably reduced to allow candidates and members to get into touch with electorates, the practice of nominating official members to the Legislative Councils should cease, Sind should be separated from Bombay, the numerical strength of the provincial Legislative Council should be increased; in the case of the Punjab, the Council should be increased, in the case of the Punjab, the Council should consist of at least 165 elected members, special constituencies should be abolished, formation of second chamber was undesirable, the system of dyarchy should be abolished, officials should not be appointed as ministers; residuary powers should be vested in the provinces; full responsible government should be granted to India on a federal basis subject to the reservation of the portfolios of defence and foreign affairs for a specified period, the Governor-General should be the constitutional head of the Government of India with powers of veto and certification in case of necessity, the province should be allowed greater freedom in the matter of raising loans for development purposes, and separation of executive and judicial functions should be immediately taken in hand.[30]

The Commission at Karachi

The Commission's next halt was at Karachi on November 11. About twenty thousand persons with black flags assembled in a maidan, opposite the railway station, greeted them with the cries, 'Simon, go back.' Twenty minutes later, the Central Committee's special arrived. Every Indian, from Sankaran Nair to the local hosts, was greeted with cries of 'shame, shame'. The Commission received a deputation from the Sind Mohammedan Association; a deputation from the All-Sind Hindu Association, and a deputation from Karachi Chamber of Commerce. It also interviewed D.I.G of Police, Sind and Chief Engineer, Llyods Barrage and Canals Construction, Sukkur.[31]

At Peshawar

The next halt of the Simon Commission was at Peshawar where it reached on November 17. About ten thousand persons, carrying black flags greeted the Commissioner with the cried of 'Simon, go back.' Processions of Hindus, Sikhs and Muslims marched through the city, singing national songs and exhorting the people to boycott the 'purely white' Commission. There were numerous rows of posters like, 'Simon, go back'; 'Take the reactionary Bolton Away......' 'Bolton Raj is worse than Martial Law.' A huge meeting of the people was held under the Presidentship of Sardar Ram Singh of Bannu, and the following resolution was unanimously passed.

'This meeting of the Frontier people condemns the appointment of the All-White Commission and the half-education reactionary Committee composed entirely of Sir Bolton's henchmen to boycott it in view of the better experience of cooperation with the Bray Committee. It further dissociates itself from all witnesses.' Abdur Rab Khan, Abdur Rahim Khan, Habibullah Khan, Dr. Jawahar Singh, Amir Chand Bombwala, L. Piara Ram, Pandit Om Prakash, Pir Shahinshah and others supported the resolution. The meeting dispersed amidst 'Bandemataram,' 'Sat Sri Akal,' 'Allah-O-Akbar' and 'Simon, go back'. The Commissioners and the members of the Central Committee paid a visit to Khyber and Jamrud where the Afridi chiefs initiated visitors into mysteries of frontier raids. In his welcome address the chiefs stated that they had learnt that the Commission was engaged in an important enquiry and if there was to be any transference of power in India, the frontier tribesmen must not be forgotten. They claimed their share of whatever benefits were to be conferred on India. John Simon, speaking to tribesmens' delight in *Pushtu.*, thanked them for their splendid hospitality and for the safety in which the party had travelled in the Khyber territory. He was also pleased to find them in a peaceful manner.[32]

In North-West Frontier Province, the Commission sought interviews and recorded the views and opinions of the Inspector-General of Police, Deputy Commissioner of Peshawar; Lieutenant Taj Muhammad Khan, a retired military officer; a deputation from the Provincial Hindu Conference; Khan Bahadur Abdul Ghaffar Khan, Khan of Zaida (spokesman), and eighteen others and a deputation from the Advanced Hindu Party. The two non-official deputations which appeared before the conference put forward the views of reactionary elements in the North-West Frontier Province. The deputation of Khans who claimed to be the natural and hereditary leaders of the people and were the chiefs of the various tribes, suggested the creation of legislative council in the North-West Frontier Province with the same powers as were enjoyed by the legislatures of the other provinces. They did not demand any drastic change in the administration, and insisted that only one-third of the members of the legislature should be elected, while the remaining two-thirds should be nominated by the Chief Commissioner. The Khans expressed their apprehension of the elective system on a wide scale, because it disorganised the existing state of society. An other deputation examined by the conference was led by Rai Bahadur Thakur Datta who claimed to represent the views of the Hindus of the Frontier Province. The deputation opposed the extension of reforms and of the elective system to the province. They urged that strategic and political reasons as well as financial difficulties were against a change. They also maintained that constitutional changes which weakened the executive authority, would be dangerous to the peace of the empire. They were anxious to uphold the influence of the Khans who had been the bulwark and important safeguard against the unruly elements in the province. They held that as long as the dominant community had not reached a stage of political advancement where politics was dissociated from religion and religion from the affairs of public life, provincial autonomy would not be acceptable to the Hindu. They were, however, agreeable to the setting up of an advisory council, leaving further advance to the central government through periodical enquiries. They claimed in the assembly two seats for Hindus and two for Muslims, and advocated judicial amalgamation with the Punjab, the repeal of the Land Alienation Act and the opening of the public services to competitions.[33]

Lajpat Rai's Death

Meanwhile, the sad news of Lala Lajpat Rai's death gained currency like wild fire in the Indian press. In fact, he could not recover from the severe hits of the police lathi-charge on him. *Hartal* was observed all over the Punjab and Delhi as a mark of respect to the fearless soldier of freedom. Prominent leaders expressed their sense of utter grief and sorrow at his untimely demise. Gandhi said: 'Lalaji's death had left a gap which it was difficult to be filled. His was a glorious death and he died a patriot. I do not believe that Lalaji is dead, but he lives. Motilal Nehru called him a 'Prince among peacemakers'. Jinnah stated, 'Lala Lajpat Rai was undoubtedly a great figure in the political world of India and whether one could always see eye to eye with him or not, he was an earnest and sincere worker. His loss at this particular moment is a great misfortune to India'. Other leaders like C.P. Ramaswami Iyer, T.B. Sapru, C.Y. Chintamani, Raja Narendra Nath, Dr. H.S. Gour, Pheroze Sethna, Malik Feroze Khan Noon, S.C. Bose, Sankaran Nair, Abdul Qadir, M.C. Rajah, Madan Mohan Malaviya and G.D. Birla sent their condolence messages.[34] All praised Lalaji's courage, sacrifice, forbearance, nobility, heroism and patriotism.

John Simon, when interviewed by the Associated Press, said, 'My colleagues and I greatly regret to learn of Lajpat Rai's death which means the removal of an ardent social worker as well as of a prominent political leader'. A public meeting under the auspices of the London branch of the Indian National Congress was held at Caxton Hall on November 25 to mourn the death of Lajpat Rai at which Colonel Wedgwood, Saklatvala and others spoke. The meeting adopted a resolution drawing the attention of the British public to the fact that the death of Lajpat Rai was caused through the policy of the Government of India, vigorously suppressing all-India demonstrations against the presence of the Statutory Commission in India.[35]

The attack of police on Lajpat Rai was also condemned in the Congress session of 1928 held in Calcutta.[36] Besides, D.P. Mishra stated in the Central Assembly of Feb. 15, 1929. 'The police has murdered Lala Lajpat Rai. This is my charge against the Government.' Motilal Nehru said, 'If in the face of this, the Government does not hold an enquiry, the result would be the conviction, that Lalaji met his death at the hands of the police, would deepen into a firm belief.[37] And when the motion for enquiry into the circumstances of Lajpat Rai's death was put to vote, the votes in favour of enquiry were 57 and against were 45.[38]

Arrival in Delhi

Meanwhile, the members of the Commisssion arrived at Delhi on November 21. There was a general hartal in the city. In Delhi University about five hundred students held a strike. Outside the station a huge crowd of 15,000 who had lined themselves along both sides of about three-fourths of a mile, raised the slogans of, 'Simon, go back.' A mass meeting of the citizens was held which was addressed by leaders like Lala Deshbandhu, Mohammed Taqqi and others. Besides, there was a huge procession of about 40,000 persons with black flags in their hands. Thus, all-round resentment was expressed by the people of Delhi.[39] The demonstrations in Delhi were a unique success, not only from the point of view of the number of people who participated in them, but also from the general sympathy that prevailed throughout the city among all classes and interest in favour of effectual boycott of the Commission.

At Delhi, the members of the Commission took evidence of Home Secretary, Officer-on-Special-Duty, Home Department; Secretary, Legislative Department; Secretary, Commerce; Secretary, Education and Health; and Secretary, Industry and Labour. They also received a deputation of Anglo-Indian and Domiciled European Association led by Lt. Col. R.B.L. Rallia Ram of Lahore.[40]

John Simon and members of the Commission arrived at Lucknow on November 30, and were received at the railway station by G.B. Lambert, Home Member; Nawab of Chhatari; the Chief Secretary; the members of the Provincial Simon Committee, headed by J.P. Srivastava, and several other civil and military officials. Out side the railway station, about ten thousand persons led by Jawaharlal Nehru and G.B. Pant had collected and cried 'Shame, Simon, go back,' 'Down with Imperialism.' Similar expressions were displayed conspicuously in the form of posters and placards on the trunks of trees and on walls.Several university students also joined the demonstration. The police *sawars* charged the peaceful processionists with batons, and Jawaharlal Nehru, G.B. Pant and many other received injuries.

Excesses of U.P. Police

Having received the news of U.P. Police excesses on the peaceful demonstrators, Motilal motored from Allahabad to Lucknow where he addressed a huge gathering. Referring to the Simon Commission, he said that 'once the country had given its verdict to dissociate itself with the white Commission at every stage, we could not go back. If the Commissioner did not like public demonstrations, the best course for them would be to bid good-bye to this country for good.' He advised youngmen to do their duty peacefully, and expressed his admiration for their peaceful and non-violent attitude who, in spite of provocation, kept quiet and obeyed the orders of their leaders.[41]

Jawaharlal Nehru said, 'The assault has sunk deep in our soul. I, along with others, was the first victim of police assaults and I warn the Government that if the police continue behaving like this, I would not wonder if young men go off our hands and do whatever they choose with the object of gaining freedom for the country.' Before the meeting came to an end, Chaudhry Khaliquzzaman thanked Motilal Nehru and Jawaharlal Nehru who had taken trouble of coming over to Lucknow. So amidst shouts of Vandemataram and Jawarharlal ki-jai, the meeting terminated late in the evening.[42]

Obviously under strict police guard John Simon and his colleagues were entertained at a tea party given by the British Indian Association of Awadh. At a distance of every yard a red-turbaned policeman was seen and all gates on the four sides of the Kaiser Bagh were closed. To express their resentment, the boycotters had covered the whole sky with black kites and balloons bearing, 'Simon go back.[43]

The following personnel represented their province. J.P. Srivastava (Chairman), Hidaya Hussain, Bisheshwar Dayal Seth, Rama Charana, Shafat Ahmad Khan, Kushal Pal Singh and H.C. Desanges. This committee advocated the abolition of dyarchy and recommended the extension of franchise to an extent which would enable the toiling masses to feel that they had a share in the government of their province. It also recommended safeguards to minorities and deprecated separate electorate. It state: 'We believe that the quickest way to bring rapproachment between the different communities is to guarantee them what they feel doubtful about.[44]

The Commission during their halt at Lucknow interviewed a few officials and received a number of deputations. The officials interviewed were: the Chief Secretary, Secretary, Local-Self-Government, Chief Engineer, Finance Secretary, Officer-on-Special Duty, Chief Conservator of Forests, Inspector-General of Police and the Collector of Kanpur. The Commission also received a deputation from the Muslims of the U.P.; a deputation from the Agra Province Zamindars' Association, Muzzaffarnagar; a deputation from the British Indian Association and a deputation from the Upper India Chamber of Commerce.[45]

Judging from what had taken place at Lahore and at Lucknow in connection with the visit of the Commission, there was every reason to believe that determined attempt was being made to suppress the boycott movement by making a physical assault on those who associated with it, including their principal leaders, and to make the country safe for the Commission.

Nehru's Statement on Lucknow Incident

A number of statements have been issued regarding the recent happenings at Lucknow. It may interest to people to have a connected account of these incidents from one who was an eye-witness to many things that happened there.

It appears that the authorities were assured by their underlings and informers that the boycott demonstrations at Lucknow would not amount too much. They were told that Muslims would not take any prominent part. And a slight difference of opinion in the Boycott Committee was magnified and made to appear as if there had been a split among the boycotters. The original attitude of the authorities was thoroughly accommodating. As soon as the news of the so-called split reached them, they stiffened their attitude: but very soon they found that there was no split and the Boycott Committee was as determined and united as ever. Immediately the authorities became accommodating and agreed to the procession on the 26th. So far as the Boycott Committee was concerned, they made it clear that they were prepared to abide by all reasonable arrangements made by the police. It was not their attention to seek conflict with the police. Their sole object was to organise a great demonstration against the Simon Commission. The procession of the 26th November was an eye-opener to the authorities. It was a vast procession whose numbers it is impossible to guess. It proved conclusively the tremendous strength of feeling against the Simon Commission and the Government that was backing this Commission. Nothing untoward happened in connection with this procession inspite of the vast numbers that took part in it, because the Police did nothing aggressive.

Tactics of Terrorism

The procession, however made it clear to the authorities that their informers who had told that there was not going to be much boycott agitation were hopelessly in the wrong. Immediately there have been a change in the attitude of the officials and they seemed to have decided to try a little bit of terrorism to cow down the people. The first of this change of attitude became visible on the 28th when another procession was to have been taken out from the Congress office. Notice of this procession and the route it was going to take, was sent to the police authorities. On the very evening of the procession, however, the police informed the Boycott Committee that they would not permit that route. The secretary of the committee told the police that it was too late for them to change their plans. The procession, therefore, gathered round the Congress Office. The city Magistrate, Mr. Ainuddin, with a squad mounted police came there and spoke to Mr. Mohan Lal Saxena, secretary of the Committee. They went into the adjoining shop and exchanged written notes which have been published. The procession formed up. It was faced by the mounted police. The procession had hardly proceeded a step or two when they were attacked by the mounted police and batons were freely used.

It is untrue to say, as has been said in the Government *communique,* that the procession tried to force their way through the police. Their idea was to assert their right to proceed and to stop it the police actually stopped them. They had in fact, stopped when the charge was made. It is stated in the Government *communique* that the people tried to get round the police by climbing over the railings of the park. This is untrue. Many people did try to climb over the railings, but this was when the police charge was made and they wanted to escape. It must be remembered that, apart from the processionists, there were many other people there and it was largely these people, who tried to escape the charge. The police, however, pursued them on the pavements, on to the railings and beat them there. The hoofs of the sowa's horses were plainly visible the next day on the pavements. Many people on the side of the procession were injured. Among them were Messrs. Mohan Lal Saxena, Pestonjee and Kishan Prasad Kaul of the servants of India Society.

It is stated by the Government that stones were thrown by the processionists: the police and s ome police officers were injured. It is impossible for any one to say whether stones were thrown or not. But it was pointed out at the time to the Deputy Commissioner, Mr. Gwynne, that if the processionists had wanted to throw stones there were piles of them lying handy on the roadside. Mr. Gwynne was also asked if he would show to any responsible member of the Boycott committee the injuries which were alleged to have been caused to the police by stone throwing. But none was forthcoming. Mr. Gwynne stated ultimately that no obvious injuries were caused. Anyway in spite of repeated requests none was shown.

That night I received a telephone message from Lucknow about the police assault and left or Lucknow the next day. I found on arrival that there was a great resentment at the police assault on the day before and the general feeling was that the Boycott Committee should have no further official dealing. There was no procession on behalf of the committee that day, that is, the 29th. But a mass, meeting had been called to celebrate Lajpat Rai Day. A *mohalla* meeting had been called at the Narahi at the back of Hazratganj.

Police Heroics

I went to this small meeting with Messrs. Khaliquzzaman, Harkarnath Misra and Govind Ballabh Pant. After the meeting was over it was proposed to go in a body to the big meeting at Aminuddaula Park. I suggested that we should not all go in a procession, as there were a number of small boys present and it might not have been easy to have an orderly procession. Our suggestion was that two or three small groups, not exceeding 12, should go and they should go individually. We further suggested that in order to avoid any traffic block or any conflict with the police, we should not go through Hazaratganj, which is the main European shopping quarter, but should proceed by unfrequented roads.

In the course of these discussions, the Assistant Superintendent of Police came up and wanted to know what we were going to do and if we proposed taking out a procession. I told him that in view of the wanton attack of the police the day before, we were not prepared to have any further dealings with them.

A little later, we formed up three groups of twelve each. Two of these groups remained standing whilst one, headed by Pandit Govind Ballabh Pant and myself, proceeded along Nawal Kishore Road. We had hardly started when we were stopped by the mounted police, and a charge was made on this group of 12. The road was practically empty at the time except for us and the mounted police. Members of our group received plenty of *lathi* blows. After a few minutes the *lathi* blows ceased and the Deputy Commissioner appeared on the scene. It is curious that both on the evening of the 28th and on the 29th when the police made an assault and used their batons, the Deputy Commissioner, Mr. Gwynne, appeared on the scene like a *deus ex machina* immediately after the occurrence. It would appear that on both occasions he was wanting in the neighbourhood for the assault to be over in order to put in this appearance. We had a long argument with the Depty Commissioner. He said that he had no objection to our proceeding in this manner we intended to do, but we must have a formal permission for it. We told him that after the police behaviour on two occasions we were not prepared to ask for any formal permission. Thereupon he suggested that he would be satisfied by an oral request, but that too, we were not prepared to make. Ultimately, he even said that he was prepared to treat our conversation as an oral request if we were also prepared to read it as such. We were unable however, to agree to this even.

Matter of Prestige

It this became entirely a matter of prestige on either side. We sat down there by the roadside with the mounted police barring our way. Meanwhile the news of this happening had spead far and wide and created a great deal of consternation at the mass meeting that was going on at Aminuddaula Park. There was a tendency for the audience to come in a body to us. This was stopped and the meeting sent a deputation to make enquires and report. Big crowds began to assemble on the Hazratganj side of Nawal Kishore Road. Ultimately after an hour's waiting, the Deputy Commissioner said he would permit our group to proceed along the route we had originally decided upon. Whether this was due to the increasing crowds or the triumph of reason, I do not know. His decision was evidently not to the taste of the Superintendent of Police, who did not like the idea of official prestige going down before the prestige of a group of 12 men. However our groups were allowed to proceed. We told the great crowd that had assembled to go back to the meeting by other roads which they did. Our three groups marched along proceeded by the mounted police as a kind of guard of honour along Hazratganj and Kaiser Bagh to the park. Incident of the evening had naturally attached a great deal of attention and our little procession which might otherwise have been unnoticed became a kind of triumphal march. The meeting itself at the park was an enormous gathering and very great enthusiasm prevailed in it.

The Secretary of the Boycott Committee had asked the police previously for a block of land along the route to be taken by the Simon Commission from station for our demonstration. The Deputy Commissioner had replied on the 29th that he would have no objection to giving this plot, but he had already allotted it to the depressed classes. Later on the 29th night some of us went to see the lands, lying round about the station. We saw that the so-called depressed classes, numbering about 30 to 40 occupying two little *shamianas* at a great distance from the Station and there was enough land among the road and in front of the Station to accommodate five or six lakhs of people. No question could possible arise as to our taking the land which has been allotted to the depressed classes.

Seduction and Allurement

We visited these people and found that they have been asked to come there to witness dancing and singing from professional singers who have been brought from Kanpur. This is locally known as *nautanki* performance. We were told that each person who had come had been given Rs.2/-. They were also provided with *ganja* and *charas*.We talked to some of these people. They knew little about the Simon Commission and those who did know something about them said that they were prepared to wave black flags etc. When they passed by.

It was clear that if the Deputy Commissioner was sincere in his offer to give us a good site, there was no lack of space. It was the easiest thing possible for him to separate us by a hundred yards or so from the depressed classes and, if necessary, to put policemen between us. Even apart from the line of the route, there was an adjoining *maidan* which though not very suitable for us, was far better than the plot of land at a distance that he had allotted.

The next morning the procession started from the Congress office at 6 with black flags etc. The procession was well-organised and marched in fours with ropes on their side to keep the lines. Behind the regular procession of a thousand or more followed large numbers of other processionists in no very regular array. It was a vast crowd on the march. Smaller processions from various *mohallas* went direct to the station. When the main procession arrived near the open space opposite the station it turned to the left to go towards the line of the route. They were stopped by the police and were asked to go to the right. The plot on the right was at least a quarter of a mile from the nearest point of the Simon route. I pointed out that it was ridiculous for us to congregate at this distance. As however, we were not allowed to proceed to the left, we remained standing there. Apart from the procession was allowed to march a little further ahead along the route but then stopped by the police. Here we stood for an hour or more. Many of the small procession and individuals gradually dribbled to the other side of the *maidan* near the line of the route.

A Rough Official

I had a short conversation with the Deputy Commissioner and pointed out to him that his allotment was grossly unfair as there was plenty of vacant land available for us in a better position. He told me gruffly, however, that he was not prepared to argue and that his orders must be carried out. A day before the police assault he had appeared as a sweetly reasonable person. On the 30th morning there was little of sweetness or reasonableness about him. Eventually, he had felt annoyed at the downfall of prestige the night before and wanted to reinstate it by aggressive and offensive behaviour.

So we stood for a long time, the main procession in several ranks on the road with a small part of it facing the left and the crowd near the line of the route and odd individuals appeared over the *maidan* to the left. It is difficult to estimate the number at present. Opinions vary greatly. Some people estimate the entire crowd as a lakh of person; other give a smaller figure. I do not think there could have been less than 50,000 people in the various open space in front of the station.

Suddenly, we saw a charge by the mounted police at the other and of the *maidan*. We were told subsequently that they had given five minutes notice to the party but had as a matter of fact charged within a couple of minutes. The *maidan* was full of little groups of people. These were driven down ruthlessly by the mounted police and beaten with *lathis*. Many people fell down and were driven over by the horses. The *maidan* was enormous place and the mounted police had a fine chance of charging at gallop which they took full advantage of. All this we saw from a distance of nearly a quarter of a mile distance which rapidly decreased because the drive was in our direction. Ultimately the mounted police reached the procession. The processionists stood firm and for a while refused to budge. Even horses were brought to a standstill by the solid phalanx of the procession. The mounted and foot police then charged with batons at the procession. Quite a prominent part in the attack was taken by the Assistant Superintendent of Police. The procession, however, did not break in spite of this, but gradually receded by still maintaining a fair measures of order. Having crossed the road we came to the plot, which had actually been allotted to us. The police charge, however, continued for another hundred yards or so.

The police then stopped the charge and took to throwing stones—a pastime in which some of the police officials on foot vigorously indulged. This was a bit too much for the nerves of the procession and they began to retaliate in kind. Numbers of stones were thus thrown by the crowd on the side of the processionists, but immediately they were asked to resist and stone throwing stopped on the side of the processionist. The procession lined up again and stood facing the mounted and foot police in a battle array, three or four deep with a distance of 10 or 15 yards separating them. Thus they stood and a little later they saw at a great distance cars being taken away from the station which presumably contained the Commissioners. After some time the procession marched back in an orderly manner to the Congress office where after a few speeches were delivered, it dispersed.

It is difficult to estimate the number of casualties, but it is clear that hundreds of persons must have been injured, though probably really grave injuries were fortunately not many. One of main line was dispersed of and several had their heads split open. On the police side one of the Superintendents was hit by a stone on his hand.

Moral of these Events

After the end of the procession the students of Lucknow University, who had taken a leading part in it and who were largely responsible for the discipline and orderliness, marched back for their university quarters. At one place they were pursued by the police. There was a similar argument between the two, the police threatening to assault the lot. The Vice-Chancellor, however, appeared on the scene and damped the ardour of the police.

Practically, the whole day little processions of students and others were seen about the city and held meetings at Aminuddaula Park.

The City observed Hartal

So far as I am concerned, I have not the slightest grievance against the Government or the officials of Lucknow. The Boycott Committee ought to give them honourable badges for the tremendous help that it received owing to their stupidity in making the boycott demonstration a magnificent success. Every thing that they did was, from the point of view of the Government, stupid and from the point of view of the boycotters extremely felicitious. It was painful of course to me and to others to see the extraordinarily callous and brutal behaviour of the police. But I suppose that is the price which we shall often have to pay. It was clear on the 30th that the police were out for vengeance. Indeed they gloated about it afterward.. But in their stupidity they did not realise that they had completely played into the hands of the boycotters. They have brought the real issue before the people before the country bereft of all sophistication and legal quibbles. That issue is that British rule in India means the policemans baton and the soldier's bayonet and the real problem is how to overcome them. Logic and reason is unhappy lost on the baton and bayonet. They will be overcome by the strength and sanction that the country develops. In this process of developing sanction we can have a greater allies than the British officials of the kind which Lucknow possesses today.

Visit to Patna

After U.P., the Commission shifted to Patna, where it reached on December 12.[46] A huge number of boycotters welcomed it and there was a partial *hartal* in the business quarters of the city. Muslim shops, however, were open and their business went on as usual. The *hartal* was mostly confined to the Hindu quarters of the city. The Bihar and Orissa Committee which consisted of seven members, *viz.*, Raja Harihar Prasad Narayan Singh, Raja Chandreshwar Prasad Narayan Singh, Raja Rajendra Narayan Bhanja Deo, Babu Lakshmidhar Mahanti, Rai Bahadur Sarat Chandra Roy, Maulvi Saiyd Mubarak Ali and Saiyid Muhammed Akthar Hussain, recommended abolition of dyarchy; responsible government in the province in which the excutive was to be responsible to the legislature and the legislature to the electorate; decentralization to the extent as to make for real autonomy; a second chamber; the formation of a separate Oriya province and safeguards for minorities.[47]

The Commission met at Patna on December 13, 1928, along with members of the Central Committee (except Kikabhai Premchand) and the members of the provincial committee and the secretaries. The following officers gave their oral evidence: Special Officer, Reforms; Finance Secretary; Inspector-General of Police; Chief Inspector of Mines; Revenue Secretary; Director of Industries; Collector of Patna; and the Ex-Settlement Officer, Sambalpur. A number of deputations were received. They were from L. Van Hoeck, Catholic Bishop of Ranchi; a deputation from Chota Nagpur Improvement Society; a deputation from the Bihar Landholders' Association; a deputation from the Bihar and Orissa Muslim Association; and the All-India Yadav Mahasabha and a deputation of the Bihar Provincial Sanatan Dharam Sabha.[48]

Meanwhile the Viceroy delivered the following speech at the dinner given by the European Association at Calcutta on December 17, 1928. "....I am sure that all sober-minded citizens of India must have witnessed with regret, and will condemn, the continued attempts to conduct unmannerly and offensive demonstrations against the Commission and their Indian colleagues. I can understand the attitude of those who, following the hitherto established tradition of boycott, prefer to hold themselves rigidly aloof from the Commission's investigation. I have often expressed my view that such a policy is mistaken and short-sighted; and ill-designed to convince Parliament of the justice of India's claim. But to substitute for this policy of abstention the procedure of noisy and dangerous public demonstration against the chosen representatives of Parliament and their colleagues is to exchange what might have been a dignified protest of responsible persons for the methods of disorderly disturbance of a mob.[49]

Thus the Commission wisely guided by John Simon has already made it plain that it has no other desire but to render a faithful account to Parliament of India's aspirations, and of the conditions under which it is sought to bring these to fruition. They are fortunate in having the assistance of colleagues from India, among whom one of your representatives Arthur Froom, has all the qualities requisite to make him a worthy of European interests.'

The Calcutta Congress, 1928

At the annual session of the Indian National Congress held at Calcutta in December 1928, Motilal Nehru, the President, hit hard on the Simon Commission and its working in India. He said, 'The solemn promises of responsible Government have found fulfilment in that colossal fraud, the Statutory Commission, which is now careering along our streets leaving bleeding heads and broken bones behind. Nothing has so clearly brought out the cold callousness of the officials on the one hand, and the utter helplessness of the people to protest themselves on the other, as the progress of this Commission from town to town. To my mind, the circumstances attending it are symptomatic of a grave organic infection and not merely of the well-known, functional incapacity of the Government. It shows the presence of the toxin of Dyerism in their internal economy. The happenings at Lahore and Lucknow are only mild eruptaions on the surface indicating the deep rooted disease within.'[50]

In the same Congress, Jamnadas Mehta said that the Indian boycott of the Simon Commission was as complete and effective as was the Egyptian boycott of the Milner Commission. He stated that Calcutta saw the beginning of the British rule and it would prove the grave of the British rule.[51]

Visit in the East

The members of the Commission continued their official tour as usual and reached Shillong on January 3, 1929. They, alongwith the Governor of Assam, detrained at Tinsukia, and visited the Doom Dooma tea gardens. Simon engaged himself in talking with the labourers in whose condition he took keen interest. W. Doughlas, the Superintendent of Doom Dooma Tea Company, provided him with an analysis chart of wages applicable to the different classes of labourers and percentage of labourers of various provinces. The party inspected the Beesakopie tea factory and also the hospital attached to that estate and also went into every detail of medical relief provided for female labourers specially.[52]

Thereafter, they motored over to Saikhyaghat, a distance about fifteen miles. Here the Political Officer, Sadiya, with about five hundred tribesmen, who had gathered there to see the 'Ambassador of the Maharani.' They thought that Queen Victoria still ruled over India, and that the Commission had come to inspect various parts of India, and then report to the 'Maharani.' The Abour tribes were represented by four distinct types; Galong, Minyong, Pasi and Padam. The other tribes present were Chalikanta, Digaru Kantis, Ifgpho, Tikhanaga and Miris. The Political Officer related the political history of these tribes since they had come under the influence of the British government.[53]

At Kohima, district headquarters of the Naga Hills, the Commission was welcomed by Naga tribesmen and their chiefs. They were entertained with every characteristic tribal dance. The chiefs of every tribe offered presents of spears, cups and dishes, head-dresses, tails and other articles which these tribesmen valued. Some ladies' petticoats and bodies were presented to Lady Simon. A horn was presented to John Simon. These tribes did not wish to be placed under any legislative council, but wished to be kept directly under the British government and allowed to carry on self-government through their tribal panchayats.[54]

The Assam Committee which consisted of seven members viz. *W.D. Smiles, Amarnath Ray, Munuwarali, Arzan Ali Mazumdar, Keramat Ali, S. Dowerah, and M.N. Boroah,* recommended as follows:

Introduction of responsible government in the province; all the subjects now classed as provincial including police, should in future be administered by ministers responsible to the legislatures, provincial legislature should be unicameral as second chambers are superfluous; universal suffrage and the control of the central government should, in the revised constitution, be restricted in respect of all provincial subjects in the same manner as it was then restricted in respect of the transferred subjects. The central government would, therefore, continue to have a certain measure of control over the provincial administration, although not so extensive as at that time; universal suffrage for all persons of not less than 25 years of age with open voting for those who could read and write; the Assam Legislative Council should consist elected members and not more than 5 members nominated by the Governor; two seats should be reserved for the European community; the representation of Assam in the Central Legislative Assembly should be on the basis of area as well as population; dyarchy should go and Khasi and Jaintia Hills should no longer be classed as backward tracts and it would be brought fully under the reformed constitution.[55]

In Assam, the members of the Statutory Commission interviewed the Chief Secretary, Inspector-General of Police; Inspector-General of Civil Hospitals and Prisons and the Conservator of Forests. It received deputation from the Assam and Surma Valley Branches of the Indian Tea Association, Assam Branch; deputation from the Goalpara Zamindars' Association, deputation from the Primitive and Backward Tribes and deputation from the Assam Provicial Muslim League. The Europeans wanted four seats in the council. There were 1,400 Europeans in Assam of whom, only 400 enjoyed the franchise. The Goalpara Zamindars' Association pressed for the transfer of the Goalpara district to the province of Bengal as their interests were not protected in the province. The Depressed Classes Deputation demanded certain social rights and privileges enjoyed by the high caste Hindus. They also demanded representation in the legislative council. The Muslim League claimed 40 percent representation in the local council and local bodies with separate electorates.[56]

The Calcutta Visit

The Commission's next halt was at Calcutta where it was accorded an angry and resentful welcome. At an emergency meeting of the Executive Council of the Bengal

Provincial Congress Committee on January 8, a committee called the Simon Boycott Committee, which included among others, J.M. Sen Gupta, S.C. Bose and Akram Khan, in order to organize *hartal* and demonstration against the Commission on January 12, the day of its arrival in Calcutta, was constituted. Only Hindu shops and business houses were closed in North Calcutta and there was a partial *hartal* in South Calcutta. All Muslim shops were kept open. Tramcars and other vehicular traffic ran as usual.[89] A mamoth meeting was held at the Shraddhanand Park. It resolved to organise the social boycott of those who dared cooperate with the Commission and to strengthen the movement of the boycott of British goods. B. Sambamurti who spoke at the meeting, said, 'The effective democracy was reflex of the nation's grim determination to repudiate the right of the foreigners to determine her destiny.' Subhash Chandra Bose declared that the Simon Commission had entered Calcutta like 'Pardanashin ladies.'[57] He announced that they would preach boycott during the Commissions' stay and urged the people to resort to social boycott of those who wanted to lower the prestige of the national flag by giving evidence before the Commission. Private schools and colleges were closed and picketing was resorted to by students in front of schools and colleges, where attendence was small.[58]

The Commission sat for oral evidence in Calcutta on January 4, 1929 and interviewed a number of provincial officials and also received a few deputations. The officials were: Special Officer Reforms; Labour Intelligence Officer; Secretary, Local-Self-Government; Commissioner, Burdwan Division; District Officer, Mymensing; Inspector-General of Police; Commissioner of Police, Chief Secretary; Finance Secretary; Chief Justice, High Court of Judicature; Finance Member and Revenue Members, Government of Bengal.[59] The deputation received were as follows: Deputation from the British Indian Association; deputation from the Central National Muhammendan Association; deputation of All-India Association of European Government Servants; deputation of Indian Officers' Association; deputation from the Bengal Depressed Classes Association and the All-

Bengal Namasudra Association; deputation from the Darjeeling Planters' Association; deputation from the Association of Chambers of Commerce of India and Ceylon; deputation from the representatives of Rural Interests from West Bengal and deputation from Kanchrapara Railway Workmen's Union. All these deputation demanded representation of their class and community. The deputation of British Indian Association emphasized that provincial autonomy subject to the safeguards of an Upper House was essential for order, progress and responsible government and the zamindars should be given at best one-third of the elected seats in the local council. The European Services Association demanded security of tenure and financial safeguards.[60]

The members of the Bengal Committee were: Abdulkerim Ghuzanavi (Chairman); W.L. Travers; A.K. Fazl-ul-Huq; Maulvi Abdul Kasem; Bhupendra Narayan Sinha of Nashipur; Maharaja Sashi Kanta Acharjya Chaudhuri of Muktagacha, Mymensing and K.G.M. Farouqi. The committee sat in joint conference with the members of the Commission and the Central Committee at Calcutta in December 1928 and January 1929 and held sittings of its own from time to time. It stated that the ultimate goal so far as this province was concerned, was complete provincial autonomy. It recommended the transfer of all provincial subjects excluding police, to the charge of popular ministers responsible to and removable by the legislature and a strong central government of a federal type capable of exercising a unifying influence over the country as a whole both by legislation and by administrative action. The provincial legislature should be bi-cameral and of a more representative character. Separate communal electorates should be retained and should be extended to all local-self-government bodies. There should be a provincial public service commission composed of members belonging to different communities.[61]

Departure for Rangoon

The Commission and the Central Committee left

Calcutta for Rangoon by the S.S. Tairea on January 27, 1929 and after a voyage of sixty hours docked at Rangoon harbour. The attempts of boycotters to organise a *hartal* in the cityfailed and business was carried on as usual in all quarters with the exception of a few Marwari shops, which were closed. Posters bearing 'Simon, go back' which were pasted all over the city were noticed.[62]

The Burma Committee which consisted of Aung Thin (Chairman), Bah Shin, Ba U, M. Eusoof, Shwe Ba, C.H. Campagnae, and M.M. Rafi, gave its recommendations as follows: 'Separation of Burma from rest of India as Burma's political connection with India is wholly arbitrary and unnatural. It was established by the British rulers of India by force of arms and is being maintained for the sake of administrative convenience. It is not an association of two peoples having natural affinities tending towards union. It is neither a combination of two willing partners. In all essential features of corporate life, Burma widely differs from India. There is nothing in common between the two peoples except their common allegiance to His Majesty, the King-Emperor, which need not necessarily place one of them under the political tutelage of the other. 'The present communal electorates should also be maintained, until conditions alter to justify their abolition. Increased representation should be given to Indians, Karens and Anglo-Indians; unicameral legislature, executive power should be vested in the Governor acting on the advice of the ministers. There should be six ministers, five of whom should be non-officials and elected members of the Legislative Council and one official. Minister shall be appointed by the Governor.'[63]

The members of the Commission interviewed Commissioner of Tenasserim, Chief Conservator of Forests, Secretary to Government of Burma, Forest Department, Finance Secretary, Finance Member, Collector of Rangoon, Chief Secretary, and Inspector-General of Police, Burma. They also received a deputation from the Burma Chamber of Commerce, jointly with the deputation from the Burma Association of Professional and businessmen, deputation from the Burmans League jointly with the deputation of the Separation League, deputation from the British Burman Association, deputation from the Karen Elders and the Karen National Association, deputation from the Provincial Tanzim Committee, deputation of representatives of Indian interests in Burma, and deputation of the Burma Landowners' Association. The deputation of Burmese Leagues wanted separation from India. They feared that if the immigration of Indian continued, the Burmese race would become extinct. The deputation of Indian interest wanted the number of Indian representatives in the Burma Council to be raised from nine to sixteen and of the representatives of Burma in the Assembly to be raised from three to nine.[64]

Reception in Madras

Meanwhile, Madras also got ready with the befitting reception to be accorded to the Simon Commission on the eve of its arrival there. A joint meeting of the Tamil Nadu and Andhra Congress Committee was held at the Mahajan Sabha, Srinivasa Iyengar, presiding. It discussed boycott demonstrations and *hartal* arrangements. The city observed a successful *hartal* on February 18 on the arrival of the Commission. Srinivasa Iyengar, Pattabhi Sitaramayya, Satyamurthy, T. Prakasam and Ramdas Pantulu joined the procession. A meeting was held at the beach and the leaders testified in brief speeches to the successful manner in which the people of Madras had conducted the demonstration. Dr. Sitaramayya said, 'The Commission had to go to Poona in the darkness of night; in Calcutta they were carried through iron barricades; but in Madras, they were being put like goods in a goods train by the harbour authorities and carried to Government House at the owners' risk.'[65]

The Commission interviewed a number of officials and the deputations, the prominent amongst them were Secretary, Provincial Committee, Chief Secretary to Madras Government, Secretary, Local-Self-Government, Labour Commissioner, Inspector-General of Police, Commissioner of Police and deputation from the South Indian Liberal Federation, deputation from the United Planters'

Association of Southern India, deputation from the Madras Presidency Oriya Association, Behrampore (Ganjam), on deputation from the Ganjam Defence League, deputation from the Hindu Religious Endowments Board, deputation from the Madras Presidency Muslim League, deputation from the Depressed classes of the Madras Presidency, deputation from the All-India Adi Dravinda Maha Jana Sabha and the Madras Arundhathi Maha Jana Sabha, deputation from the Kodava Sabha, Mercara, deputation from the Coorg Planters' Association, Mercara; Ganjam District People's Association and the South India Liberal Federation (together), Indian Christian Association, deputation from the Catholic Indian Association of South India, deputation from the Christian Depressed Classes, and a deputation of *Orthodox Brahmans.*[66]

Every deputation put forth its problems. The deputation of South India Liberal Federation stated that dyarchy was unworkable. It recommended the establishment of provincial autonomy in the provinces; the deputation of Indian Christians pressed the claim of their community to seven seats on the local legislature; the deputation of Catholic Indians advocated the retention of the existing communal electorates and demanded adequate and effective representation of their community on the legislatures—both local and central and the deputation of depressed class Christians pleaded for the extension of the same privileges to their community as were enjoyed by the Hindu Depressed Classes.[67]

At Trichur, the Namboodris presented a memorandum to the Commission. It stated, 'It will be indeed a matter of suprise to learn that a vast majority of His Majesty's subjects, belonging to our community, are still in the dark as to the benefits of British rule and to the cultural connection India holds with British Crown. They are now in such a pitiable plight that their only hope for oemancipation rests on the goodwill and sense of justice of the British Crown.'[68]

In Madras, the Committee which was elected by the Madras Legislative Council, had the following seven members:

A.P. Patro (Chairman), S. Kumara swami Reddiyar, The Kumararaja of Venkatagiri, P. Khalifullha, Daniel Thomas, P. Siva Rao and Siva Raj. The Committee held twenty-five meetings to discuss procedure and to study and form conclusions from one hundred and ninety-five memoranda sent from this presidency.[69] The changes proposed were the grant of provincial autonomy or full responsible government, the establishment of responsible government in all the civil departments of the Government of India, except those dealing with defence, foreign relation with Indian states; a declaration by the British government that full Dominion Status in the British Commonwealth of Nations was accepted as the goal of India to be achieved in a reasonable definite period, and that the automatic achievement of such status in such time might be brought about by the provision of adequate means for the Indianization of the army and other forces of defence. Besides, they recommended that immediate action should be taken on the lines of the Skeen Committee so as to have the defence forces officered mainly by Indians in the period set for the attainment of Dominion Status for India. More than one Indian Sandhurst should be opened to train Indian officers. The majority of the committee was of the opinion that there should be separation of executive and judicial functions so as to secure an independent judiciary and improved administration of justice.[70]

Visit to C.P. and Berar

The next halt of the Commission was at the capital of C.P. and Berar. Nagpur organized a successful mass demonstration on the occasion of its arrival on March 14, 1929. All roads leading to the railway station were closed, barricades having been erected. Admission to the railway station was by tickests and only one road leading to Government House was left unbarricaded.[71] The All-Parties' Boycott Committee, Youth League and the Congress organized three processions led by leaders of all parties. Prominent among the leaders were Seth Jamnalal Bajaj, Seth Govind Das, N.B. Khare, Paranjpye and Abhyankar.

The processionists occupied the allotted space in front of the railway station and about two hundred yards from the main gate, mounted *sawars* and special police lined the fencing railway route to keep the boycotters away who numbered about six thousand.[72]

The specials carrying the members of the Commission and members of the Central Committee arrived one after the other. Instantaneously, shouts of, 'Simon, go back,' 'Simon, shame,' were raised; and black flags with the inscription, 'Go back,' 'Lathi Commission not wanted,' waved when the members of Commission and Central Committee motored towards their official destination. After the members had left, the leaders addressed the boycotters who formed a mass meeting and criticised the action of the members of the Central Committee in having betrayed the national cause and national honour.[73]

The oral evidence started on March 14. Present were the Chairman, John Simon and all the members of the Commission (except Lord Burnham and Attlee) and of the Central Committee (except Kikabhai Premchand and Zulfiqar Ali Khan) and the secretaries. The prominent government officials interviewed were the Chief Secretary to the Government of the C.P. and Finance Secretary. Besides, they received a deputation from the Muslims of C.P. and Berar; deputation from the All-India Depressed Classes Association and a deputation from the Central Provinces and Berar Non-Brahmin Political Association. The Muslim deputation complained that they got seven seats out of fifty elected seats in the local legislative council and claimed more seats in order that Muslim repesentation might be adequate and effective; the depressed classes' deputation wanted separate electorates in order to secure adequate representation in legislatures and the C.P. Non-Brahmin deputation demanded voting rights and entry into temples of the Depressed Classes.[74]

From Nagpur, the Commission moved to Delhi. Thirty-six prominent Sikhs gave a banquet in honour of John Simon and his party at Maidens Hotel on March 23. Sunder Singh Majithia, their well-known representative, said that inspite of the promises given and hopes forth by the highest authorities both in England and India for safeguarding the rights and interests of the Sikh community, the reforms scheme ignored not only their special claims, but even denied and placed them in a position which his community would never accept. John Simon assured them that the Commission would look facts fair in the case.[75]

A memorandum was also submitted to the Commission by the Government of India. Starting with a short sketch of the existing reformed constitution, it dealt with the communal representation in the legislatures and local bodies, the representation of commerce, industry, labour, education and other interests in the provincial and central legislatures, the system of administration in the North-West Frontier Province, and the province of Delhi and Andaman and Nicobar islands, the formation of separate Andhra province, Tamil province and Kannada province; amalgamation of the Oriya-speaking peoples, and the transfer of Sylhet from Assam to Bengal.[76] In the second volume, the memorandum stated about the position of High Courts, the superior civil service in India, division of sources of revenue between the central government and the provincial government, financial relations between the Government of India and the provincial governments, memorandum on the development and working of representative institutions in the sphere of Local-Self-Government. Memorandum on the progress of education in British India between 1916-1926, question of introduction of reforms in Baluchistan, and the system of administration in Ajmer—Merwara. Besides it also mentioned about the position of the Governor in regard to Indian States not in direct relation with the Governor-General-in-Council, the Public Service Commission, the status and position of India in the British Empire, the Depressed Classes, the state and industry, and the rates of pay in the new provincial services.[77]

During a few months' stay here, the Commission toured whole of India, met and interviewed prominent persons and received memorandum from numerous communities and associations and thus gathered information for its report.

Thereafter, it sailed for England on April 13, 1929. Vernon Hartshorn in an interview with the representative of the *The Times of India* stated that the Commission had made an exhaustive investigation into the present system of government in India. He added that in making its report to Parliament, the Commission would be entirely uninfluenced by black flags. The recommendation would be made regardless of what happened in the Assembly or outside. 'Very sorry to leave, but glad to go.' With this or similar expression, John Simon greeted every one present at Ballard Pier in Bombay.[78]

Scenes reminiscent of the arrival of the Simon Commission in Bombay, Lahore, Lucknow and elsewhere in India, were witnessed in London, when John Simon and his colleagues arrived there. A hostile demonstration was staged in the Hyde Park under the joint auspices of the London Branch of the Indian National Congress, the Anti-Imperialist League and the Workers' Welfare League of India. [79] A procession headed by S. Saklatvala was forbidden to march to Victoria Station. Several of the demonstrators who were ordered to disperse, offered satyagraha and were forcibly removed, and according to the correspondent of the *Civil and Military Gazette,* the police took away banners and smashed them. 'To hell with Simon Commission' was typical of the flags carried by the Hyde Park demonstrators, several of whom when ordered to disperse attempted, 'satyagraha' and were forcibly removed. Four persons, i.e., Sanyal, Dr. Banerjee, Dadvo and R. Lovell were arrested on charges of obstructing public. T.P. Sinha, Assistant Secretary of the London Branch of the Indian National Congress, in an interview with *Reuter*, said, "We will not demonstrate against any individual member of the Statutory Commission, but we will continue to do so whenever they meet in an official capacity."[80]

Thus it is evident that the opposition to the Simon Commission did not end here. In the House of Commons on April 29, 1929, when a man in the galley threw a bundle of leaflets on the floor of the House and shouted, 'Down with the Simon Commission.' Later, a woman rose and shouted

'Down with the Government.' She was removed from the House. The leaflets read, 'To Hell with the Commission,' 'Down with Imperialism,' 'Release Indian Comrades.' The leaflets were signed, 'London District Committee of the International Classwar Prisoners' Association.' The House was startled and overwhelmed by this unexpected intrusion.[81]

At this point, the India Office also presented a memorandum to the Indian Statutory Commission.[82] It said about the relationship between Indian Office and the Government of India, the India Office in relation to the civil services in India, international status of India, the structure of Indian Government finance, financial relations between the central and provincial governments, and the financial relations between His Majestry's Government and the Government of India.[83] Finally the Commission submitted its Report in 1930.

References

1. The full team consisted of Sir Sankarran Nair, Sir Hari Singh Gour, Sir Arthur Froom, Dr. Abdullah Suhrawardy, Sir Kikabai Premchand, Nawab Ali Khan, Sardar Singh Uberoi, Sir Zulfikar Ali Khan and M.C. Rajah.
2. *See* Codogan, Edward, *op.cit.,* p. 114.
3. *Times of India,* October 13, 1928. Among notable passengers by the Majola were Lady Irwin and Mrs. Crerar, wife of Sir James Crerar, Home Member, Government of India.
4. *Ibid.*
5. *Ibid.*
6. *Bombay Chronicle,* October 13, 1928.
7. *Ibid.*
8. *Ibid.*
9. *Times of India,* October 15, 1928.
10. Indian Statutory Commission, Oral Evidence, Bombay, Vols. I and II.
11. *Ibid.*
12. Reforms Office, Miscellaneous F. 26, 1928.
13. Report of the Bombay Provincial Committee.
14. *Ibid.*
15. *The Tribune,* October 23, 1928.

16. *See* Order of the District Magistrate, Lahore, quoted in *The Tribune* October 31, 1928.
17. *The Tibune,* October 31, 1928.
18. *The Tribune,* November 1, 1928.
19. *The Tribune,* November, 2, 1928.
20. *Ibid.*
21. *Ibid.*
22. *Young India,* November 8, 1928.
23. *Ibid.*
24. *Ibid.*
25. *The Tribune,* November 9, 1928.
26. *Ibid,* November 10, 1928.
27. Indian Statutory Commission: Oral Evidence.
28. He was Secretary and represented the Sikhs.
29. He represented the European interests.
30. *The Tribune,* November 16, 1928.
31. *The Tribune,* November 14 and 15, 1928. The Muslims of Sind insisted on separation of Sind before the Joint Free Conference. The Hindus oposed the separation of Sind and supported joint electorates.
32. *Times of India,* November 20, 1928. Nawab Mohamed Samad Khan of Khyber was the Afridi chief.
33. The deputation consisted of 8 persons from Peshawar, 5 persons from Dera Ismail Khan, 4 from Hazara, 4 from Kohat and 4 from Bannu. *See* the Report of the NWFP Committee.
34. Quoted in *The Tribune,* November 19, 1928. Gandhi also stated that with Lalji's death, a great plane has set in India's solar system.
35. This resolution is quoted in *The Tribune,* November 27, 1928.
36. It was the forty-third session of Indian National Congress. For reference *see* its proceedings.
37. Both Pandit D.P. Mishra and Pandit Motilal Nehru spoke with deep emotions about the death of Lala Lajpat Rai in the Central Assembly. Proceedings are quoted in *The Tribune,* November 17, 1929.
38. *Ibid.* The division was as follows: 57

    (a) For enquiry, elected Indian members 55; nominated non-official 2

(b)	Against enquiry:	45
	officials	26
	others	19

Only one elected Indian voted with the government.

39. *The Tribune,* November 23, 1928.
40. Indian Statutory Commission, Oral Evidence, Delhi.
41. Misbehaved themselves during the last three days at Lucknow, See *The Tribune,* December 4, 1928.
42. *The Tribune,* December 4, 1928; *See* full text of Pandit Jawaharlal Nehru's speech on Lucknow incident.
43. *Ibid,* December 8, 1928.
44. Report of the U.P. Committee.
45. Indian Statutory Commission, Oral Evidence, United Province, Vols. I and II.
46. *Times of India,* December 14, 1928.
47. Report of the Bihar and Orissa Committee, pp. 529-90.
48. Indian Statutory Commission, Oral Evidence, Vols. I and II.
49. Speeches by Lord Irwin, Vol. I, pp. 493-96.
50. *See* the Proceedings of Indian National Congress, Calcutta session, 1928. Pandit Motilal Nehru presided.
51. *Ibid.*
52. *Times of India,* January 5 and January 11, 1929.
53. *Ibid.*
54. *Ibid.*
55. Report of the Assam Committee, pp. 592-611.
56. *Ibid.*
57. *Times of India,* January 15, 1929.
58. *Ibid.*
59. Indian Statutory Commission, Oral Evidence, Vols. I and II.
60. Indian Statutory Commission, Oral Evidence, Vols. I and II.
61. Report of the Bengal Provincial Committee.
62. *Times of India,* January 31, 1929.
63. Report of the Burma Committee, pp. 510-25.
64. Indian Statutory Commission, Oral Evidence, Burma.
65. *Times of India,* February 20, 1929.
66. Report of the Madras Committee, Vol. I.

67. Report of the Madras Committee, Vol. II.
68. Indian Statutory Commission, Report of the Madras Committee, Vol. II G.O.I., 1920.
69. *The Tribune,* March 16, 1929.
70. *Ibid.*
71. Indian Statutory Commission, Oral Evidence, Central Provinces.
72. For reference *see Times of India,* March 25, 1929. The hosts included Sir Sunder Singh Majithia, Raja Sir Daljit Singh, Sir Jogendra Singh, S.B. Shivdev Singh and Sardar Sobha Singh.
73. Memoranda submitted to the Indian Statutory Commission by the Government of India, Vols. I and II, 1930.
74. *Ibid,* Vol II, 803.
75. *See Times of India,* April 15, and *The Tribune,* April 16, 1929 1929; The Commissioners were accorded a warm send off by representatives of the non-Brahmin Party, members of the Muslim Federation, the Bombay Chamber of Commerce, the Bombay European Association and ministers of the Government of 1929.
76. *The Tribune,* April 30, 1929.
77. *Ibid.*
78. *Ibid.*
79. India Office Memoranda submitted to the Indian Statutory Commission, pp. 1573-1604.
80. *Ibid.*

6

Oral Evidence: A Glimpse

The Commission then rose late in the afternoon, having held the longest sitting since its public enquiry.

Interview of Miles Irving

Lahore—2nd November, 1928

The Joint Free Conference met at 10 o'clock this morning. Mr. Miles Irving, who had been collecting data for the Commission in the Punjab, and Khan Bahadur Muzaffar Hussain Khan, Election Commissioner, were examined.

Mr. Miles Irving said that the Punjab Government had expressed no opinion regarding the communal composition of the Council of the future. He would not, therefore, express any opinion on the subject.

Sir John Simon said that they only wanted to get a picture of the working of the Reforms in respect of communal division and franchise.

Mr. Irving gave figures showing that, while Mohammedans were more in population in the Province, their voters were 44 per cent of the total. Sikhs who formed only 11 per cent of the population had 24 per cent of the total and Hindus, who formed 33 per cent., had 33 per cent of the total. He further pointed out that though the urban population was 11 per cent and rural population 89 per cent, urban voters were 70 per cent and rural voters 88 per cent of the total.

Sir John Simon said that the rural area had not got representation among voters according to their mathematical proportion. But Irving further added that, if the existing qualification as regards assessment of land which applied to urban areas were applied to rural areas, it would practically double the Mohommedan and Sikh votes in rural areas, but would not improve the position of Hindus to the same extent. He told Captain Sikander Hayat Khan that no member in the Punjab Council could be said to represent the small landowner.

He agreed with Dr. Narang that the majority in the Punjab Council belonged to the agricultural classes and that the Land Alienation Act stood in the way of non-agriculturists buying lands and becoming rural voters.

Mr. M. C. Rajah pointed out that, though there were about three millions of depressed classes in the Punjab, they had no representative in the Council. Sir John Simon said that while the hardships of the depressed classes were not the same in the Punjab as in some other Provinces the point raised by Mr. Raja was important.

Evidence of J.G. Beazley

Mr. J. G. Beazley, Secretary to the Government in the Transferred Departments, was the next witness examined.

Mr. Cadogan opened the examination by asking whether it was a fact that there was no communal representation on District Boards and whether there was a system of adjustment to secure a fairly equitable representation of the various communities. Mr. Beazley replied in the affirmative but added that there had been a demand for communal representation. The Deputy Commissioner was the Chairman of all the District Boards in the Province except two. If there was a desire among 50 per cent of the elected members to have a non-official as Chairman, the Deputy Commissioner always stood out.

Recently, the Government enquired of some District Boards whether they wished to have non-officials as their Chairman and every one of them replied that they did not wish to have a non-official as Chairman. When a Deputy Commissioner was Chairman, the Control and supervision were effective.

Mr. Beazley also said that the Chairman were non-officials in all the Municipalities except in three. Under the present system of government, there was an effective system by which the central authority could exercise control over the Municipalities and District Boards.

Nawab Muzaffar Khan

Lahore—3rd November 1928

Giving evidence on this day Nawab Muzaffar Khan, who had acted as Election Commissioner, explained how voters' lists were compiled, and votes registered in the Punjab. He was of opinion that the voters' lists in the Province were fairly accurate. During the last Council election 305,873 votes were polled. In one constituency, votes recorded was 75 per cent of the total number of voters.

Sir John Simon said he was glad to hear that the percentage of votes polled was gradually increasing.

Continuing Nawab Muzaffar Khan said that on the occasion of the last elections 1,190 women voted for a constituency out of a total of 21,000. He attributed the small number to the fact that women suffrage had been introduced but a short time before the elections. In the case of Moslem women, purdah proved to be a handicap. Another reason was that separate polling booths could not be set up for women.

Sir John Simon said that in England in the past there had been cases of bribing voters, but conditions had improved considerably. He asked whether cases of bribing voters had occurred in the Punjab ? Nawab Muzaffar Khan replied that there were cases of feeding voters, but this was due to the fact that in rural areas there were no shops, and besides Indians were a very hospitable people.

Sir John Simon asked whether the Commissioners would receive hospitality if they went to villages ? Witness : You are welcome visitors : but hospitality is extended even to unwelcome visitors (Laughter).

Nawab Muzaffar Khan admitted that in many cases, candidates for the Assembly had no personal touch with voters owing to the vastness of the constituencies. They generally canvassed through agents.

Punjab Labour Board's Evidence

A deputation of the Punjab Central Labour Board was

next examined. The deputation urged that, if franchise was not made universal, every member of a registered Trade Union should be given the right of voting for the Provincial and Central Legislatures. The Deputation was headed by Mr. M. A. Khan, their President and the General Secretary of the General Workers' Union of N. W. Railway.

Their examination was opened by Mr. Vernon Hartshorn to whom they said that under the present Government, both for the Provincial and the Central Legislatures, voting qualifications were determined by age, education and ownership of property, and thus the great masses who formed the major portion of India's population were barred from taking any part in the constitution of the Government to make the future Government more representative. It was essential that general adult franchise should be adopted and if the present circumstances did not allow of this, property qualifications should at least be so relaxed as to cover a fairly large proportion of the population to make representation in real spirit.

So far as labour was concerned, every member of a registered Trade Union should be given the right of voting for the Provincial and Central Legislatures. *Achhoot* (untouchables) organisations and tenants paying about Rs. 2 monthly as rent should also be given this right. Women aged 35 and those educated up to a certain standard, and not less than 22 years of age, should also be given the right of voting. The Deputation urged the introduction of joint electorates with multiple transferable vote; but the allotments of seats should be fixed according to the population of each community. One-fourth of the total seats should be reserved for labour : half by nomination (to be made by labour organisations) and half by election in special constituencies created for the purpose.

Mr. Hartshorn wanted to know the strength of the Trade Unions.

Mr. Khan replied that registered Trade Unions had a membership of about 500,000 and unregistered about 1,000,000.

The Deputation urged the appointment of a separate Labour Minister in each Province, to be nominated by the

Governor along with the other Ministers. He should be in charge of all matters relating to the welfare of labour, the peasantry and the untouchables; their education, health and sanitation, and he should see to the proper operation of all laws touching the interests of labour, such as the Trade Unions Act, the Workmen's Compensation Act, the Trades Dispute Act, etc.

Question : Do you not think these will involve too much work on one Minister ?

Answer : At present Ministers have larger portfolios.

The deputation urged the appointment of courts of arbitration in each Province, with the tribunal consisting of three representatives of labour, three of capital, two of the Government and two of the public. In case of disputes between labour and capital not being settled within two months' time, the tribunal should have right of interfering in the matter and giving the final award.

The Deputation stated that the present Councils consisted of members of the bourgeois, and landlord classes. In the case of labour employed by Government the employees should be given an equal partnership in the management, control, direction, and finance of the Department concerned through their representatives nomination by their registered Trade Unions. It should be made obligatory on employers to open day and night schools and colleges, at their own expense, according to the requirements of labour. Such education should be compulsory and free of charge for the labour classes.

Dr. Narang : Supposing I own a small factory with 50 workmen, should I open a college for labourers ? Witness : You join with another employer for this purpose.

The Deputation urged the grant of various privileges for labour such as stability of service, a living wage and old age pension.

Lahore 15th November 1928

Hindu Deputation's Evidence

The Joint Free Conference took up non-official evidence to-day, entering upon to most controversial stage of its inquiry in the Punjab. A Hindu deputation waited on them in the morning and a Moslem one in the afternoon. The Hindu deputation was led by Pandit Nanakchand. The other members of the deputation included the Hon'ble Rai Bahadur Lala Ramsaran Das, Rai Bahadur Motisagar, Rai Bahadur Durgadas, Pandit Bishen Narain, Rai Bahadur Sewakram, Mr. Purilal Jaganath, Mr. Agnihotri, Professor Gulshan Rai and others. The deputationists represented the National Reform Party in the Punjab Council and the Provincial Hindu Sabha and the National Democratic League. Professor Gulshan Rai submitted his own memorandum.

Dr. Gokulchand led the examination for the Provincial Committee, followed by Chaudhuri Zafarali, Sardar Ujjal Singh, Mr. Roberts and Captain Sikander Hayat Khan while from the Central Committee Sardar Shivdev Singh Uberoi, Sir Zulfiquar Ali Khan, Dr. Suhrawardy, Sir Arthur Froom and Sir Hari Singh Gour examined the witnesses.

After both the Provincial and Central Committees had examined the deputation, Sir John Simon briefly examined the witnesses in order to elicit their point of view clearly. It appeared that the conference had agreed beforehand to adhere to a strict allocation of time between the wings, and thus out of two hours and a quarter, the Provincial and Central Committee took one hour each while Sir John occupied daily quarter of an hour. Strict adherence to the time table minimised largely the tension which the evidence that was tendered often tended to create. In spite of the considerable restraint shown by all sections of the conference there were frequent occasions when feelings threatened to run high. Sir John Simon controlled the proceedings with tact and firmness.

One important feature of the day's proceedings was the disclosure made to the Conference at Poona evidently in camera and by one of the members of the Bombay Government that one way of reconciling the demand of the Muslims for separate electorates and of the Hindus for joint electorates would be to provide for a panel of Muslim candidates to be elected purely by a Muslim electorate from whom the Joint Electorate shall be free to elect Muslim representatives. Sir John Simon said that it was claimed for this scheme that while permitting joint electorates with reservation of seats for Muslims it did at the same time assure that any representative returned by the joint electorate would be a representative acceptable to the Muslim community and not merely a sham representative.

Sir John Simon said he held not views no the merits of the scheme. He only wanted to know the views of the deputation.

Pandit Nanakchand, leader of the Deputation, said that he had not considered the scheme and could give no off-hand answer, while one member of the deputation intervened and said that he thought it to be a good scheme.

Sir John Simon said the leader of the deputation had exercised his discretion wisely in not giving an off-hand reply as it was an intricate question. He continued in reply to an eager statement of another deputationist that he liked the scheme. "I would not be in a hurry to approve it."

To Sir John Simon who pointed out that the declaration of no reforms except on the basis of abolition of all communal principle, went contrary to the Nehru report, Pandit Nanakchand said that the Nehru report was a compromise scheme drawn in emulation of the Government with a view to enlist the support of Muslims. He was opposed to any compromise. That was his party's view also. They would even ask for withdrawal of the present reforms if communalism was continued.

Dr. Gokulchand Narang : What is the view of your party in regard to political advance ?

Pandit Nanak Chand

Pandit Nanakchand : We are in favour of Dominion Status provided there is complete abolition of the communal principle in the legislatures in the local bodies, in the services etc., in all parts of India and provided also there is no discrimination of any caste or religion in matters of distribution of civic rights or the imposition of civic disabilities. Granted these two conditions we are in favour of advance to Dominion Status. But in case communal representation is retained in any shape or form and in any part of India, we are not in favour of any advance.

Dr. Narang : It is not stating a broad proposition ?

Pandit Nanakchand : No, we state it as our considered and deliberate opinion. In our opinion communal representation has intensified communal bitterness and is responsible for the frequent riots, intruders and bloodshed which have taken place since the reforms.

Sir John Simon : Do you consider communal representation responsible for these things ?

Pandit Nanakchand : Yes, I can give authority for this statement from the opinions expressed by the leaders of the Hindu, Muslim and Sikh communities.

Sir John Simon suggested that Pandit Nanakchand might supply the "conference" secretariat with his citations of authority.

Continuing Pandit Nanakchand stated that with the introduction of the communal principle under the Montagu Reforms in regard to legislatures it had been extended to municipalities in order to secure Muslim predominance over other minority communities; and it was the deliberate opinion of the Hindus of the Punjab that communal representation was not extended to District Boards for the chief reason that if it was introduced the Hindus would have gained more seats and the Muslims would have lost some seats. He also maintained that the National Union Party in the Punjab Council was really a Muslim Party though it included some Hindus. To call the party a Rural or Agricultural Party was a misnomer. It was a camouflage.

Pandit Nanakchand dissented from the evidence of Mr. Emerson, Chief Secretary in regard to the statement that appointment to the services on communal lines had not affected efficiency. In the witnesse's opinion it had.

Dr. Narang : What is the result ?

Pandit Nanakchand : It leads to inefficiency and corruption. Recently, when certain public servants were prosecuted they offered a communal defence. If he was a Muslim, he alleged that the charge was due to Hindu machinations, and if he was a Hindu he alleged vice versa.

Sir Mahomed Shafi as counsel for the accused in a case in which a public servant was charged, put forward this communal defence.

Lord Burnham : I am sorry to intervene. But, I appeal to the Chairman whether statements about individuals should be allowed to be made to the conference unless supported by authority.

Pandit Nanakchand : I can give authority in support of my statement. I can tender to the conference a report of the arguments of Sir Md. Shafi in that case.

Lord Burnham : I only appealed to the Chairman.

Sir John Simon : It is understood that in a grave constitutional inquiry of the sort in which the conference is engaged it is not desirable to make mention of individuals. In this case, a reference has been made to the arguments said to have been used by Sir Md. Shafi in his capacity as counsel. What counsel says in his capacity as counsel cannot be used to prove anything. I would ask the official shorthand writer to strike off the reference to Sir Md. Shafi.

Pandit Nanakchand : I am sorry, Sir, to have made a personal reference.

Continuing, Pandit Nanakchand said : We are not in favour of any political advance unless the communal principle is totally abolished, as we consider that any power given would be used not for the advancement of the country but for the domination of one community over another.

Dr. Narang : Is the provision in the Government of India Act that none shall be disabled from entering service by reason of creed, etc., acted up to ?

Pandit Nanakchand : No.

Dr. Narang : Do you favour an amendment of the Government of India Act to secure that none shall be disqualified for the highest post by reason of caste, creed etc. ?

Pandit Nanakchand : Yes.

To a further question Pandit Nanakchand said that the Land Alienation Act was one illustration of communal legislation. The local Government notified certain castes and communities as members of agricultural tribes. The notified castes and communities included persons who held no land and who did not subsist on land and who were in no way agriculturists. And persons who owned lands and who subsisted on land and who were agriculturists for generations were excluded from those who were members of notified agricultural tribes.

Lala Harkishenlal had sought to introduce a Bill to exempt from the operation of the Land Alienation Act, acquisition of lands for industrial purposes, but it was defeated by the votes of the so-called members of the agricultural tribes.

Dr. Narang : Lala Harkishen Lal's Bill was only for giving effect to the recommendation of the Industrial Commission but it was still defeated.

Pandit Nanakchand continued : The Money-Lenders' Bill is another illustration of class legislation. It was an effort by the Muslims to destroy the commerce and trade of the Hindus and Sikhs. It affected not only the Hindus and Sikhs, but also Muslims who were not members of agricultural tribes. Twenty-six Muslim military officers had memoralised the Government against that Bill. Sikhs not belonging to agricultural tribes had also protested against the Money-Lenders' Bill in a conference held at Hoshiarpur.

Sir John Simon to Dr. Narang : What is your suggestion I understand that you regard these pieces of legislation as illustrating communal legislation. But what is your further point ? Do you suggest that the Parliament should repeal some acts of the local legislature, or do you suggest any amendment to the Government of India Act ? How far are these questions relevant to the constitutional inquiry?

Dr. Narang : We want an amendment of the Government of India Act to debar legislatures from undertaking any legislation which is discriminatory in character with reference to caste, creed or birth. Raja Narindranath has submitted a draft clause which embodies this idea.

Sir John Simon : I understand the point. The British Commissioners are fully alive to this point.

Pandit Nanakchand : There is a similar suggestion in the Nehru Report also.

To Dr. Narang Pandit Nanakchand said : I would recommend the adoption of the majority of the declarations contained in the Nehru Report for embodiment in the constitution. The depressed classes are an expropriated class in this province. I want all disabilities in regard to them to be removed and I want that they should be placed on the same footing with high caste Hindus and Muslims. I am not in favour of separate electorates or reservation for the depressed classes, as it would only lead to their exploitation by interested persons. I am opposed on principle to all reservation. Mr. Emerson, Chief Secretary, is wrong when he suggests that high caste Hindus are responsible for the condition of the depressed classes. We have four societies in the Punjab working for the amelioration of the depressed classes. Brahmins and depressed classes interdine in the Punjab. In the D.A.V. College which is a premier institution, depressed class boys are admitted freely. Recently Brahmin cooks refused to cook for depressed class boys, and wanted to make a difference, and they were bodily dismissed by the management. The Hindus in the Punjab Legislative Council have sought to remove the civic and political disabilities of the depressed classes but opposition has been met with from Muslims and the Government.

Continuing, Pandit Nanakchand said he would recommend increase of seats in the Punjab Council to 150.

Dr. Narang : Do not Hindus who are in a minority in the province want any safeguards ?

Pandit Nanakchand : No. They are prepared to make a sacrifice in the interest of democratic advance.

Dr. Narang : Do you want abolition of communal representation in every province ?

Pandit Nanakchand : Yes the politics of one province react on the politics of another province. In the Punjab the politics of the United Provinces react on its politics.

Continuing, Pandit Nanakchand said : It is my personal view that whenever any Hindu is appointed as a Minister, he should be really a representative Hindu. He would suggest that a convention be established by which a panel of Hindu names should be submitted to the Governor by the Hindu members of the Council from which the Governor should select his Minister. He would like the same policy to be followed in selecting Muslim and Sikh Ministers. It would be necessary to retain this principle for sometime until communal feelings which were now violently manifested subsided. "I am in favour of joint responsibility of Ministers to the legislature. I also favour transfer of law, order and justice to the Central Government. In my opinion the Central Government should retain powers of superintendence and direction over the local Government.

Lala Jagannath Agarwala here explained the point of view of the deputation. He said : Our considered view is that the Federal system of government is not suited to this country. We want a unitary form of government with certain autonomy to the provinces. The history of India shows the necessity of a strong Central Government.

Pandit Nanakchand then explained why the Hindus wanted certain safeguards in regard to the defence of India. He said' 'We would point out that the Punjab is practically a Frontier Province. Next to the North-West Frontier, it will have to bear the brunt of any invasion. Considering that we have a virile and easily inflammable Muslim population and also in view of the fact that the Muslims of the province have a tendency to look to Afghanistan and other Muslim countries for protection as evidenced by the Hijrat Movement of 1922 and also considering that the Hindus have a large stake in the Punjab, we want certain safeguards. We want abolition of the convention and rule by which certain Hindu sections classified as non-martial races, are not recruited to the Army.

Chaudhari Zafarullah

Chaudhuri Zafarullah : Why do you claim that communal representation is responsible for communal tension when in a large number of municipal committees and in the District Boards Joint Electorates prevail ? Is it not a fact that a riot took place at Rawalpindi and joint electorates exist in Rawalpindi Municipality ?

Pandit Nanakchand : My point is that owing to the introduction of communal representation, communal leaders and newspapers have come into being poisoning the atmosphere in the Punjab and rendering it difficult for the Hindus and Muslims to live peacefully together.

Chaudhuri Zafarullah : In the Punjab both separate electorates and joint electorates are being tried side by side.

Pandit Nanakchand : But in order to secure return of communally-minded men communal leaders and papers have created an atmosphere in which arson, loot and riots have become frequent occurrences.

Chaudhuri Zafarullah : But in separate electorates one Muslim would stand against another Muslim candidate. It is only that a Muslim who appeals most to the bigotry and communal passion of the Muslims that gets returned. The same is true of the Hindu candidate also.

Chaudhuri Zafarullah : May not the same thing happen in joint electorates ?

Pandit Nanakchand : It might happen for some time, but it will be a temporary phase. You presuppose only one Hindu and one Muslim contesting. In fact, there will be many Hindus and many Muslims contesting.

Chaudhuri Zafarullah : Is it not a fact that under the Minto-Morley Reforms under joint electorates, the struggle always was boiled down to a struggle between the Muslim and non-Muslim candidate ?

Pandit Nanakchand : I do not know that it was so.

Dr. Narang : Under the Morley-Minto Reforms, it was by indirect election.

Pandit Nanakchand : My friend, the Hon'ble Lala Ram Sarandas, reminds me that in one election the Muslim candidate, Mr. Yusuf, beat him by one vote.

Chaudhuri Zafarullah : Is it the view of all Hindus that there should be no advance unless there be abolition of the communal principle ?

Pandit Nanakchand : That is our view.

To Sir John Simon, Pandit Nanakchand reiterated that it was the considered opinion of the deputation that there should be no advance unless there was complete abolition of the communal principle. The deputation opposed even joint electorates with reservation. The deputationists also wanted that the communal principle should be eliminated from the services and all other bodies.

To Chaudhuri Zafarullah, Pandit Nanakchand said that he relied on the report of the Co-operative Department for his proposition that communal appointments resulted in inefficiency.

Chaudhuri Zafarullah : In that report the Inspector says that inefficiency is due to the reluctance of bank directors to appoint *Bania* accountants although they are best qualified and to their preference for members of the agriculture tribes. It is not the Government that appoint.

Pandit Nanakchand : It illustrates my point all the same.

Referring to the Money Lenders' Bill, Pandit Nanakchand said that when a similar bill was sought to be introduced in the Assembly, its introduction was opposed by the Government of India. But in the Punjab, the local Council passed the Bill into law. But the Governor withheld assent.

To question by Chaudhuri Zafarullah, Pandit Nanakchand said that he objected to imposing a disability on the depressed classes which would prevent them from acquiring land. There was no statutory prohibition, but there was the customary law which was enforceable by the law courts which prevented them from acquiring lands. He was opposed to that disability on its fundamental aspect.

In the Punjab villages, the feudal system prevailed which was opposed to democracy. According to the feudal system prevailing in the Punjab villages, non-proprietors had to pay certain levies if they performed marriage or other ceremonies.

Continuing Pandit Nanakchand said : I am not opposed to adult franchise, but I would not recommend it for the legislation immediately. I would recommend adult franchise in the elections to the local boards and municipalities in the first instance. I favour lowering of the franchise to a certain extent, but I have not worked out the details. I would give votes to literates. I would also advocate increased representation for the urban constituencies. In fact, I would make no distinction between the rural and urban constituencies. I would suggest increased representation for the University, Commerce and Industries. I would suggest special representation for income-tax payers.

Chaudhuri Zafarullah : Are not Muslims who form 44 per cent only of the voters in a minority against the Hindus and Sikhs combined ?

Sir John Simon : The witness is entitled to point out that one must not merely take the total percentage, but must also look into the strength of the respective constituencies.

Sir John Simon then took the Nehru Report and pointed out that according to the statistics and maps given in it, Muslims predominated in West Punjab, Hindus and Sikhs predominated in the East Punjab, and there was also a mixed zone.

To Dr. Narang, who invited attention to a passage in the Nehru Report in explanation of the statistics, Sir John Simon said : "This is not the first time, I assure you, that I have looked into it."

Pandit Nanakchand then explained that he favoured the provision of special educational facilities to all backward communities whether Muslims, depressed classes, or any other communities, as he believed that education was the foundation of democracy. Pandit Nanakchand then said that his party in the Council consisted of 19 members, of whom four were members of agricultural tribes. They were not present in the deputation and one or two of them had possibly not seen or approved of the memorandum before its submission to the Commission.

To Mr. Roberts, Pandit Nanakchand said that he had not considered the question of the transfer of commerce to the Central Government.

To Sardar Ujjal Singh, Pandit Nanakchand said that although there was no communal representation in the district boards, the constituencies were so grouped as to secure predominance of certain communities in ward. It amounted to a form of communal representation.

To Sardar Uberoi, Pandit Nanakchand said : We suggested transfer of Law and Order to the Central Government, because we think that it would secure immunity to these departments from communal influence. We had experience in the Punjab of attacks on judges of the High Court and on the constitution of the High Court on communal grounds, which were not calculated to ensure independence. It is our belief that if they were transferred to the Central Government they would be more free from communal attacks.

To Sir Zulfiquar Ali Khan Pandit Nanakchand said that he was opposed to reservation for any community in regard to the services.

Sir Zulfiquar : Are you then against Indianisation ?

Pandit Nanakchand : No. I do not want reservation for any community. I would certainly employ British citizens who are domiciled Indian subjects if they are more fitted than other Indian nationals. He also said that are conference of Hindus held in Lahore during the last visit of the Commission a resolution was passed that even the present reforms may be withdrawn if the communal principle was not abolished. It indicated the strength of the Hindu feeling on the question. Pandit Nanakchand also said that if as a result of the appointments on the basis of efficiency only, Muslims were appointed to 100 per cent of the posts he would not oppose it.

Dr. Suhrawardy : Do you not think that more than communal representation, the caste system is a greater impediment to national advance ? Is not the caste system an enemy of Hinduism ?

Pandit Nanakchand : To the extent that caste is an impediment to national progress, we are seeking to abolish it.

Dr. Suhrawardy : Has not caste been the bane of India since the times of Asoka and Vikramaditya ?

Dr. Narang : In the times of Asoka, caste was abolished.

Dr. Suhrawardy : I want to put my questions. I have only very little time.

Sir John Simon : I do not want any complaint to be made. It is the conference as a whole that has agreed to rationing of time, and it is not open to a member to complain after agreeing to the decision.

Dr. Suhrawardy : I make no complaint Sir. I was only thinking loudly.

Dr. Narang : I would like to make it clear, Sir, that I agreed to the time limit only because there was no help for it.

Sir John Simon : As practical men engaged in practical work, we cannot but ration the time.

Dr. Suhrawardy : Will you agree that no objection was raised to the introduction of communal representation in the Punjab ?

Pandit Nanakchand : It was a blunder.

Dr. Suhrawardy : Do you know that communal representation was introduced in Bengal in 1999 with the consent of Mr. Gokhale, then Congress leader ?

Pandit Nanakchand: He was wrong.

Dr. Subrawardy: Do you know that the Lucknow Pact conceded to Muslims separate electorates ? Pandit Nanakchand: It was a great blunder.

Dr. Suhrawardy : I would invite your attention then to a greater blunder. Is it not a fact that the late Sir Surendranath Bannerjea introduced it in Bengal in the Calcutta Corporation against my opposition ? Is it not also a fact that Deshbandhu Das conceded to Moslems separate electorates in his Bengal Pact ?

Pandit Nanakchand : My reply is that it is not surprising that Hindus in their anxiety to wrest power from the Government should imitate Government's methods and seek to secure alliance of Muslims by promising them what the Government had promised. Pandit Nanakchand then explained that he referred to abolition of caste. He was only referring to civic and political disabilities imposed by caste. He was only referring to social and religious customs.

Sir John Simon : For instance, you were not thinking of admitting depressed classes freely into temples.

Pandit Nanakchand : No.

To Sir Aurthur Froom, Pandit Nanakchand said that the clause in the Instrument of Instruction to the Governors regarding non-differentiation of classes etc. was inadequate.

Sir John Simon : Your point is that you want a clause in the constitution so that any aggrieved party might be able to challenge any act of legislature in a court of law if he thought that any legislation was ultra vires ?

Pandit Nanakchand : Yes.

Sir John Simon : May I invite your attention to the statement in Raja Narindranath's memorandum that joint electorates cannot be forced on any minority community against its will. It is not your party's view ?

Pandit Nanakchand : No.

Sir John Simon : May I point out that your party's view is not consistent with the Nehru Report recommendations on the communal question ?

Pandit Nanakchand : In our opinion the recommendations of the Nehru Report contain a compromise in order to please Moslems. We are opposed to any compromise as we do not think it would be in the interests of a democratic Government.

Professor Gulshan Rai explained that if Law and Order were transferred to the Central Government, the Deputy Commissioner might be deprived of his revenue functions and might act under the supervision of the Governor in his capacity as agent of the Central Government.

Sir John Simon : Will it ensure prompt help of the police on occasions when they might be required in connection with transferred subjects.

Prof. Gulshan Rai : I think so.

To Sir John Simon Pandit Nanakchand explained that he complained that certain class of Hindus described as non-martial class were excluded from the Army. His complaint was not that all Hindus were excluded. The Khatris, who furnished Generals to Ranjit Singh's army were treated as non-martial classes.

Dr. Hari Singh Gour : Why are you against political advance in case there is no abolition of the communal principle ?

Pandit Nanakchand : Because it would lead to more bitterness to give reforms while retaining the communal principle.

Sir John Simon then asked : Have you considered in what manner the chief objection to the joint electorates can be met ? The chief objection is that it will not secure the return of truly representative Muslims. In Poona, it was suggested to us that wholly communal electorate may be asked to choose a panel of representatives from whom the electorates might make their choice. I have formed no views in regard to the merits of the suggestion. Have you thought about it ?

Pandit Nanakchand : No, I cannot express any off-hand opinion.

One member of the delegation here remarked that it appeared to be a good suggestion.

Sir John Simon : I will not be in a hurry to approve it. Mr. Nanakchand has exercised discretion wisely, in not giving an off-hand answer.

Prof. Gulshan Rai then put forward his view that no amount of communal representation would solve the question and recommended the solution which had found favour with Lord Delamere.

Sir John Simon said he was thankful for the suggestion. This concluded the examination of the Hindu deputation, and the conference adjourned for lunch.

The Muslim Deputation's Evidence

On the Conference reassembling after lunch, the Muslim deputation led by Sir Mahomed Shafi, appeared in support of the memoradum submitted by the Shafi section of the All-India Muslim League. The deputation comprised nearly twenty members, chief amongst whom were Sir Mohommed Iqbal, Sir Umar Hayat Khan and others.

To Sir John Simon, Sir M. Shafi said, the views of the deputation were enumerated in the memorandum submitted to the "Conference." He was prepared to answer questions in elucidation of the memorandum.

To Chaudhuri Zafarullah, Sir M. Shafi said : Communal representation was introduced simultaneously with the introduction of elections in regard to legislatures. The Minto-Morley Reforms were put in force in January, 1910, and from that time communal representation has been in force. I played my humble part in connection with these reforms. I was one of the six Mohommedans who were invited to confer with the sub-committee of the Executive Council of the Viceroy. Communal representation was introduced with the concurrence of Mr. Gopala Krishna Gokhale, who was the leader of the Congress.

Sir Mahomed continued : I, as the General Secretary of the Punjab Provincial Moslem League had a good deal to do with all elections which took place under the Minto-Morley Reforms. In the Punjab we had joint electorates. In every election it used to happen that at the initial stage several Hindu and Muslim candidates stood, but at the final stage the struggle was always between one Hindu and one Muslim candidate.

Sir M. Shafi added : The Hindus did not oppose communal representation when it was introduced under the Minto-Morley Reforms or later even. In 1916 when the Congress and the Muslim League were the only two important political bodies, there was an agreement arrived at in Lucknow in 1916 conceding Muslims separate electorates. It gave the Muslims in Bengal and the Punjab separate electorates; and in the Montford Reforms, though the Government of India recommended fifty per cent of the seats for Muslims, the Joint Committee of Parliament gave the Muslims of Bengal only 40 per cent, which is what the Lucknow Agreement recommended.

Chaudhuri Zafarullah : When did the opposition to separate electorates commenced ?

Sir Shafi : In 1922 there was no opposition to separate electorates right till the end of 1922 December. On the contrary, in the United Provinces during the period of his office my friend, Mr. Chintamani, Minister extended the principle of separate electorates in regard to local boards and municipalities with the concurrence of the Hindu majority in that council. It was in December 1922, that the first session of the All-India Hindu Mahasabha was held in Gaya under the presidency of Pandit Malaviya. At the Gaya session only, Shuddhi and Sangathan were preached. In August 1923, there was a special session of Hindu Mahashabha at Benares. There also Shuddhi and Sangathan were preached. It was for the first time in the session of the Hindu Mahashabha held at Belgaum in December 1924, that a voice was raised against separate electorates ?

Sir John Simon : Is it in 1922 or 1924 that opposition was first voiced against separate electorates ?

Sir M. Shafi : In December 1924. But I divide the period into two parts. One is the period which begins from December 1922. It is our considered opinion that Shuddhi and Sangathan and the demand for abolition of separate electorates and all parts and parcel of one and the same movement. If I am not mistaken the opposition to separate electorates really began with the return from England early in 1924 of Lala Lajpat Rai and the publication of Lord Olivier's letter in the London "Times" against communal electorates.

Chaudhuri Zafarullah : Will joint electorates lead to communal harmony ?

Sir M. Shafi : No, not at all. In our view joint electorates are bound to lead to frequent recurrence of friction between the two communities. As true Nationalists, we are opposed to joint electorates.

Continuing, Sir M. Shafi said : In the separate electorates a Hindu stands against a Hindu and a Muslim against a Muslim. Whatever bitterness may be caused will not last. In joint electorates, it will actually be reduced into a struggle between the two communities' candidates. Instead of promoting communal harmony joint electorates are calculated to lead to friction and increasing communal bitterness. In our view joint electorates are detrimental to the cause of nationalism in the highest degree.

Further questioned Sir M. Shafi said : In joint electorates with reservation Hindus will try to secure election of a dummy Muslim candidate with the support of Hindu voters. Muslims will make similar efforts. These attempts may or may not entirely succeed. But, I am certain that the result of joint electorates will be the composition of legislatures in a manner which will make the legislatures a laughing stock in the country. Sir M. Shafi then said : Mr. Chintamani, a Hindu leader, has borne testimony in his evidence before the Reforms Inquiry Committee of which I was a member that separate electorates, instead of creating communal tension, fostered better relation and mutual goodwill and co-operation. It is on that account that he extended separate electorates during his term of office.

Chaudhuri Zafarullah : It is contended that communal representation is responsible for communal tension.

Sir M Shafi : How can it be ? Shuddi and Sangathan and Tanzim and Tabligh are responsible for communal tension.

Sir M. Shafi then explained that under the Morley-Minto Reforms, out of six elections to the Punjab Council only in one election was a Muslim returned by the University. Sir Fazli Hussain was the successful candidate, but even then he was returned because Sir M. Shafi, as Sir Fazli Hussain's counsel, took objection successfully to the nomination of a Hindu candidate, Raja Harnam Singh, on the ground that he was not a British Indian subject. In the Punjab University, graduates elected two members to the Senate, but since Lord Curzon's Act not one Muslim had been returned.

Sir John Simon : I am a graduate of the Oxford University. In how many elections do you think a liberal has been returned ? (Laughter).

Sir M. Shafi : But may I point out that in England all are Christians and there is only political difference, and not communal difference. Sir M. Shafi then said that Muslim representation in the municipalities and local boards was not proportionate to their population strength.

Sir M. Shafi then explained the genesis of the Land Alienation Act of the Punjab. He said that in Rawalpindi it was during the period of one settlement that large areas of land had passed from the ownership of agricultural tribes into the hands of money-lenders. In consequence grave political danger arose. The Commissioner of Rawalpindi urged on the Punjab Government the desirability of a measure like Land Alienation Act. It protected agricultural tribes whether Hindus, Muslims or Sikhs.

Sir John Simon : I have studied the legislation carefully, and I can appear for an examination on the subject.

Sir M. Shafi : I know Sir John, how carefully you study questions.

Sir John Simon : We are not going into the merits of that legislation. Sir M. Shafi : I am opposed to any such provision.

Raja Narindranath

To Raja Narindranath, Sir M. Shafi said that he included in the term "Depressed classes," all pre-Aryan aborigines who numbered sixty millions. He did not object to the inclusion under that terms all pre-Aryan aborigines, whatever their present creed.

Raja Narindranath : Is it on the ground that Muslims were in a minority that the Muslim deputation led by the Aga Khan in 1908 urged on Lord Morley separate electorates?

Sir M. Shafi : That may be one of the reasons. Whatever be the reasons, I want separate electorates for two fundamental reasons. The first is that joint electorates will lead to friction in the conditions existing in India and is detrimental to the cause of nationalism, and the second reason is that it is only through separate electorates that truly representative legislatures can be secured.

Raja Narindranath : Can you cite one case in which in any country separate electorates have been retained at the instance of the majority community while the minority community does not want it ?

Sir M. Shafi : I have not studied all constitutions.

Raja Narindranath : It is only in the case of a few countries that separate electorates are retained ?

Sir M. Shafi : It may be, but I know of no country in which the parliamentary form of Government has been introduced as in India and conditions are so intricate and complex as one finds them in India. We must decide upon the form of representation which is suited to the actual conditions prevailing in the country.

Raja Narindranath : Will you give the other minority communities the same weightage which you want for the Muslim minorities ? Sir M. Shafi : Yes.

Raja Narindranath : In the United Provinces Muslims are only 14 per cent and enjoy thirty per cent representation in the provincial legislature, and 33 $\frac{1}{3}$ in the central legislature. Will you give the Sikhs who are 14 per cent the same weightage in the Punjab ?

Sir M. Shafi : The distinction which is sought to be drawn between the Hindu and Sikh is artificial. One might as well draw a distinction between a Shia and a Sunni amongst the Muslims. But as long a weightage is given to Sikhs out of 45 per cent, after providing 55 per cent to Muslims, I have no objection. A distinction is sought to be drawn between Sikhs and Hindus for political reasons, just to deprive Muslims of their small majority.

Raja Narindranath : Will you give weightage to minority communities in the services also ? Sir M. Shafi : I will give my personal view, as the League has not expressed its view. I would only give representation to communities according to the population strength in the service.

Raja Narindranath : In the United Provices Muslims have 47 per cent representation in the services. Would you stop recruitment to the services of Muslims until other communities secure their percentage of representation ?

Sir M. Shafi

Sir M. Shafi : No. In the United Provinces, Muslims are more largely represented in the services, because they are educationally advanced. Percentage on the population basis is the minimum and not maximum.

Raja Narindranath : In the United Provinces and the Central Provinces both Hindus and Muslims are equally situated in regard to educational standing, etc. Will you put obstacles in the way of Muslims if they are over-represented in the Punjab ? Sir M. Shafi : I will put no obstacles. In the Punjab, qualified Muslims are to be found for the highest post in the Government. I would lay down the minimum standard of efficiency, and if that qualification is obtained then I will give representation to communities which are not represented.

To a further question, Sir M. Shafi said that he was responsible for the policy of the Government of India, which laid down that in recruitment to the higher services two-third of the vacancies might be filled on merits, and one-third might be filled so as to give representation to unrepresented communities, and that he agreed with that policy.

Sir John Simon : Sir Mahomed, may I ask you a clear up one point ? Under the Minto-Morley system, there was no communal electorate in the Punjab. It would not be therefore correct to say that with the Minto-Morley Reforms a wholly communal system was introduced?

Sir M. Shafi : No. My point was that it was under Minto-Morley system that election to the legislatures was introduced and that with that communal representation was introduced.

Sir John Simon : I quite agree. In the Punjab under the Morley-Minto system not one member was returned by a communal electorate ?

Sir M. Shafi : Yes.

Sir John Simon : May it not be said to be because it was intended to be applied only to the minority community, and Muslims were in a majority in Punjab ?

Sir M. Shafi : I do not know what can be said to be the real explanation. I was one of the deputation of 1906 which waited on Lord Minto and we then put our case. I have got the reference.

Continuing Sir John Simon Said : In Bombay four additional seats were reserved for Moslems to be returned by the Moslems of the whole province. It was in addition to the right of Muslims to contest seats in joint electorates and to exercise their votes.

Dr. Suhrawardy : In Bengal we had five seats reserved like that.

Sir M. Shafi reiterated his viewpoint that with the introduction of election to legislatures communal representation was introduced in some parts of India simultaneously.

Replying to Dr. Narang, Sir Mahomed Shafi said : My friend asks me about the existence of the two Muslim Leagues. He knows only too well that the League split only the question of boycott of the Commission. As long as the Commission's labours are not concluded the split may continue, but as soon as the Commission's labours are over the League will be united again. We have no other material difference.

Sir M. Shafi said that Ahmediyas also were represented in the deputation. Continuing Sir M. Shafi said that the ideal of constitutional advance which the League placed before itself was Dominion Status. Sir M. Shafi then stated his view that India should be entitled to adequate representation in the League of Nations.

Dr. Narang : Will the two communities be able to live peacefully under provincial autonomy and separate electorates ?

Sir M. Shafi : Yes.

Dr. Narang then suggested that the Hindu Sabha was only a social body and Shuddhi and Sangathan were planks in the social programme.

Sir M. Shafi : The Hindu Sabha is a socio-political religious body. I can supply the proceedings of the Sabha in support of the view.

Sir John Simon said he would be glad to receive a copy of the proceedings.

Sir M. Shafi advocated adult franchise for provincial legislatures, but not for the Assembly at present.

Continuing Sir M. Shafi said : I do not think communal representation will retard political advance. On the contrary it will secure fulfilment of the principle of all democratic Governments that the Legislature should be truly representative. Sir M. Shafi then said that Muslims were the predecessors of the British Rulers in India, and not the Sikhs as Dr. Narang contended was the case in the Punjab.

To Sardar Ujjal Singh, Sir M. Shafi said that the Lucknow Pact was a political bargain between the two organisations. He refused to speculate on the possibilities of a bargain based on joint electorates.

To Sir John Simon Sir M. Shafi said that Muslims were of the opinion that under the existing conditions communal electorates were essential to secure real representation. But it might be dispensed with when the time came when the whole nation was welded together.

Sir M. Shafi then reiterated that good relations between the communities could be mentioned only with the retention of separate electorates.

To Sardar Ujjal Singh Sir M. Shafi maintained that the Sikhs were essentially part of Hindus. To Raja Narindranath and Sir M. Shafi said that he was prepared to give separate representation to Indian Christians and the Depressed Classes.

The Hon. Raja Nawab Ali Khan : Out of 26 district boards with joint electorates in how many do Muslims possess more seats than their population strength ?

Sir M. Shafi : In a few they have more seats but in the majority their representation is less than their population.

The Hon'ble Raja Nawab Ali Khan then gave the figures of the excess representation of Muslims in Dera Ismail Khan, Mianwali, Rohtak, Gurgaon, Karnal, Hissar, Jullunder, Ferozepur, Lahore, Amritsar, etc.

Sir M. Shafi challenged the accuracy of the figures.

Dr. Narang later pointed out that these figures were taken from the Government note.

The Hon. Raja Nawab Ali Khan : Is it your view that the Muslims in the Punjab and Bengal should get representation according to population strength and in other provinces the proportion of the Lucknow Pact might be retained ?

Sir M. Shafi : I will agree to give the Hindu minorities the same weightage which they are prepared to give to Muslim minorities.

Dr. Gour : Were you a party to the Delhi Muslim proposal?

Sir M. Shafi : I did not agree to them, as they were finally decided.

Dr. Gour : Mr. Jinnah and you agreed to joint electorates?

Sir M. Shafi said that what transpired at the Delhi meeting in the first instance was confidential. What happened therein was contained in a leaflet.

Sir M. Shafi gave a copy of the printed leaflet to Dr. Gour.

Sir M. Shafi said the Delhi meeting was not representative.

To Dr. Gour Sir M. Shafi maintained that separate electorates were necessaly to safeguard Muslim interests and to secure a truly representative Government.

To Dr. Gour, who mentioned that the scheme of panel of Muslim candidates from whom representatives might be selected by joint electorates, Sir M. Shafi said that he had not considered the proposal and could give no opinion.

Replying to Sardar Uberoi, Sir M. Shafi maintained that Sikhs and Hindus were indistinguishable.

Sardar Uberoi : Was any Sikh elected to the Punjab Council before they were given separate electorate ?

Sir M. Shafi : I think one was elected.

Sardar Uberoi : One for the whole province ?

Replying to Dr. Suhrawardy, Sir M. Shafi said that under the Lucknow Pact Muslims in the Punjab were not getting their due share of representation. He did not object to more representation to Sikhs as long as it came out of the 45 per cent allotted to Non-Muslims and the 55 per cent representation for Muslims was left untouched. Continuing Sir M. Shafi said that it was true that Muslims although in majority in the Punjab were heavily indebted, and that their majority in the province was illusionary. In the big riots which took place at Lahore and Rawalpindi, the Sikhs sided with the Hindus.

Sir M. Shafi repeated that he would give separate representation to Christians and Depressed Classes. The Frontier Province would be enjoying Reforms even now if it had been a separate province.

To Sir John Simon, Sir M. Shafi said that he shared the view expressed in the Montford Report that Muslims regarded separate electorate as a settled fact. It was only under separate electorates that their interests would be adequately safeguarded. He reiterated again that it was introduced with the concurrence of Gokhale, and until 1924 December no voice was raised against it.

Dr. Narang pointed out that in April 1923 opposition was raised to separate electorate.

Replying to Lord Burnham and Lord Strathcona, Sir M. Shafi said that Dyarchy had worked in the Punjab smoothly but he wanted advance all along the line both in the Provincial and Central Governments. Considering the pros and cons he was of the opinion that Dyarchy should not be extended.

In conclusion, Sir M. Shafi said that if communal electorates were abolished it was their considered opinion that not only should there be no advance, but the Reforms should even be withdrawn. Muslims wanted Dominion Status only, if their rights were safeguarded. Muslims also wanted that freedom of religious worship and practice should be secured to all communities.

This concluded the evidence of Sir M. Shafi and the "Conference" rose for the day.

Sir John's Reaction

Lahore—6th November 1928

The Simon Joint Free "Conference" met half an hour

earlier to dispose of to-day's witnesses in good time. A deputation of the Punjab Zamindars' Association, headed by Major D. Vanrenen, placed before the "Conference" the case of Zamindars in the Punjab.

At the outset Sir John asked Major Vanrenen whether he would prefer to be questioned or whether he would make a statement.

Major Vanrenen preferred to make a statement in the course of which he said that money-lenders were responsible, to a large extent, for the economic backwardness of the zamindars. He complained that judges did not properly administer the law with the result that cases were decided to the detriment of the agriculturists.

Sir John objected to the remark and said that he could not permit reflections of that character on the judiciary.

To Sir John, Major Vanrenen said that his association recommended the abolition of the official bloc in the Council and the widening of rural constituencies.

Q : Do you think the depressed classes should be represented by election ?

A : They should form constituencies of their own.

Q : You say that the system of competitive examination is not suitable for India. What method your association would recommend for filling the public services ?

A : By qualifying examinations.

Capt. Sikandar Hayat Khan pointed out that if the recommendations of the Zamindars' Association were carried out, the rural population would get 89 per cent representation on the Council and the urban population 11 per cent.

Witness said that he would change the definition of the "urban population." He would call all towns with more than 5,000 population as urban areas.

Chaudhuri Sultan Ahmed, member of the deputation, replying to Capt. Sikandar Hayat's question, said that there was no restriction on non-agricultural classes buying land in the colony areas.

Examined by Chaudhuri Chhotu Ram, Major Vanrenen

said he was for the principle of 'joint responsibility' of Ministers. He did not feel any necessity of retaining representation in the Council of special interests like the Punjab University.

Q : Would you retain the present classification of constituencies into rural and urban ?

A : These must remain separate.

Q : Would you like income-tax to be made a provincial subject ?

A : Certainly.

Q : Would you apply the same principle to assessment of land revenue as is applied in the case of income-tax ?

A : Yes, but gradually.

To Raja Narindranath, the witness said that one of the main principles of their association was to uphold the Land Alienation Act. They had very few non-agriculturists on their association.

Raja Narindranath : You agree that the Land Alienation Act is based entirely on a caste test ? In a province which consists of peasant proprietors, don't you think the bureaucratic system is better than a democratic system ?

Witness was indistinct, but was heard to say that officials were not impartial.

Raja Narindranath : This is the first time I have heard an indictment against the impartiality of officials. What is the population of the agricultural tribes in the Punjab ?

Witness : I do not know.

Q : Will you take it from me, it is little more than half the population.

Witness : No. I will take it from the book : (Laughter).

Q : If the official *bloc* is removed, your representation which is already 75 per cent, will proportionately increase and become preponderant ?

A : I think the agriculturists all over the world are sensible.

Raja Narindranath : You say, your association consists

of all communities and has no communal feelings. Yet, your association is not able to decide the question of representation of minorities, and opinion, you say, is divergent on the point ?

Witness : That is my personal opinion.

Raja Narindranath further pointed out that there were middle classes among the rural agricultural classes, and among the urban agricultural classes communal feeling was predominant as also in the Punjab Council.

Sir John Simon remarked it was agreed that there was a good deal of communal feeling in the country. Was that the point the Raja wished to make ?

The Raja replied that he wished to show that there were many lines of divisions in the Punjab, more than in any other province, and yet the witness wanted to advance forward.

Sir John Simon : One cannot use cross-examination for persuading witnesses.

Dr. Narang : Are you a member of an agricultural tribe?

Witness : Not of the scheduled tribes.

Q : Would you not extend the same privilege that applies to you to those who are agriculturists by profession ?

Witness : That will give them a chance to overcome the Land Alienation Act while we stand for this Act.

Dr. Narang : You want to restrict this privilege to men like yourself and not extend it to Punjabis ? Major Venrenon did not reply.

Further examined by Dr. Narang, the witness said the association contained big landlords and tillers of the soil. The latter formed a very large proportion. He would agree to a graduated system of land revenue.

Q : You say you want separate electorates for Zamindars as such. Is it consistent with the interests of various communities holding different religions to have jointly a separate electorate as zamindars ? Witness : Yes, it is.

Dr. Narang further mentioned that the zamindars at present had 50 out of the 70 elected seats showed that their influence was more potent than the influence of money-lenders.

Witness : In general constituencies, yes.

Mr. Owen Roberts pointed out that the Country League to whose memorandum the witness was a signatory had opposed widening of the franchise, while the Zamindars' Association, Punjab, had urged extension. Was it that in this matter, the Punjab Zamindars dissociated themselves from the Country League's proposition which applied to the whole of India ?

Witness : That is so.

Sir H.S. Gour's Reaction

Sir H. S. Gour : Zamindars are people who easily fall a prey into the hands of money-lenders and you want the usury law to be extended to them as a class ?

Witness : That is so.

Q : When these people come into the legislatures, how will they manage other people's affairs when they cannot manage their own ?

Witness : All are not ignorant and illiterate.

Sir H. S. Gour : Yet you don't believe in freedom of contract ?

Sir John Simon : Even in England the Money Lenders' Bill is an undoubted interference with free contract.

Witness : Zamindars require some protection in financial matters.

Sir H. S. Gour : Would not you let the zamindar have unfettered choice of selecting the best man for the legislature ?

Witness : Zamindars are forced to make a selection.

Sir H. S. Gour : Then they are devoid of judgment.

Witness : They are subject to influences both of money-lenders and officials.

Sir H. S. Gour wanted the witness to define what was meant by "stake in the country" but did not press as the witness did not answer.

Sir John Simon said that the view of the witness was that agriculturists being 80 per cent should have preponderence of authority.

Sir H. S. Gour : Do you recognise that the central and provincial legislatures should have the best brains ?

The Witness : No; we want men of average intelligence.

Sikh Deputation's Evidence

The Sikh deputation was headed by Sir Sundar Singh Majithia and included Professor Jodh Singh, Sardar Man Singh, Lieut. S. Raghbir Singh, Sardar Mohan Singh, Sardar Tej Singh and Capt. Lakhan Singh.

Sardar Ujjal Singh conducted the main examination. He observed. Yesterday it was stated that the Sikhs were not a distinct community and were part and parcel of the Hindus. Is that true ?

View of Sundar Singh

Sir Sundar Singh replied : Whatever the rival community might say, facts are facts namely, that throughout the Sikhs have been a distinct community. Their interests are not identical in religious or social matters with the interests of any other community and in the Punjab Council they, for instance, voted with Muslim members on the Money-lenders Bill and on a number of other matters. I myself was returned to the pre-Reform Council by Muslim help, the understanding being that there should be one Sikh.

Sir John Simon said that facts regarding the Sikhs were recorded clearly in the Montford Report, and they need not hold a historical discussion on the facts recorded in the Montford report.

Sir Sundar Singh : Even the Nehru Report has considered us a distinct community.

Sardar Ujjal Singh

Sardar Ujjal Singh : Can the party system be developed on communal electorates ?

Witness : Parties in the Council have been on communal lines and so long as separate electorates exist the party system is not possible.

Further examined, he said if separate electorates remained, he would not extend them to local bodies where he would experiment with joint electorates. He did not see how the Chief Minister could select his ministry if the council was formed on a communal basis and all communities were to be represented on the Cabinet.

Sardar Ujjal Singh asked the opinion of the witness on the claim of the minority to have representation on a population basis.

Witness : The majority want practically to have the statutory right to govern the country. The Sikhs were the rulers of the Punjab before the British and did not give up the Punjab without struggle. Do you expect we shall let ourselves be subordinated to any community's rule ?

Chaudhuri Zafarullah : You would like to rule ?

Witness : We want the rule of all communities jointly.

Sardar Ujjal Singh : You will call the rule of one community as communal raj and not Swaraj.

Witness : It will be a curious Swaraj.

Sardar Ujjal Singh's further question regarding the position of Sikhs was answered by Professor Jodh Singh who said that the Muslim Minister had in the teeth of Sikh opposition passed the Gurdwara Bill with the help of Muslim votes and another instance was that the Sikhs as voters in the local bodies were larger in proportion to their population, and yet the Muslim Minister sent round a circular asking constituencies to be so arranged as to neutralize the effect of this voting advantage and secure a majority for Muslims. These were glaring instances.

Explaining to the President the position of his community in regard to communal representation Sardar Jodh Singh said if the principle of communal representation was entirely removed from the constitutional structure of British India, then the Sikh community was prepared to abandon separate electorates for Sikhs in the Punjab.

Sir Sundar Singh Majithia recommended for his community, in case of retention of the communal principle, thirty per cent representation in the council and local bodies and thirty per cent representation for Hindus and forty per cent for Muslims. "My reasons for recommending this", he said "are first of all we are only in the Punjab, and as such we have everything, our hearts and homes in the Punjab and in this place we should not be placed in any detrimental position. We have not the satisfaction of being in a majority in other provinces. We are a military community and have fought battles for the Empire and have sacrificed for the upkeep of the Government. Our community's strength in the past has been nearly one-sixth of the whole population. We pay in the Punjab something like 40 per cent of the canal and land revenues."

Proceeding, Sir Sundar Singh said representation in excess of the population strength was not unknown in India. In Bihar and Orissa although the Muslim population was 10 per cent of the whole population they had 20.4 per cent representation. Witness did not wish the provinces to be constituted as independent sovereign States. As an ex-Member of the Governor's Executive Council he stated Dyarchy had worked fairly satisfactorily in the Punjab.

Chaudhuri Zafarullah asked the witness what he would do in those provinces where there were only two communities, one in a majority and the other in a minority.

The witness replied that in those cases the majority would remain a majority, but the minority community would have a majority in another province, and thus there would be balance of power.

Q : You say franchise should continue on the same basis as at present. Is it due to the fact that the voting power of the Sikhs will be lowered if the franchise is extended ?

A : No. The widening of the franchise will lead to difficulties in elections.

Sardar Jodh Singh

Sardar Jodh Singh said their experience in Gurdwara legislation had shown that universalisation of the franchise would not increase the percentage of voters. Increase would come about when the standard of education was increased.

Proceeding Sardar Jodh Singh said they wished to have a system of proportional representation on the single transferable vote in local bodies. There should be a second chamber in the provinces. A minimum efficiency qualification should be fixed, and the Provincial Public Services Commission should see that proportionate representation was maintained in the services.

Dr. Gokulchand Narang asked whether bloodshed would result on the introduction of joint electorates.

Sir Sunder Singh : No. Have a trial in local bodies and if the system succeeds there, try it in other spheres.

Sardar Jodh Singh, replying to another question, said at present Muslims had an effective majority in the council. The Hindus were divided into three groups.

The Chairman at this stage said it was depressing for those who wished to study Indian politics to find that among Indians much interest was taken in communal disputes.

Dr. Narang said his object in discussing the communal questions was to expose them and to show how ridiculous and disastrous in character communalism was.

Dr. Suhrawardy drew attention to the deputationists that Sikhs had joined the Muslims in the Council on various occasions, and that their complaint of the standing tyranny of the Muslim majority. He asked : Is it not a fact that with the help of the official bloc you were defeated ? Sardar Jodh Singh : I doubt.

Later Sardar Jodh Singh said if the Sikhs succeeded in getting special representation, they would not mind if Muslims got special representation in the other provinces here they were in a minority.

Dr. Gour (to Sir Sunder Singh) : Do you think since the introduction of communal representation communal tension has grown ?

A : It has grown.

Witness asked the Chairman whether the question was put to him in his capacity as ex-Member of the Governor's Executive Council in which case he would not express any opinion. The Chairman said it was put to the witness in his capacity as a gentleman who studied politics.

Dr. Gour : How far in your opinion the introduction of separate electorates has contributed to the growing the tension.

A : They have accentuated the tension.

Q : Is the growth of communal representation in the services conducive to the growth of inefficiency in the services ?

Witness : Yes.

Proceeding, the witness replied that if the communal principle was altogether removed from every sphere of administration in India, the Sikhs were prepared not to urge representation in the service, but would stand on their own legs.

Replying to Sir Zulfikar Ali Khan's question, the witness said that serious communal riots within the last seven or eight years had been caused on account of communalism.

Sir John Simon on Communalism

After lunch, Sir John Simon said difficulties in the Punjab connected with communalism were increased by the existence of the important Sikh community. He said figures showed that Sikhs were 11 per cent of the population, 24 per cent of the voters and wanted 30 per cent seats in the Council. The Mohommedans were 55 per cent of the population and 43 per cent of the voters and the Sikhs would give them 40 per cent of the seats. The Hindus were 33 per cent of the population, 32 per cent of the voters, and the Sikhs would allot them 30 per cent of the seats. Thus, while the Hindus practically got what they were entitled to both on population and voting strength, the Sikhs would benefit at the expense of the Muslim community.

Sir Sundar Singh said he had reduced the Hindus' seats also by 3 per cent, but as they happened to be a minority, the Sikhs had to get seats from the majority.

Sir John Simon : I am only making an elementary mathematical observation.

Witness : The Sikh problem is confined to the Punjab only and owing to our special position, we want special consideration.

Sir John Simon : I appreciate the special importance of the Sikh community, but according to your proposal, if you add the Hindu and Sikh seats, they will have more seats than the Mahomedans.

Witness informed Sir John Simon that one of the main reasons why the Sikhs, though they were only 11 per cent of the population, had among them 24 per cent of the voters, was that in the rural districts Sikhs were occupiers of more land than members of any other community.

Sir John Simon said the witness had complained that the constituencies for district boards had been arranged by the Muslim Minister to their detriment but membership of boards showed that there were 186 Sikh members against the 141 seats. They would be entitled to get according to the formula, which showed that the Sikhs had been able to hold their own and won these seats probably at the expense of the Hindus.

Witness replied that Sikhs were strong in the central districts. Hindus had not large landed interests like Sikhs.

Sir John Simon said the witness had told Sir H. S. Gour that communal representation had contributed to the communal riots. He did not wish to pursue the matter as the communal argument could not occupy the whole of political and public interest; but he wished to ask certain questions.

Q : Do you think riots were due to the reason given by you to Sir H. S. Gour, or do you think the position was that in previous times when the prospect of more rapid advance to self-government seemed very distant, the different communities were less jealous to try and get full political representation ? Do you think that, now that in recent years the prospect has opened out of constitutional and responsible advance, the different communities are becoming increasingly eager, so to say, to improve their position before the later stages are reached; or is there nothing in that ?

Witness : It may be so, because previously the Government was carried on by officials.

Sir John Simon : The opportunity for influencing political action now is more ?

Witness : Also for getting representation in the services.

Sir John Simon : You mean that through adequate representation in the legislature you are able to put pressure to secure adequate representation in the services and so the wheel goes round and round ?

Witness : We cannot drive away from our mind that we were rulers before the British, and cannot be relegated to the position of dependence on a majority community.

Sir John Simon further pointed out that it was striking that yesterday morning the Hindu deputation was opposed to constitutional advance if communal representation was not abolished all over India, and Sir Mahomed Shafi in the afternoon powerfully and emphatically demanded that joint electorate be not substituted for separate electorates, while the Sikh deputation was opposed to radical advance without the removal of the circumscribing adverse conditions. What were these conditions ? Sir John Simon continued : Don't you think every community in this province must realise and do its utmost (I make this suggestion with the greatest humility) to cultivate the spirit of give and take ?

Witness : That is what we want, but it must not be to deprive the Sikhs of their legitimate rights.

Examined by Lord Burnham, the witness said that the Sikh deputation arrived late in England and the Selbourne Committee regretted that they could not reopen the matter at that stage.

Q : You mean to go again to England ?

A : Certainly, we must press our claim before the Parliamentary Committee.

Major Attlee was informed by the witness that they wanted Governors to be appointed to all provinces from England, and later on from this country itself.

Major Attlee said he could not understand how they reconcile their plan of representative Government with the suggestion that Ministers be selected not from the party having the largest following, but from opposition quarters as well. How then could joint resposibility be ensured ?

Professor Jodh Singh replied that they had advocated the abolition of separate electorates throughout the country. But if this was not done, then the Council should be elected on communal basis. How would men be selected to form a Ministry and represent the interests of all communities when they were elected by one community and not as the representative of the general body of citizens ? They must have members from various communities, and ask them to work as Ministers in a spirit of compromise.

Major Attlee remarked that he only wanted to emphasise the question of Parliamentary machinery.

Witness told Lord Strathcona that they did not favour the handing over of law and order to the provinces.

After the deputation withdrew, Sir John Simon observed that he forgot to mention that according to revenue figures, 50 per cent of the land revenue in the Punjab was paid by Muslims, 23 per cent by Hindus and 26 per cent by the Sikhs.

National Unionist Party's Evidence

Chaudhuri Chotturam's Evidence

Rai Sahib Chotturam, member of the Punjab Committee, went into the witness box to lead the deputation from the National Unionist Party of the Punjab Council, otherwise known as the "Ministerial Party."

Examined by Sir John Simon, he said the party was open to all castes and creeds, so long as their programme was accepted. It had 5 Hindus and one Sikh member. Though Muslims were in a majority there was nothing to prevent non-Muslims being in a majority. Its policy was to advance the interest of the backward areas. He told Sir John Simon that no one could be a member of their party and at the same time a member of another party in the Council.

Explaining their chief demands one by one, Chaudhuri Chotturam said that they wanted provincial autonomy. Residuary powers should rest with the Provincial

Government and the official *bloc* at least as a voting factor should be removed.

Sir John Simon remarked that a great many people seemed to attach enormous importance to residuary powers; while on the other hand the point to settle at this stage was one of the principle of the constitution.

Witness replied that if residuary powers were to be given these should be left with the Provincial Government.

Continuing, Chaudhuri Chotturam said they wanted collective responsibility for Ministers. Distribution of subjects between the Central and Provincial Governments should be such as to enable the Provincial Government to redistribute and readjust the present burden of taxation in a fair and reasonable manner.

Sir John Simon : Are you complaining against the present situation or enunciating a principle for the future:

Witness : The latter.

Sir John Simon : I understand that you want such powers in financial matters as would enable the council to adjust the burden in rural interests for instance.

Witness : That is so.

Continuing Chaudhri Chotturam said that at present the Provincial Government could not change the principle applied to land revenue assessment, while his party would like to see it correspond to the income-tax assessment. The Government of India would not allow any change.

Views of John Simon

Sir John Simon : Your view is that in future the Punjab Council which would no doubt contain a preponderant rural element and would have a Ministry responsible to the House should have the power to reduce or increase land revenue assessment. And when members are predominantly rural, do you think it likely that such a council would support reduction of land revenue or encourage constant remission?

Witness : Our past record shows that we will be reasonable.

Sir John Simon : You think it will make no material

difference if the person responsible for land revenue, instead of being an irremovable Executive Councillor, were a Minister belonging to the party directly responsible to the House ?

Witness : It won't make any difference. I expect in the course of the next forty years that the basis of land revenue would be changed to correspond ultimately to income-tax. Chaudhri Chotturam proceeding stated that there should be nothing in the constitution barring the Provincial Legislature from passing an economic measure like the Land Alienation Act and any measure which might be necessary in future to protect any section of the population whether urban or rural.

Sir John Simon : Do you think any cross-examination would change your view on that ? (Laughter).

Witness : Yes, if I am convinced.

Finally, on the question of franchise the witness advocated lowering it both in the case of the land-owner and tenant to a payment of Rs. 10 land revenue or the occupation of land assessable to a land revenue of Rs. 10.

Lord Burnham : Your proposal to assimilate land revenue to income tax would mean that land revenue would be a tax on the profits of agriculture ?

Witness : Yes.

Raja Narendranath remarked that the witness wanted a larger power of taxation. He stated that any person could join his party, but was it not a fact that the real pivot on which the programme hung was the Land Alienation Act for which the Unionist Party stood ? How could others join the party ?

Witness : We also say that the basis of taxation should be changed.

Sir John Simon : You say it should be changed in an equitable and fair manner to which everyone could subscribe. (Laughter).

Raja Narendranath asked the witness how the urban party approximated to capitalists, and the rural to the Labour

Party when the Unionist Party consisted only of members of agricultural tribes who would not include agricultural labourers who depended on daily wages?

Witness : All peasants are labourers.

Raja Narendranath pointed out that though the Central Legislature had power to repeal local Acts, the Land Alienation Act was not repealed. Was not the then existing guarantee quite enough ?—Witness thought it might suit. To Raja Narendranath, witness replied that he wanted more, namely, statutory provision preventing such legislation by any legislature.

Dr. Narang : You want the Provincial Government to be so independent of the Central Government as to have no power of control or direction ?

Witness : Yes. In all matters except those reacting on the sphere of the central or other Provincial Governments.

Dr. Narang : You would like to give them greater autonomy than Indian States are enjoying at present ?

Witness : It is difficult for me to say that.

Sir John Simon : I am obliged to Dr. Narang for bringing the point out. In constitutional structures, this distribution of powers sometimes takes one form, and sometimes another. In some constitutions like that of South Africa, the Central Legislature has an overriding power. That is, strictly speaking, not a Federation at all. Another instance is of the Imperial Parliament technically possessing the power to repeal acts passed by a subordinate Parliament. The Government of India Act is constructed on that principle, and the Central Legislature can repeal laws in force in any part of British India. The second class of cases is where you dole out power so much for the Central Government and so much for the provinces and the powers exercised by one authority cannot be exercised by another. The case of Canada is very nearly that. The next question is when you have distributed all power, what about the unnamed power ? In some instances these rest in the centre and in some with the provinces. But all this is a matter of structure at the last stage. The first thing we must settle is whether the right principle is the principle by which the Central Legislature has overriding power or whether it is one in which there is distribution of powers.

Dr. Narang, resuming, asked the witness what safeguards he provided against misrule by majority and of abuse of power.

Witness : The Governor can dissolve the Council.

Sir John Simon intervening asked the witness to take the case where a dangerous situation had developed, and the Provincial Government wanted the assistance of the military which according to the witness, was to be in the charge of the Central Government. If there was a rigid distribution of powers and provinces were made absolutely self-contained how would the Central Government intervene ? These points must be considered in constituting-building.

Witness said that they would have to apply to the Central Government for military assistance.

Chaudhuri Chhoturam told Dr. Narang that he would abolish the Governor-General's veto in respect of provincial legislation and keep only the Governor's veto.

Dr. Narang's Reaction

Dr. Narang next pointed out that Chaudhri Lalchand, ex-Minister, had advocated joint electorates with reservation of seats. Witness disagreed, and said that could be adopted only by general agreement between the communities themselves.

Dr. Narang next pointed out that the proceedings of the Council showed that they in the Punjab had gone far beyond the communal question, as they had advocated sectional preference, caste preference, and even territorial preference.

Dr. Narang asked whether these were cleavage on a communal basis?

Witness did not agree.

Dr. Narang next pointed out that the memorandum of the party consisted of men of rural extraction, and that there was an unending conflict of views betwen them and the other party in the Council. Dr. Narang pointed out that if they had Ministers responsible to the House the majority, namely, the party of the witness must rule, and this party had a never-ending conflict with the other party, which meant that the majority could when in power, tyrannise over the minority. What safeguard would he give to the minority, to protect itself from tyranny?

Witness : The Council can revolt against them if they indulged in tyranny, and they would not be elected next time. There is in addition the Governor's power to dissolve the Council.

Dr. Narang asked why they wanted power ? Was it because of the tyranny of the existing rule, or because of their desire to apply the principle of self-determination ? If they would not give safeguards for minorities, then the present rule was good enough. Witness did not think the argument held good.

Dr. Narang said the witness did not want the Central Legislature to interfere with such a measure as the Land Alienation Act. But would he call it an economic measure when its application depended on exigencies of birth and no one not born as such, could become a member of an agricultural tribe ?

Witness replied that economic measure was one which would safeguard the economic interests of a section of population which was backward, and could not look after their own interests without help.

Sir John Simon brought this controversy to a close by remarking that they thoroughly understood the pros and cons of this matter.

Examined by Chaudhri Zafarullah, Chaudhri Chotturam stated that to the Central Government could be assigned control of foreign affairs, Indian States, customs, railways, posts, telegraphs, etc.

Sir Hari Singh Gour : You want assessment of land revenue on the principle on which income-tax is assessed? In other words you want the establishment of freeholds in the Punjab ?

Witness agreed.

Replying to Sir Arthur Froom's question, Chaudhuri Chotturam said that in the matter of raising provincial loans, there should be some sort of understanding between the Central and Provincial Governments.

Sir Arthur Froom said it was essential in order to avoid any two provinces trying to raise loans simultaneously, and thus spoiling each other's chances.

Military Classes' Deputation

The deputation of the martial races in the Punjab headed by Sir Umar Hayat Khan next presented their case to the Commission.

Sir Umar briefly stated their case. He said that no less than 480,000 members of martial races went to War from the Punjab. (Sir John : that is a wonderful record). But when the reforms were given to the country, they were forgotten. They wanted at least 25 seats in the Punjab Council.

Sir John : One of the members of the Punjab Reforms Committee is an ex-army officer ?

Sir Umar : He is not here as our representative. He is representing the landowners.

Sir John : Do you want a separate constituency for every occupation as well as religion ?

Sir Umar : In combined constituencies we might get one or two seats; but they are inadequate.

All the members of the Punjab Martial Classes' deputation then withdrew except Sir Umar Hayat Khan, who led the next deputation of the Punjab Chiefs' Association. The short time which was spent in calling the other members of this deputation was spent in the examination of Sir Umar Hayat Khan on the memorandum which he had submitted in his personal capacity.

Sir John asked him to make a statement on his memorandum. Sir Umar Hayat Khan said that in the olden days friends and loyal subjects of kings were admitted to high positions; but the British Government invited every one through election with the result that the Government was always defeated. For the smooth carrying on of Government, therefore, some friends of the Government should be admitted to the Councils. In the present legislatures, the friends of the Government had no place. Their number would go on diminishing.

Sir John said it was true that in the Central Legislature there was a tendency for critics to be numerous and for supporters of the administration to be small in number.

Witness urged that both in the Central and Provincial Governments there should be second chambers so that mistakes made in the lower houses might be rectified.

Punjab Chief's Case

Views of Sardar Mohan Singh

Sir Umar Hayat Khan and Sardar Mohan Singh acted as spokesmen of the Punjab Chiefs' Association. Sir Umar Hayat said that there were about 500 members of the Association who were big landholders, having thus a great stake in the province. Their principle was to stand or fall with the British Government. They felt that their big properties would suffer if anything happened to the Government. "We are friends of the administration whatever administration there may be" said Sir Umar, (Laughter) Sir Umar complained that they were not getting their due share in the administration. Previously, their sons used to get high positions in the services, but during the last two or three years this had been made difficult. Experience had shown that their sons proved better than the ordinary B.A.'s because they possessed administrative qualifications.

Sir John said that there might be another view taken of great families, that as they possessed land, influence and leadership, they could seek election through ordinary constituencies.

Sir Umar Hayat Khan said if they were given three seats in the provincial and one in each of the central legislatures, they would be satisfied.

Examined by Dr. Narang, Sir Umar stated that the Army career was thrown open to every body. He cited the case of the Bengali Regiment which proved a failure.

Dr. Narang asked him whether he would allow the non-martial classes to improve gradually?

Witness : Directly you bring in the wrong class you weaken the Army.

Sir Umar agreed that if members of the Chiefs' Association were divided among constituencies of the Punjab, there would be ten of them at least per constituency.

Dr. Narang : At the elections you have ten aristocrats. Therefore, the poor money-lender does not count at all.

A : Probably, every one of those ten is heavily in debt.

This finished today's examination and the Conference rose at 6 p.m.

Lahore—8th November 1928

Having recorded what would perhaps rank as the most conflicting controversial evidence on a given subject in any part of India the Simon Joint Free Conference were able, to-day, to divert attention from non-official to official evidence.

Today's evidence was confined in the morning to the Executive Councillors, Sir Fazli Hussain and Mr. Stow, and in the afternoon, to the three Ministers. But while the Executive Councillors were examined together, the three Ministers were heard one by one as they had sent in separate notes.

Depressed Classes' Deputation

Before the Conference met, a contingent of 500 members of the depressed classes' men from various parts of the Punjab, had arrived—all red-turbaned and dressed in white—and wished to meet Sir John Simon. Sir John's time being fully occupied, he was unable to witness the demonstration but received a small deputation of six of them led by Mr. Rajah.

M.C. Rajah's Views

Sir John Simon received the deputation's address and assured them that though he could not hear them publicly, he was giving his best consideration to their case and that Mr. Rajah was there giving all the facts and figures and devotedly representing the cause of the depressed classes.

The depressed classes deputation, said in the course of their memorial that they belonged to an ancient race which ruled India, about 5,000 years ago, prior to the invasion of India by the Aryans. The Aryans, whose present descendants were called high class Hindus, had all along been treating them with the most inhuman brutality, so that their unlucky community, numerically large as it was, is now little more than a mere name. In spite of the fact that there were some highly-educated and capable men in their community, they were not given any honourable status in society nor the right of ownership or anything. They had not even the right to safeguard their individual lives.

In fact this deplorable condition of the mute millions of the depressed community was due to the horrible treatment meted out to them by high-class Hindus in consequence of the pronouncements of the ancient Aryans, which were embodied in the *Manu Smriti* and a lot of other Hindu scriptures of that ilk.

The deputationsists next stated that they did not wish to be called Hindus but 'Addharmis' and in the next census they should describe themselves as 'Addharmis.' They did not want Swaraj in India under present conditions, as it would mean practically a monopoly by caste Hindus.

They enumerated their demands as follows :—

Necessary arrangements for the better education of Addharmis (untouchable) boys and girls; separate representation in all public bodies and the Legislature; a share in all public services, including the police, civil and military; a Minister in every province; equal rights of using all District Board public wells with other communities; equal rights of ownership of any property—dwelling houses and common fields—with other communities and proscription of the *Manu Smriti* and all such Hindu scriptures in which contemptuous references are made to the race and community. References to the community by the term of Shudra, the memorial urged, should be strictly forbidden. Land in the new colonies should be distributed just as it is done in the case of other communities.

Lala Harkishen Lal's Evidence

After this function the Conference met and examined Sir Fazli Hussain and Mr. Stow. The examination was in camera. The Conference next heard Lala Harkishen Lal who was the first Minister of Agriculture under the Reforms.

Simon on Dyarchy

Sir John Simon : What is your view of the working of dyarchy; has it been successful or unsuccessful ?

Witness : Well, Sir, there was no dyarchy. It was no dyarchy; it was a quadrarchy or unitary government.

Sir John Simon: You don't want me to adopt that word (laughter); but whether it was a four-footed thing or single footed thing, do you consider it worked ?

A : It worked, I should say, to a large extent.

Sir John Simon : I put a leading question though it is a bad thing to do. Do you think the influence and help which the Governor gave in this province was of assistance in making it work ?

Witness : I think the Governor's attitude was very helpful, and so was the attitude of the people who had to work it.

Sir John Simon : There has not been, we are glad to find, in this province, a constant succession of votes of censure on Ministers ?

Witness : One was tried, and it failed.

Sir John Simon : Is it legitimate, to ask you in a very plain way, as to what in your view should be done now ?

Witness : The King Emperor in 1918 said he would like to see India work to full responsible government and it was said in the despatches that the present concession was a substantial instalment. Well, so far as the provinces are concerned, I think a second instalment ought to be fully said and the debt liquidated; while so far as the Government of India is concerned, I should fix up one instalment now, and one later.

Sir John Simon : Your view is that speaking with experience of the province, the time has come to take a step forward in this province to go to the full length of provincial autonomy.

A : To be definite, it should not be power in the hands of the Governor, for that would also be autonomy, but I want power in the hands of Ministers.

Sir John Simon : Would you be in favour of extending the powers of the Governor in regard to veto, supposing autonomy were granted ?

Witness : No, because autonomy would mean joint responsibility of the Ministers. I would not accept the Governor's powers of overruling the Cabinet except in exceptional cases.

Mr. Cadogan : What would those exceptional cases be ?

Witness : Times of trouble, turmoil and disorder. When there is a war the Government of India would dictate terms.

Col Lane-Fox: Would you like to see law and order transferred to Ministers ? Several witnesses have suggested against such a course when there is a strong majority of one community.

Witness : The Minister under the present system does not have to deal with the matter. He cannot dictate anything to the police in the early stages of an enquiry. There may be some influence exercised. When I was Minister, we found these matters rested with the subordinate magistracy and the police.

Col. Lane-Fox : Anyhow, you are nor afraid ?

Witness : I am not.

Dr. Narang : You think all these wrangles about communalism will disappear ?

Witness : Is there trouble now ?

Captain Sikandar Hayat Khan : Are you in favour of extension of franchise to tenants ?

Witness : Yes.

Q : You are not in favour of adult suffrage ?

A : I am in theory, but for the sake of management, I will begin by a property qualification and gradually work up to adult suffrage.

Q : Would you like an automatic provision in the constitution to secure ultimately adult suffrage ?

Witness ? Yes, if sufficient time is fixed, otherwise as the Council sees fit.

Sardar Ujjal Singh : Will you have separate communal electorate ?

Witness : No, I will have joint electorate.

Q : Under provincial autonomy, should we give control to the Central Government such as retaining the Governor General's vote ?

Witness replied that this point required detailed examination. In some cases this vote would be necessary, but he would reduce it to a minimum.

Sardar Ujjal Singh : Supposing separate electorates are kept alive in the Council, would you like them to be extended to local bodies ?

Witness : As I told the Muddiman Committee, I won't kick at it, but I would remove it even from the local Council.

Chaudhuri Chotturam : Did you get on well with your colleague ?

Witness : Very well. I was dining with him three nights a week. (Laughter).

Q : What about the Secretaries ?

Witness : With the Secretaries, I got on well except with one head of department.

Q : Was there any friction ?

Witness : Absolutely none except difference of opinion.

Sir John Simon : Most people have differences of opinion. We have also in this conference. (Laughter). Sir John Simon suggested that questions be restricted to the constitutional points involved.

Sir H. S. Gour : Why do you oppose communal electorates?

Witness : The chief reason is that responsible government and communal electorates are a negation of each other. There cannot be any responsible government based on political views if people are divided and the members of Council are divided on religious grounds.

Sir H. S. Gour : Is the answer based on theoretical or practical grounds ? Did you find as Minister that the decisions of the Council were affected by communal considerations ?

Witness : Sometime, not always.

Sir H. S. Gour : Under general electorates would you give reservation of seats ?

Witness : No reservation of seats.

Q : You will leave the minorities to work out their own salvation ?

Witness : The minorities are created. There are no minorities. They have been created on the basis of religion on economic ideas. From the political point of view there are no minorities and majorities.

Sir H. S. Gour : There are people not so politically minded. For instance, are the depressed classes likely to have a representative returned ?

Witness : I stand for adult suffrage. They can come in through the general electorates.

Q : Do you think under adult suffrage the same class of intellectual men would come into the councils ?

Witness : I do not know of a higher standard in this country. We have the best men nowadays, and that standard would be maintained.

Sir H. S. Gour : Would busy people like you care to contest such constituencies ?

Witness : It all depends on the strength of the Council. I would like the membership to be 200.

Sir Arthur Froom : You are a big banker. Your view would be valuable. Would you have the Finance Department of the Punjab entirely separate from the Central Government?

Witness : In ordinary cases, the provinces should be allowed to borrow independently; but in the case of a stringency, the Government of India might be consulted.

Sir Arthur Froom : Supposing there was independence, you will have eight provinces bringing out a loan at the same time.

Witness : We find every day that the Imperial Bank tries to beat us and we are trying to escape that. Where the Imperial Bank lends at 6 per cent, we cannot afford to. I do believe the Finance Department would be wise enough to see the resources of the country. I do not fear they will cut each other's throats.

Sir Arthur Froom : The question is bigger. The fear is that without central control there might be a race to be in the field first.

Witness : In the London money market, people who are not really active have to wait with good schemes; while others more active get financed quickly. There is no suggestion that there should be central control over the London Money Market.

Sir Arthur Froom : I do not quite agree that the cases are alike. What about the rate of interest ?

Witness : That would depend upon the internal resource of the province. At present, the Government of India cannot do equitable service to the provinces and the Government of India's requirements have preference.

Sir Arthur Froom : Provincial loans are raised on the security of the Government of India.

Sir John Simon intervening pointed out that provincial governments may raise loans on the security of the provincial finances if allowed by the Government and that in the Punjab this had been done in two cases.

Sir John Simon : I feel some difficulty in this matter. In London the different departments of state cannot go into the London Money Market without going through the Treasury.

Witness : Local bodies in England can borrow independently from the Treasury. The Provincial Governments here would correspond to the local bodies in England for this purpose. Then again there are already port trusts, improvement trusts, and municipal corporations borrowing in the market independently of the Government of India.

Sir John Simon : Your point is, if there are 9 or 10 Provinces in India and also the Central Government, the whole system being Federal, you think each provincial unit should be free to raise its money by a loan without any co-ordination by the Government of India?

Witness : Theoretically it is possible, but in practice just as bankers put their heads together, the provinces may have to put their heads under the guidance of India.

Sir Arthur Froom : What I want to ask the witness is whether without co-ordination he will not find that he will have to pay more for his money.

Witness : Possibly yes. We may have to pay more.

Sir John Simon thanked the witness who then withdrew. This finished the Commission's Lahore programme.*

---

* See the Evidence in the volumes of Indian Statutary Commission.

7
Turning of the Tide

Simon Commission

Suddenly, on 8 November, 1927, the British Prime Minister sprang a surprise upon the Indian Public by announcing the decision of the British cabinet immediately to constitute the Commision. The motive was apparent to everybody. The life of the British House of Commons would expire in 1929, and there was a growing probability that the new election would return the Labour Party to power. It was generally held in Britain that a Labour Government would be more sympathetic to Indian demands, and perhaps go further in conceding reforms, than would be compatible with the vested interests of Britain in India. It was, therefore, considered safer to appoint the Commission forthwith and thus forestall the Parliament.The exclusion of Indians from a body which was to prepare the future constitution of India was so unnatural and unreasonable, that the Viceroy, Lord Irwin, while making the announcement in India on the same day, was at pains to defend the composition of the Commission. He said, in effect, that 'the two chief requisites of a member of the Commission are that he should be unbiased and unprejudiced. An Indian member cannot be expected to possess these two qualities'. For, "the desire, natural and legitimate, of the Indian members to see India a self-governing nation, could hardly fail to colour their judgment of her present capacity to sustain the role.") Further, the Parliament would instinctively fool that the opinion of Indian members "in more than one case represented views to which the holder was previously committed". The Viceroy, however, agreed that Indians have every right to ask that "their solution of the problem or their judgment on other solutions which may be proposed should be made an integral factor in the examination of the question and be given due weight in the ultimate decision". This was to be effected by two-fold means suggested in the Prime Minister's announcement. First, "the Central Indian Legislature (as well as Provincial Legislatures) would appoint a Joint Select Committee, chosen from its elected and nominated unofficial members, which would draw up its views and proposals in writing and lay them before the Government had presented proposals to the Parliament on the basis of the Report submitted by the Commission, these proposals should be referred to a Joint Committee of both Houses, and facilities would be given to the Indian Central Legislature to present their views before the Joint Committee be delegations who would be invited to attend and confer with the Joint Committee.[1]

The Indians held that the reasons advanced by the Viceroy for excluding the Indians were too puerile to merit serious consideration. For, if desire for self-government could bias the judgement of the Indians, the desire and interest of the British to keep control over India were more likely to warp their judgement about the future constitution of India. The so-called opportunities given to Indians to place their views were worse than useless.

The announcement about Simon Commission was received with profound disappointment and indignation by all political leaders in India, irrespective of their party affiliations, and they unanimously decided to boycott the Commission. Never before, within living memory, did the Indian political leaders hold a common view on such an important political issue.[2] The general attitude of the Indians towards the Commission was thus eloquently put by Sapru in his Presidential Address at the annual session of the All-India Liberal Federation: "I do not think a worse challenge has been thrown out ever before to Indian nationalism, and notwithstanding the profuse assurances in Mr. Baldwin's speech and the yet more profuse assurances in Mr. Ramsay MacDonald's speech, Indian nationalists of the Moderate School have been compelled to ask if the only way of recognizing the spirit of co-operation is by telling Indians that their lot is to be none other than of petitioners, that they cannot be trusted to participate in the responsibility of making recommendations to Parliament for the future of their country, and that all that they may aspire to is to put their proposals before the Commission which may accept them or reject them, and again to repeat the same process of persuasion, arguement and discussion before the Joint Committee of Parliament. Now, if this is what is meant by co-operation, if this is the new idea of equality of status on which we are to be fed, if our patriotism is a prejudice and if the patriotism of the seven Members of Parliament is to be treated as impartial justice, then we Liberals feel justified in telling the Government here and in England, "You may do anything you like in the assertion of your right as supreme power, but we are not going to *acquiesce* in this method of dealing with them. Neither our self-respect nor our sense of duty to our country can permit us to go near the Commission."[3]

The manifestoes and proposal to boycott the Commission were endorsed by numerous public meetings all over India. It came as a rude shock to the Indians that men like Ramsay MacDonald and Lord Olivier, who had supported the grant of Dominion Status to India in their public speeches and writings, should have been party to the betrayal of India's cause.

While the idea of boycotting the Simon Commission was adopted by all political parties, the Indian National Congress suggested some practical measures to make it effective. These included (1) mass demonstrations all over India on the day the members of the Commission set foot on this country, and similar demonstrations in every city on the day it was visited by them; (2) refusal of the legislatures to elect their own Committees to co-operate with the Commission of helping their inquiry in any war; (3) rejection of the demand for grant in connection with the Commission; and (4) social boycott of the members of the Commission. Thus the Congress organizations made the boycott a great success. On 3 February, 1928, the day of the arrival of the Commission in Bombay, complete *hartal* was observed in all important towns in India, and huge demonstrations marched in processions waving black flags and carrying banners with the words, "Go back, Simon", inscribed on them. Of the numerous public meetings of protest held on that day, the one held in Bombay was the most memorable.

On 16 February, 1928, Lala Lajpat Rai moved a resolution in the Central Assembly to the effect that as the scheme of the Commission was unacceptable to the house, it would have nothing to do with it at any stage and in any form. The resolution, supported by an overwhelming majority of elected members, was passed amid cries of *Bande Mataram*.

Attempts by Indian Leaders to Draft an Agreed Constitution

In a speech in the House of Lords on 7 July, 1925, Birkenhead referred to the contention of the Swarajya party that no constitution framed by the British would be acceptable to them, and said: "Let them produce a constitution which carries behind it a fair measure of general agreement among the great peoples of India. Such a contribution to our problems would nowhere be resented. It would, on the contrary, be most carefully examined by the Government of India, by myself, and, I am sure, by the Commission, whenever that body may be assembled."

The same challenge was renewed by Birkenhead while moving the constitution of the Statutory Commission in November, 1927. He said: "I have twice invited our critics in India to put forward their own suggestions for a constitution. That offer is still open."

The Indian leaders now decided to accept the challenge. Preliminary discussions between the Hindu and Muslim leaders for the settlement of outstanding differences between the two communities in regard to the future constitution of India having been carried out in a friendly spirit with great chance of success, the question was taken up by the Indian National Congress in its Madras session in 1927. It passed a resolution authorizing the Working Committee to confer with similar committees appointed by other organizations, potitical, labour, commercial and communal; to draft a Swaraj constitution for India; and to place the same for consideration as approval before a special convention to be convened in Delhi not later than March, 1928, consisting of the All-India Congress Committee and the leaders and representatives of the other organizations mentioned above, and elected members of the Central and Provincial legislatures.

The idea was fully approved by the All-India Liberal Federation and the Muslim League and the Working Committee of the Congress issued invitations to a large number of organizations, including the following:[4]

National Liberal Federation; Hindu Mahasabha; All-India Muslim League; Central Khilafat Committee; Central Sikh League; South Indian Liberal Federation; All-India Trade Union Congress; General Council of All-Burmese Associations; Home Rule League; Republican League; Independent Party in the Assembly; Nationalist Party in the Assembly; Indian States Subjects' Association; Indian States Subjects' Conference; Indian States Peoples' Conference; Anglo-Indian Association; Indian Association of Calcutta; Parsi Central Association; Zoroastrian Association; Parsi Rajkiya Sabha; Parsi Panchayat; All-India Conference of Indian Christians; Southern India Chamber of Commerce; Dravida Mahajans Sabha; and the Landholders Associations of Oudh, Agra, Bihar, Bengal and Madras.

Many of these organizations sent representatives to the Conference which held its first meeting on 12 February, 1928, at Delhi, under the chairmanship of Dr. M. A. Ansari. But it was soon apparent that there were sharp differences between the Muslim League on the one hand and the Hindu Mahasabha and the Sikh delegations of the other, over matters which each of them considered vital. Thereupon the Conference, in its session of 19th May, 1928, appointed a small committee under the chairmanship of Motilal Nehru to consider and determine the principles of the constitution for India. The Committee submitted its report on 10 August, 1928, and it was considered by the All Parties' Conference held at Lucknow from 28 to 31 August, 1928.

The important recommendations were moved as seperate resolution and votes were taken on each. There was some hitch on the resolution demanding Dominion Status for India. The Congress in its Madras session (1927) had adopted independence as the goal, and the younger section, headed by Jawaharlal Nehru, opposed the resolution and demanded a constitution based on full independence. They submitted a statement to this effect and abstained from voting. The resolution was passed *nem con.* It was unanimously resolved that there should be joint electorates without reservation of seats for any community in the Punjab, provided that the franchise was based on adult suffrage and it was open for reconsideration after ten years. Subject to this the Report was adopted with only one dissentient voice.

The Report envisaged a sovereign Parliament consisting of a Senate and a House of Representatives, with powers analogous to those of the Dominions.

The Constitution provided for a Federal System with residuary power vested in the Central Government, joint responsibility of the ministry to the Legislature, a single Chamber in the Provincial Councils, and a Committee of Defence.

Regarding the all-important communal representation, the Nehru Committee made the following recommendation, which were accepted, subject to the Punjab agreement mentioned above:

"I. There shall be joint mixed electorates throughout India for the House of Representatives and the provincial legislatures.

II. There shall be no reservation of seats for the House

of Representatives except for Muslims in provinces where they are in a minority and non-Muslims in the N. W. F. Province. Such reservation will be in strict proportion to the Muslim population in every province where they were in a minority and in proportion non-Muslims, where reservation is allowed to them shall have the right to contest additional seats.

III. In the provinces.

(a) There shall be no reservation of seats for any community in the Punjab and Bengal;

(b) In provinces other than the Punjab and Bengal there will be reservation of seats for Muslim minorities on population basis with the right to contest additional seats;

(c) In the N. W. F. Province there shall be similar reservation of seats for non-Muslims with the right to contest other seats.

IV. Reservation of seats, were allowed, shall be for a fixed period of ten years.

The Constitution adopted by the All Parties Conference, hereafter referred to as the Nehru Constitution was, however, a stillborn child. The Conference had decided to place the new constitution before a representative Convention in Calcutta, and it met on 22 December, 1928. The Muslim League and a section of the Khilafat Committee led by M. A. Jinnah refused to accept the communal settlement incorporated in the Constitution on the bases of compromise between the Muslims and other communities. Jinnah moved, by way of amendments, the incorporation of the following in the Nehru Constitution:

1. The Muslims should have one-third representation on the Central Legislature.
2. The Punjab and Bengal Legislatures should have Muslim representation on the population basis for ten years in the event of adult suffrage not being granted.
3. Residuary powers should be vested in the Provinces

and not in the Centre.

After an acrimonious debate Jinnah's amendments were lost, and he left the Convention in protest. Next day the Sikhs also withdrew, and two days later, the Convention was adjourned *sine die* on 1 January, 1928, the eighth day of the session. Jinnah, now joined the groups of Muslims led by the Aga Khan and Sir Muhammad Shafi, and organized a united opposition which held an All Parties' Conference in Delhi on 1st January, under the Chairmanship of the Age Khan. It endorsed Jinnah's amendments, demanded separate electorates for Muslims in various legislatures and other statutory self-governing bodies, constitution for Sindh as a separate Province, and raising the status of Baluchistan and N.W.F.P. to that of other Provinces.[5]

Apart from the Muslims, some sections of the Sikhs, non-Brahmins and Backward and depressed communities also did not fully approve of the Nehru Constitution, and even the Christians, while expressing general approval, were for opinion that indeed non-sufficiently safeguard the interest of minorities. In the other hand, it should be emphasized that eminent Muslim Leagers like Dr. Ansari, Sir Ali Imam, the Raja of Mahmudabad and many other approved of the Nehru Constitution and the scheme for communal representation adopted in it. The same thing may be said of the other minority communities and organizations. Besides, the All-India Liberal Federation, an all-India political body next in importance only to the Indian National Congress, gave its blessings to the Nehru Constitution.

The discussion following the publication of the Nehru Constitution and criticisms directed against it revealed the all-important facts, that on the question of immediate grant of Responsible Government, the whole of India stood united, the difference being only in respect of details.

The sentiment of complete imdependence, however, gradually gained ground. As mentioned above, the Indian National Congress had declared independence as India's goal in the Madras Session in 1927. Since then it was reaffirmed in the Provincial Conference of the Punjab,

Delhi, and U.P. The younger section led by Jawaharlal Nehru and Subhash Chandra Bose organized an Independence League and carried on active propaganda in favour of independence.[6]

The nation-wide sentiment for independence also found expression in the annual session of the Indian National Congress in Calcutta in December, 1928. In view of the strong sentiment held on the subject, Gandhi, by way of compromise, suggested that the Dominion Status be accepted, provided the British Parliament accepted the Nehru Constitution in its entirety within a year. He therefore moved the following resolution:

"This congress having considered the Constitution recommended by the All-Parties' Committee Report welcomes it as a great contribution towards the solution of India's political and communal problems and congratulates the Committee on the virtual unanimity of its recommendations, and whilst adhering to the resolution relating to Complete Independence passed at the Madras Congress, approves of the Constitution drawn up by the Committee as a great step in political advance, specially as it represents the largest measure of agreement attained among the important parties in the country.

"Subject to the exigencies of the political situation, the Congress will adopt the Constitution if is accepted in its entirety by the British Parliament on as before the 31st December, 1929, but in the even of its non-acceptancy by that date or its earlier rejection, the Congress will organise a campaign of non-violent Non-co-operation by advising the country to refuse taxation and in such other manner as may be decided upon.

"Consistently with the above, nothing in this resolution shall interfere with the carrying on in the name of the Congress of the propaganda for complete Independence."

But even though Gandhi declared that he would join the movement for independence in case the ultimatum given by the Congress was rejected, his proposal was vigorously opposed by the younger section led by Jawaharlal Nehru and Subhash Chandra Bose. An amendment was moved by the latter to the affect that the Congress would be content with nothing short of independence. The amendment was lost by 973 votes to 1350, but the large number of voters cast in opposition to veteran leaders like Gandhi and Motilal Nehru showed the rising strength of the left wing in the Congress.

The year 1929

1. New Activities

The compromise resolution of the Calcutta Congress put a stop to active political agitation by the Congress in 1929. But it was a lull before the storm which broke out in 1930 in the shape of Civil Disobedience Movement and continued, with an interval, till 1934. Before describing the events that led to that great trial of strength between the Congress and the Government, it is necessary to refer briefly to some other activities during this period, which formed other outlets, as in were, for national ardour and enthusiasm.

In the first place, there was a revival of revolutionary activity which will be discussed in detail in Ch. XXII. It will suffice to states here that considerable stir was created in the political circle by the murder of Mr. Saunders, Asst. Superintendent of Police, Lahore (for the assault on Lala Lajpat Rai in 1928 which was believed to have caused his death), throwing of bombs in the Assembly Hall at Delhi (1929), Lahore Conspiracy Case leading to a hunger strike and the martyrdom of Jatin Das (1929), the Chittagong Armoury Raid and fight at Jalalabad Hill (1930), hanging of Bhagat Singh and his two comrades (1931), and murder or attempted murder of a large number of officials, both Indian and European. The railway train carrying the Viceroy, Lord Irwin, from South India met with a bomb accident near New Delhi on 23 December, 1929, The Viceroy narrowly escaped.

The death of Jatin Das also gave a fillip to the youth movement. Throughout 1929 youth and student organizations grew up all over India, and congresses and conferences were held at Calcutta, Poona, Madras, Ahmedabad, Lahore, Nagpur, Amraoti, and several other places. In December, 1929, an All-India Congress of Students was held at Lahore, presided over by Pandit Madan Mohan Malaviya.

There was also wide-spread labour unrest caused mainly by the communists and ending on the Meerut Conspiracy Case.[7] There was also a big split in the Trade Union Movement caused by the appointment of a Royal Commission on Labour with Mr. Whitley as Chairman. Profiting by the sad experience of Simon Commission, two Indians were offered seats on the Whitley Commission. These were N. M. Joshi of Bombay, the father of the Trade Union Movement in India, and Chamanlal of Lahore, who at once accepted the offer. Both of them, however, belonged to the Right Wing of the Labour Movement, and when the All-India Trade Union Congress met at Nagpur in November, with Jawaharlal Nehru as President, a resolution boycotting the Whitley Commission was carried amidst shouts of "Down with Joshi and Chamanlal." The Right wing members, offended at the insult to Joshi, walked out of the Congress and, later, set up a separate organization called "All-India Trade Union Federation."

Congress Politics

A sudden change in the views of the two Nehrus—father and son—was the most interesting phenomenon in the Congress camp. In Bengal, the repeated defeats of the Ministry led to the dissolution of the Bengal Legislative Council in May, 1929. Pandit Motilal Nehru, the leader of the Congress party in the Legislative Assembly, instructed the Bengal Congress party to fight the elections. This they did with the result that the Congress party came back with added strength, and some of the Nationalist Muslims, defeated in the election of 1926, regained their seats. But suddenly, on 15 July, 1929, the Congress Working Committee passed a resolution calling upon the Congressmen to resign their seats. There were many surprising features in it. In the first place, no attempt was made to invite the opinions of the Congress parties in different legislatures, nor was any notice given to them of the proposed change. Secondly, even Motilal Nehru acquiesced in the resolution, though only two months before he had encouraged the Bengal Congress party to fight the election and enjoined upon them to recapture some of the Muslim seats. The All-India Congress Committee, to which the question was referred for final decision, met on 26 July, 1929, *rescinded* the resolution, and referred the whole question to the Congress. But the coalition of Motilal Nehru and Gandhi in favour of the boycott of the Council plainly showed the emergence of Gandhi and his creed once again into active politics of the Congress. The election of Pandit Jawaharlal Nehru as the President, who had been a devoted follower of Gandhi, but since his return from, Europe in December, 1927, he called himself a Socialist and joined the left wing. He and Subhash Chandra Bose led this wing, maintained the Independence League, and openly opposed Gandhi in the Calcutta Congress. But after he accepted the Presidentship of the Congress, he became a consistent and unfailing supporter of Gandhi.[8] Thus Subhash Chandra Bose and Nehru parted company, and the former remained the sole leader of the younger section and the left wing of the Congress.

The Viceroy's declaration of 31 October, 1929

As a result of the General Election in Britain in 1929, the Labour Party came into office. Ramsay MacDonald, the Prime Minister, invited the Viceroy, Lord Irwin, to London for consultation. Evidently, by a sort of pre-arrangement, Sir John Simon wrote to the Prime Minister, asking for the extension of the terms of reference of his Commission so that the methods for the adjustment of future relationship between British India and the States might be fully examined by the Commission. Simon further suggested that after the publication of the Commission's Report, a Conference should be arranged between the representatives of His Majesty's Government and representatives of British India and the States, for the purpose of seeking the greatest possible measure of agreement for the final proposals to be submitted by the Cabinet to the Parliament. The Cabinet agreed to both the suggestions, and Lord Irwin returned to India. Shortly after his arrival he issued a statement on 31 October 1929. It referred to the Cabinet's acceptance of Simon's proposals and the summoning of a Conference on the lines proposed by him. But the most important part of his statement is the following declaration: "I am authorized, on behalf of His Majesty's Government, to state clearly that, in their judgement, it is implicit in the declaration of 1917 that the natural issue of India's Constitutional progress, as there contemplated, is the attainment of Dominion Status."

This declaration was strongly criticized by a powerful section of the British Press, and both the Conservative and Liberal Parties opposed it in both the Houses of Parliament. In India, however, the Declaration was welcomed by all the political parties, and the most prominent leaders, including Gandhi and Motilal Nehru, issued a statement offering co-operation to evolve a Dominion Constitution for India. Both the combined protest by the Tories and Liberals had done its work.[9] The Labour Party did not command absolute majority in the House of Commons and could carry on the Government only with the support of the Liberal Party. So when Gandhi, Nehru and other interviewed the Viceroy on 23 December 1929, and sought for a definite assurance that the Dominion Status would be granted to India, the Viceroy was unable to give it. Gandhi thereupon declared himself definitely for independence, and thereby after nearly seven years regained his position of undisputed supremacy in the Congress. "I have burnt my boats" said he.

The Congress Session of 1929 at Lahore

The Congress met at Lahore on 29 December 1929, in a tense atmosphere. There was an intense fervour throughout the country over the impending declaration of independence—a fervour increased, rather than kept down, by the indiscriminate arrests of political workers by the Government. The choice of Jawaharlal Nehru, an embodiment of youthful ardour and indomitable enthusiasm for independence, as President, lent a special glamour to the vast concourse assembled at the Congress pandal. The resolution which embodied the spirit of the vast audience read as follows:

The turning of the tide (1928-30)

"This Congress endorses the action of the Working Committee in connection with the manifesto signed by party leaders, including Congressmen, on the Viceregal pronouncement of the 31st October relating to Dominion Status, and appreciates the efforts of the Viceroy towards a settlement of the national movement for Swaraj. The Congress, however, having considered all that has since happened and the result of the meeting between Mahatma Gandhi, Pandit Motilal Nehru, and other leaders and the Viceroy, is of opinion that nothing is to be said in the existing circumstances by the Congress being represented at the proposed Round Table Conference. This Congress, therefore, in pursuance of the resolution passed at its session at Calcutta last year, declares that the word 'Swaraj' in Article I of the Congress Constitution shall mean Complete Independence, and further declares the entire scheme of the Nehru committee's report to have lapsed, and hopes that all Congressmen will henceforth devote their exclusive attention to the attainment of Complete Independence for India. As a preliminary step towards organising a campaign for Independence, and in order to make the Congress policy as consistent as possible with the change of creed, this Congress resolves upon complete boycott of the Central and Provincial Legislatures and Committees constituted by the Government and calls upon the Congressmen and other taking part in the national movement to abstain from participating, directly or indirectly, in future elections, and directs the present Congress members of the Legislatures and Committees to resign their seats. This Congress appeals to the nation zealously to prosecute the constructive programme of the Congress, and suthorises the All-India Congress Committee, whenever it deems fit, to launch upon a programme of Civil Disobedience, including non-payment of toxes, whether in selected areas or otherwise, and under such safeguards as it may consider necessary."

There is no doubt that the revival of Civil Disobedience in the Lahore Congress was Gandhi's handiwork. He was of the opinion that the best way of preventing it was to canalize the resurgent spirit of youth into a non-violent campaign. As he stated: "Civil Disobedience alone can save the country from impending lawlessness which will not listen to speeches, resolutions, or conferences, but believes only in direct action."

The adoption of independence as the goal of India was hailed with defitting solemnity. As the clock struck midnight on December 31, and the date of ultimatum and spiritually", and ended with the enunciation of the future policy in the following words:

"We hold it to be a crime against man and God to submit any longer to a rule that has caused this fourfold disaster to our country, We recognise, however, that the most ineffective way of gaining our freedom is not through violence. We will therefore prepare ourselves by drawing, so far as we can, all voluntary association from the British Government, and will prepare for civil disobedience, including non-payment of taxes. We are convinced that if we can but withdraw our voluntary help and shop payment of taxes without doing violence even under provocation, the end of this inhuman rule is assured. We therefore here by solemnly resolve to carry out the Congress instructions issued from time to time for the purpose of establishing *Purna Swaraj*."[10]

Thus, every Indian was to make a declaration of complete independence and take a pledge of loyalty to the Indian National Congress and to the sacred fight for India's liberty.

The independence day was solemnly observed, and evoked great enthusiasm all over the country. But the ink with which the declaration was written had hardly dried when Gandhi issued a statement in his paper, *Young*

India, which, by no stretch of imagination, could be made compatible with the declaration, to which every Indian was asked to subscribe.

He enumerated eleven specific items of redress and appealed to the Viceroy in the following words: "This is by no means an exhaustive list of the pressing needs, but let the Viceroy satisfy us with regard to these very simple but vital needs of India. He will then hear no talk of Civil disobedience; and the Congress will heartily participate in any Conference where there is a perfect freedom of expression and demand."[11] One might rub his eyes in wonder and ask himself,—is it the same Gandhi who refused to attend the Round Table Conference save on the express promise of the grant of Dominion Status?

Again, however important might be the specific reforms demanded by Gandhi, does it lie in the mouth of those who were pledged to fight for *Purna Swaraj* or complete independence, to bargain over certain administrative reforms under the British Government and promise to abandon the fight as soon as some reforms were conceded. It is imposible to discover any consistency between Day declaration on any rational basis.

Evidently, Gandhi's statement did not attract serious notice as the country was passing through excited times. Arrests were going on and Subhash Chandra Bose and eleven other were sentenced to imprisonment for a year. The undertrial prisoners in the Meerut Conspiracy Case were committed to the Sessions. A large number of Congress members had decide the mandate to resign the seats in the Legislatures.

The Working committee met again at Sabarmati on February 14-16, and passed the following resolution on Civil Disobedience:

"In the opinion of the Working Committee, Civil Disobedience should be initiated and controlled by those who believe in non-violence for the purpose of achieving *Purna Swaraj,* as an article of faith, and——welcomes the proposal of Mahatma Gandhi and authorises him and those working with him who believe in non-violence as an article of faith to start Civil Disobedience. The Working Committee further hopes that, in the event of a mass movement taking place, all those who are rendering voluntary cooperation to the Government, such as lawyers, and those who are receving so-called benefits for, it, such as students, will withdraw their co-operation or renounce benefits as the case may be, and throw themselves into the final struggle for freedom."

The Working Committee thus authorised only Gandhi and his followers in faith to start Civil Disobedience. But the A.I.C.C., which met at Ahmedabad on 21 March, 1930, i.e., after Gandhi had begun his march for Dandi, not only endorsed the resolution of the Working Committee, but somewhat widened its scope. They expressed the hope "that the whole country will respond to the action taken by Gandhi" and undertake such Civil Disobedience as to them may seem proper and in the manner that may appear to them to be most suitable".

The Indian Statutory Commission

By far the most exciting event of the year 1928 was the announcement made on the 8th November 1927 of the composition of the Statutory Commision under the Reforms Act. Up to the date of the announcement proposals and suggestions had been based largely on the assumption that the Commission would be of mixed composition. The departure from tradition and practice in this respect took the country by surprise, and was met with unyielding opposition from all sides. (See Register 1927 Vol. II)

A widespread call for boycott went round. The politicians of all classes rushed headlong into one camp, and before many days had passed, almost every responsible leader and many public bodies had committed themselves to an ademantine opposition to the Commission and a complete boycott of all its proceedings.

It will be remembered that among the resolutions passed at the session of the All India National Congress in Madras in December 1927 was one urging a nationwide *hartal*, that is the closing of shops and general abstention from business, on the day when the Commission landed. A large number of other organisations, such as the National Federation, the Muslim League and the Hindu Mahasabha, also passed resolutions to the same effect. The Legislative Assembly and some Provincial Councils also joined in the boycott and refused to co-operate with the Commission, though subsequently all of them, excepting the C.P. Council, declared for co-operation largely with the help of official and nominated members. The elected members of the Councils, however, almost solidly stood for boycott. The only parties and organisations in India which offered to co-operate did so because they sought some sectional gain by betraying the national cause. There was a minority of Moslems who were thinking of communal rather than national interests; a section of denationalised Christians who thought that Christianity and British Civilisation were synonymous; an unrepresentative group from the depressed classes, among some of whom, unfortunately, subection to Brahmin India has bred servility in the British India.

On the 15th January 1928 the Working Committee of the Congress, in co-operation with other organisations, held an All-Party Conference at Benares which declared a *hartal* for February 3rd, the day the Commission was to land in Bombay. The following is the authentic version of the proceedings of the conference :

The All Parties Boycott Conference

"At the invitation of Dr. Ansari, Chairman of the All-India Congress Committee a conference of the representatives of the various political parties was held in Benares on Jan. 15th at 2 p. m. Among those present were Dr. Ansari, Pandit Madan Mohan Malviya, Sir Tej Bahadur Sapru, Maulana Abul Kalam Azad, Mr. J. M. Sen Gupta, Messrs. Sachidananda Sinha, C. Y. Chintamani, Bipin Chandra Pal, Pandit Iqbal Narain Guru and Prof. P. K. Telang of the Home Rule League, Dr. Moonjee, Mr. J. N. Basu of the Liberal Federation, Calcutta, Mr. Kiran Sankar Roy, Secretary, Bengal Provincial Congress

Committee, Mr. Sampurnanand, Secretary, U. P. Provincial Congress Committee, Mr. Krisnaram Mehta, editor of 'The leader.' Maulvi Masud Ali Nakvi, Babu Gaurishankar Prasad of the National Liberal Federation, Chaudhuri Bihari Lal representing the depressed class, Shauaeb Qureshi, Mr. Bhargava and Pandit Jawaharlal Nehru.

"The conference discussed the boycott of the Simon Commission and the various methods for giving effect to it.

"It passed the following resolutions unanimously :—

"This conference representing various political parties is unanimously of opinion that the Statutory Commission must be left severely alone by the people.

"(1) In pursuance of this resolution, a *hartal* should be observed all over India on the day the Statutory Commission lands at Bombay, the *hartal* to be observed from morning till the time of the meeting referred to in clause 2.

"(2) Public meetings should be held all over India on February 3rd at 4.30 p.m. At house meetings the following resolution should be placed for adoption :—"This meeting of the citizens of (here name of the place should be mentioned) places on record its condemnation of the appointment of the Statutory Commission, in utter disregard of Indian opinion, and its firm resolve to have nothing to do with that Commission in any form and any stage of its work; it calls upon all the elected members of the council of State, the Assembly and the Provincial Councils and in particular the representative of this (town, province etc) to do everything that lies in their power to oppose and prevent the formation of a committee of the legislature in connection with the said Commission; this meeting places on record its opinion that the constitution of India should be framed by Indians and strongly supports the proposal for a special convention to frame such a constitution."

On the 3rd February 1928 the members of the Statutory Commission landed at Bombay. Here, as well as elsewhere, perfect and peaceful *hartal* was observed and monster meetings were held. As a demonstration of the united nation-wide desire to boycott the Commission and repudiate the autocratic assumption behind sporadic incidents elsewhere complete success. In Madras a large crowd mobbed tram cars and private persons and gathered in great numbers outside the High Court where they quickly got out of control necessitating the police to open fire injuring a number of men of whom two afterwards died. In Calcutta most of the trouble was caused by a large crowd who tried to prevent motor buses and tram cars from plying. The students of the Presidency College, it was alleged, assaulted their Principal and came into conflict with the Police who assaulted and injured a number of students and passerby.

Barring the above two regrettable happenings the *hartal* was a success in other places. The Indian business community, with very rare exceptions, suspended work with striking unanimity—petty shopkeepers as zealously as the biggest firms—notwithstanding the considerably greater hardship the *hartal* imposed upon them. The accounts received from all quarters showed that the principal towns wore the aspect of cities of the dead, so thorough was the cessation of all locomotion or other normal activity.. The general public was so fully resolved to make the boycott a success that the efforts in some places of non-indigenous agencies controlling the means of communication to create a semblance of activity proved futile. Everywhere the members of the Commission went they encountered receptions with black flags and shouts of "Simon, go back."

From Bombay the Commissioners came straight to Delhi where they arrived on the 4th February. Two days after, i.e., on the 6th February, Sir John Simon, as Chairman of the Commission, issued a statement in the form of a letter to the Viceroy delineating the procedure to be adopted by the Commission. The following is the full text of the letter:—

Simon's letter to Viceroy

"Your Excellency,—In your speech to the Central Legislature on Thursday you laid renewed emphasis on the full discretion as to methods which has, from the beginning, been left in the hands of the Indian Statutory Commission; and I myself as Chairman on landing in India next day, authorised to issue a statement on behalf of the Commission that it hoped without delay to announce the line of procedure which it would propose to follow. Evidence accumulates that throughout India there is much uncertainty as to the manner in which we may be expected to exercise our functions, and even considerable misunderstanding as to what we to exercise our functions, and even considerable misunderstanding as to what we conceive those functions to be. While we receive many messages of welcome and encouragement, we note that speeches are being made and resolutions passed which are based on a complete, though doubtless genuine, misconception of our intentions. It is my plain duty therefore as Chairmand to set out forthwith the true position as we regard it; and since on the preliminary visit there is not likely to be any formal sitting of the Commission when a statement could be made, I venture to address this letter to Your Excellency.

Suggestion for Joint Conference

"We understand that the Government of India and the Local Governments have been engaged for some time past in preparing the material which they might put before the Commission. We have not seen these documents and do not know how fare they may consist matters of fact, and how far of matters of opinion or whether they deal with past events or with suggestions for the future. But whatever they are, instead of dealing with them by ourselves, we wish to propose that they and the evidence given in explanation or amplification of them should come before a joint free conference over which I should preside, consisting of the seven British Commissioners and a corresponding body of representatives chosen by the Indian Legislatures just as we ourselves have been chosen by the British Parliament. We put forward the plan of a joint free conference not only because we should welcome the assistance of colleagues from the Indian Legislatures, but because we think it is only right and fair, and in the truest interests of India and Britain alike, that opportunity should be provided for such memoranda and testimony to be scrutinised, and if necessary, elucidated from the Indian side on free and equal terms. We suggest therefore that the two Houses of the Central Legislature should in due course be invited to choose from their non-official members a joint committee which might conveniently be seven in number, and that each local legislative council should be asked to constitute a similar body. The Indian side of the conference would consist, when central subjects are being dealt with, of those first named. In a province, the Indian wing would primarily consist of the provincial members, but in order that the Central Joint Committee may not have a partial view of the material put before it, we should be glad if arrangements could be arrived at which would enable its members or some of them to be present as an additional element at the provincial sittings.

"We have no wish to dictate the composition of the Indian wing to the conference in more details, and we should greatly prefer that the precise scheme should be reached by agreement between the different elements in India concerned. Our main object will be met so long as the arrangement is one which secures that the Indian side of the Joint Conference includes on appropriate occasions those who are able to speak for the provincial councils. Just as the joint committee would speak for the Central Legislature, and so long as the members representing India sitting with us do not amount to an unwieldly number. We assume of course that just as we ourselves are a body selected from all the British parties and both the Houses of Parliament, so our Indian counterpart would be so far as may be truly representative.

"Two matters remain to be dealt with—the question of evidence other than that above referred to and the question of report. I wish to deal candidly and clearly with both.

"Some of us have had considerable experience of the method of joint conferences as applied both to industrial and political questions; and it is quite clear to us that each side of the conference will require from time to time to meet by itself. We see no reason however why evidence from public and representative bodies and from individuals should not normally be given to the conference as a whole, just as evidence presented by or on behalf of the various Governments would be. If a case arises when this general plan cannot be followed, I should make no secret of it and would ask my colleagues in the joint free conference when, as I hope, they learn to have faith in my sense of fairness, to accept from me such account of the matter as I can give them on behalf of the Commission, with due regard to the reason why the testimony has been separately received. I imagine that the Indian side may find occasions when they would think it well to act in the same way.

"A Completely Independent and Unfettered Body"

"As regards the report, it is, I feel necessary to restate the true function of the Commission and its place in the general scheme which you announced last November. The Commission is in no sense an instrument either of the Government of India or of the British Government, but enters on the duty laid upon it by the King-Emperor as a completely independent and unfettered body composed of members of Parliament who approach the Indian Legislatures as colleagues. It is not an executive or legislating body authorised to pronounce decisions about the future government of India. Before these decisions can be reached, the full process, of which the present investigation is a first step, must be completed including the affording of opportunity for the views of the Indian Legislature, amongst other bodies, of being presented by delegations in London to the Joint Parliamentary Committee. The present Commission is only authorised to report and make recommendations; and in this report we desire to include a faithful account of opinions and aspirations prevalent in India, and of the concrete proposals for constitutional reform so far as these are put before us. The British Commissioners therefore are bound to be solely responsible for the statement of the effect upon their own minds of the investigation as a whole. We shall report to the authority by which we have been constituted, just as (if the Conference is set up) the Joint Committee would, we presume, be entitled to report its conclusions to the Central Legislature. It is obvious that those documents should be prepared and presented simultaneously. There are wellknown constitutional means by which the document emanating from the joint Committee and presented to the Central Legislature can be forwarded to and made available for the British Parliament; but if the Indian Joint Committee would prefer it, we would make its report an annexe to our own document, so that both might be presented to the King-Emperor and made public at the same moment.

"Above all, I would urge that one of the merits of the method of joint conference is that besides securing due recognition of equal status, it provides the opportunity for that free exchange of views and mutual influence which are best calculated to promote the largest measure of agreement that is possible.

"Our present visit is preliminary; and the sitting of the joint free conference, it is set up, would not begin till October. But we make public our suggestions at once, not only in order to clear the air, but in order to show ourselves available for any conference about any matters of procedure which this statement does not adequately cover. The Commission is of course bound to carry through its task in any event, and discharge to the full the duty cast upon it; but we are undertaking this duty only after having made it known that the method of collaboration on honourable and equal terms is open, and that we put it forward in all sincerity and goodwill. We will only add that in making these proposals we are confident that we are correctly interpreting the intention of the British Parliament.

"The carrying out of our proposals will require at a

latter date that the Council of State, the Legislative Assembly and the Local Legislative Councils should be moved to elect their representatives who would take part in the Joint Conference, and the Commission will be glad if the Government of India will take such steps as seem appropriate for this purpose in due course."

Leaders Joint Statement

The above statement of Sir John was subjected to a very careful and indeed anxious consideration for two hours by the leaders of all parties at a conference held in New Delhi on the next day, the 7th February. After a good deal of thoughtful discussion all the party leaders came to an absolutely unanimous and unequivocal decision, repeating their declaration and advice that India should have nothing to do with the Commission at any stage or in any form.,

The leaders maintained that Sir John Simon's offer did not remove their fundamental objection to the constitution and scheme of the Commission and hence their decision to stick to the boycott policy in spite of Lord Irwin's veiled threats, and Sir John Simon's cajolery.

The trend of the discussion at the Leaders Conference was unmistakable and there was not one among them who could view the Simon offer with favourable eye. Mr. Jayakar's signature to the manifesto issued by the leaders after the Conference, left no room for doubt as to his attitude, whatever might have been the criticisms against him. The inclusion of Raja Ghaznafar Ali Khan of the Punjab was significant *inasmuch* as it served to prove that the Punjab in spite of Sir Mahommed Safi's activities was for boycott. The unambigous statement of the all-party leaders gave a clear indication of the country's determination to boycott the unwanted Commission. The following is the text :

"We have most carefully considered the line of procedure indicated in the statement of Sir John Simon issued to-day. But our objection to the Commission as constituted by it. In the circumstances, we must adhere to our decision that we cannot have anything to do with the Commission at any stage or in any form."

(Sd.) Dr. Ansari, Mr. Srinivasa lyenger, Maulana Abul Kalam Azad, Maulana Mahomed Ali.—(Congressmen). Lala Lajpat Rai, Pandit Madan Mohan Malaviya, Mr. N.C. Kelkar—(Nationalists) Mr. Jinnah, Sir P. Thakurdas, *Moulvi* Mahomed Yakub, Raja Ghaznafar Ali Khan.—(Independents).

There is no need to describe in detail the experience of the Commission in the many different places which they visited. At Delhi in the historic debate on the boycott of the Simon Commission in the Assembly they experienced that the country's verdict was against them. From Delhi they went on to Calcutta, then to Madras and other places in the Madras presidency and North again to Lahore and one or two other places in the Punjab. Practically everywhere they encountered similar reception. After finishing their preliminary visit they left the shores of India on the 31rd March 1928.

The Leaders' Statement

On the 20th February the following statement was issued over the signatures of Pandit Motilal Nehru, Mr. S. Srinivasa lyengar, Pandit Madan Mohan Malaviya, Mr. M.A. Jinnah, Lala Lajpat Rai and Sir Purshottamdas Thakurdas : —

"On the morrow of the momentous decision recorded last night by the Assembly, we desire to issue a statement to our constituencies and the public at large.

"For several past months and in particular since November last repeated warnings were given to the Government here and in England, to the extent to which it is possible now for Indian opinion to find expression in the English press, against the injustice, unwisdom and inexpediency of appointing under the provisions of the Statute of 1919 an exclusively British Parliamentary Commission. These warnings have gone unheeded, both in India and in England. Indeed, an almost distorted version of the Indian situation has been sedulously presented to the British Parliament; and the public and newspapers in England have generally wholly misled or misrepresented the Indian situation. The responsibility of the Government of India, including as it does three Indian members, in giving an incorrect perspective of the Indian situation is if anything greater; for we cannot believe that Lords Birkenhead and Winterton could have made the statements which they have made in Parliament and on other platforms, without receiving an estimate of the Indian situation from the Government of India.

"The minatory attitude of Lord Birkenhead, as evidenced by the speech he made in England a report of which arrived during the progress of the debate in the Assembly, and the cablegram of Mr. Ramsay MacDonald to Mr. Vernon Hartshorn, besides showing up His Majesty's Government and the Leader of the Opposition, prove that they had made up their minds to enforce their decision at all costs, without even waiting for the result of the debate in the Assembly, and have succumbed to the anti-Indian propaganda proceeding from well-known sources in India and England.

"We repeat that the responsibility of the Government of India in the matter is great. They have shown by their conduct that they have no touch with the realities of the situation, that they are totally cut off from avenues of correct information, and that they are unable correctly to appreciate or interpret Indian feeling to His Majesty's Government and that they carried on the entire struggle with the Legislature in the spirit of propagandists, and that they have placed prestige above predence. We regret to observe, that even the Commission have adopted propagandist methods to create an impression in England and India, that they have received every encouragement in India; whereas the fact is that barring a section of Mahomedans and a few others, they have been entirely out of touch with and have failed to establish any contact with the people of this country or their representative in the Assembly.

"The Government and the Commission, instead of being at this juncture a unifying factor, have been counting upon the division of opinion in India. We desire to give a clear warning, that this policy is doomed to failure. Indeed, it has already failed, though we recognised that in a country situated as India is, there are bound to be some people who are likely to yield to the expediencies of the hour.

"Our attention has been drawn to a cablegram sent to *The Times* and other newspapers, asserting or insinuating that methods of undue influence and intimidation were employed in securing Moslem votes in favour of Lala Lajpat Rai's resolution; and that Hindu officials exercised undue influence on Mahomedan members in their constituencies to vote for it. We unreservedly and emphatically repudiate such charges, and declare that they are simply not true. We treat them as part of the anti-Indian propaganda which has been for months past carried on mischievously both in an insidious and in an open manner.

"We claim to be in close touch with our people and with our constituencies; and we unhesitatingly assert that we have correctly and faithfully interpreted the feeling of the vast bulk of our countrymen by recording our votes against the Simon Commission.

"We regret to have to observe that the British Parliament was misled into the decision which it took in November last by those whose duty it was to interpret faithfully Indian feeling; and the agents of Parliament having committed an egregious blunder in this respect, have counted upon Sir John Simons' tact and ability to come to their rescue. We have been blamed for having rejected Sir John's letter to the Viceroy with undue haste. We discussed it carefully for several hours. It was not difficult for any one of us who had read the debates in the House of Commons to foresee the line which Sir John was likely to take and which he did ultimately take. It was foreshadowed in the Anglo-Indian Press on the arrival of the Commission. In point of fact, some of us had heard from reliable sources in England of the line which he was going to take.

"We have given our utmost consideration to the

announcement made by H.E. the Viceroy, the speeches in Parliament made by the Secretary of State, the Prime Minister and others, and to the speech made by Lord Birkenhead on various occasions since the debate in Parliament. They do not disclose any equality of status or power or opportunities to Indian Committees. The two letters of Sir John Simon addressed to the Viceroy and to Sir Sankaran Nair, laying down the line of procedure have made it abundantly clear that in truth no such equality is vouchsafed to Indian Committees. The recording of some evidence *in camera*, the inability of Indian members to vote at the proceedings of the Commission, the power reserved to the Chairman to allow or not to allow members of the Central Committee to examine witnesses in province, and the secondary place assigned to the Indian Committee's report, make it abundantly plain that the Committees can at best play a subordinate part. We desire to draw attention pointedly to the fact that even the proposals of the Responsivist Party which had not been endorsed by other parties have not met with any response from the Commission. For these reasons those parties which would under conditions of equality of status, power and opportunities have agreed to work in co-operation with the Commission, have felt in their duty to hold aloof from the Commission. The Congress Party has always stood out for a round table conference, and it is obvious that it could not be expected to agree to a Commission of such a character.

"We feel therefore that the responsibility for the situation so created must rest (1) on the Government of India (2) the British Government and (3) the Commission.

"In the circumstances, we appeal to public men of all parties and to all political organisations in India to unite together (1) in settling sectional or communal differences, which we have every confidence will be settled soon to the satisfcation of all parties (2) prepare a draft constitution with the maximum amount of agreement, and to adopt it at a Convention and (3) to work for its establishment.

"We also appeal to the Legislative Councils of the

United Provinces, Bengal, Bombay, Punjab and Bihar and Assam to follow the example of the Legislative Assembly, and of the Central Provinces and Madras. We dare not appeal to the Council of State."

The Commission's Statement

The following is the statement of the Commission inviting the submission of statements or memoranda from official and non-official sources, and was issued to the press early in March 1928 :

"The Indian Statutory Commission invites the submission of written statement or memoranda both from official and non-official sources, from representative associations, local bodies and responsible individuals on any of the enquiry which it is about to undertake. Before the Commission returns to India in October, the programme of its sittings in various centres will have to be drawn up, written statements or memoranda now called for should be prepared and sent to the offices of the commission as soon as possible in order that the commission may appreciate the main issues to be raised and the proposals to be urged before it hereafter and in order that it may make arrangements beforehand for the orderly conduct of its subsequent enquiry. Such written statement or memoranda, as are ready before the commission leaves India on March 31st, should be sent by registered post addressed to "The Indian Statutory Commission, camp, India". After this date the Commission to "The Indian Statutory Commission, New Delhi," office, New Delhi from which office they will be transmitted to the office of the Commission in England.

"Twelve copies of each memorandum are required in the first instance. Further copies may be called for thereafter if the proposed Indian committees are set up in time.

"It is most desirable that these memoranda should be delivered to this offices of the commission as soon as possible and in any event not later than June 1st. If for any special reason particular documents cannot be delivered till later, the commission will be glad to be informed of the circumstances, and will do its best to deal with them. But the organisation of the commission's enquiry makes it essential that written material much of which has doubtless already been prepared, should be promptly presented.

"The terms of reference under which the Commission is acting are as follows :—

"It is "to enquire into the working of the system of Government, growth of education and development of representative institutions in British India and matters connected therewith" and it is "to report as to where and to what extent it is desirable to establish the principle of responsible government or to extend, modify or restrict the degree of responsible government then existing there including the question whether the establishment of second chambers of the local Legislatures is or is not desirable."

The Commission has already had the advantage of informal interviews with important and representative bodies and deputations both at Delhi and in several provinces and has been much assisted by these interviews in appreciating the nature of some of the main questions which it will shortly begin to investigate.

"The Appendix to this notice contains a list of some of these topics (though the list does not profess to be exhaustive), and written statements or memoranda are also invited on any other subject within the Commission's terms of reference. It will be understood that those who submit memoranda are not expected or required to deal with all the subjects mentioned in the Appendix but only such of them or with such other subjects as specially concern the case they are putting forward.

"The Commission attaches special importance to written material which it is now inviting, for in many cases the memorandum will speak for itself, while in other cases the Commission after considering the memorandum (with the assistance of the Indian Committees, if these are appointed) will intimate whether it desires to hear oral evidence in support of the memorandum, and will endeavour to make the most convenient arrangements as to when this oral evidence shall be taken.

"Every memorandum should be dated and signed by or on behalf of those who present it, and should give the address to which any communication from the commission regarding it should be sent. As already stated, there will be many cases in which the memoranda submitted will themselves sufficiently convey to the commission the views of those submitting them, but in cases in which it is desired to tender to the commission oral evidence in support of any memorandum, the document should end with a address of the witness who will be ready to come forward if required for examination and cross-examination.

"Memoranda submitted in representative capacity should contain the nature extent and membership of the organisation submitting them. When a statement is put forward on behalf of a class of person, the commission wishes to have sufficient indication of the number of individuals who actually authorise it.

"The following appendix is also published :—

"Note (A)—For the purpose of illustrating the meaning of the main heads below some of the questions arising under each are given.

"Note (B)—Replies need not deal with the whole field covered by the heads, but should be limited to the particular matters to which it is desired to draw attention.

"Note (C)—Suggestions for the future are invited, as well as observations upon the structure and working of the existing constitution of British India. The Commission will be specially glad to receive any draft constitutional scheme which has been worked out beyond the stage of merely general propositions.

(1) *The representative system as applied to British India, e.g.,* (a) basis of the franchise (b) methods of election, (c) methods whereby particular interests, communal, local, social and economic may obtain adequate representation on local self-governing provincial and

central representative bodies (d) the relationship between representatives and constituents, (e) growth of parties (f) growth of informed public opinion, (g) nomination of officials and non-officials, as additional members of elected bodies.

The suitability of existing areas for legislative and administrative purposes and for the growth of representative institutions, e. g. : (a) local self-governing (b) provincial including discussion of proposal for extension of self-governing institutions to other areas than the nine provinces and of proposals for division of the existing provinces.

"The local self-governing bodies (municipalities, district boards, etc.) and their relationship with the provincial government, e.g. :—(a) constitution (b) function (c) relationship with officials of the Provincial Government (d) control by the Provincial Government (e) finance.

"Provincial Governments, e.g. :—(a) constitution (b) working of dyarchy; (c) position and powers of the Governor (d) Position of Ministers in relation to Governor and Members of Executive Council (e) relationship of Ministers to each other and the question of collective responsibility, (f) the growth of the party system in the Provincial Councils, (g) the working of particular departments, (h) classification into Reserved and Transferred subjects, (i) desirability of second chambers, (j) question of provincial autonomy [see also 6 (a) and (b)] (k) finance of Provincial Governments and financial control (l) financial relations between Reserved and Transferred sides of the Government, including the question of joint or separate purse.

"The Central Government :—(a) Constitution (b) position and powers of the Governor-General (c) relationship of the Governor-General to his Executive Council (d) relationship of the Governor General to the Legislative Assembly and the Council of State (e) position of the Executive (f) question of the responsibility of the Executive to the Legislature (g) relationship between two houses.

"Relations between the Central Government and the

provincial Governments, e.g., in regard to (a) extent to power of superintendence, direction and control to be exercised by the Central Government (b) classification of subjects as central and provincial (c) financial relationship between the Central and the Provincial Governments, including the Meston Settlement..

"Courts and judiciary—Constitutional problem in relation to such vital matters as (a) Law and Order in British India (b) justice in British India (c) Defence of India (d) Social progress in British India (e) Federation in India and (f) the status and position of India in the British Empire and the relationship between the Central Government, the Secretary of State and the British Parliament.

"The position of the services, e.g., (a) Indian Civil Services (b) other All-India services, (c) provincial services, (d) the question of recruitment and of Public Services Commission and (e) Indianisation.

"The growth of education : The Commission will shortly be making a special announcement as to this branch of the enquiry, but it does not wish the preparation of memoranda on this important topic to be delayed. Documents dealing specifically with it should be marked "growth of education" in the top left-hand corner.

Simon's second letter to Viceroy

On the 27th March Sir John Simon wrote another letter to the Viceroy with the intention of clearing two points which arose during his provincial tour, but more for the purpose, it seemed, of disabusing the public mind from some reports circulated by a press agency, that Government was thinking of nominating a Committee to sit with the Commission. Sir John stated that Burma, Punjab and the Council of State had accepted joint free conference, while the Assembly and the U.P. Council had taken the contrary view only "by small majorities" and he was hopeful of success in other Councils. Therefore he made another paper concession, namely that every Provincial Committee will have the same right as the Central Legislative Committee of presenting its report for being printed as appendices. The second concession was that Provincial Committees could depute some of their members for the final conference before the Commission leaves India. The fundamentals were left altogether untouched. The following is the text of the letter :—

"It is now seven weeks since the Indian Statutory Commission made public, by means of my letter addressed to you on the 6th February, the outline of the scheme for conducting the enquiry which the Commission will undertake in October next by method of joint free conference of which the Indian Committees would form one wing while the Commissioners the other. In the interval the scheme proposed has been accepted as a basis for co-operation by the Council of State and by the Legislative Councils of Burma and of the Punjab, while the Legislative Assembly and the United Provinces Council have, by small majorities, adopted resolutions in a contrary sense. Other legislative bodies in India are likely to be considering the matter before the Commission returns, and we think that it would be useful to clear up two points of possible ambiguity which have been brought to our notice in the course of our preliminary visit before we leave at the end of this month.

"(1) We have been asked whether a Provincial Committee after the close of its sittings with us in the Provinces, would have an opportunity of summarising its own views in a report which we might consider before arriving at our own conclusion. Our reply is that if, at the end of the sittings of the joint conference in any Province, the Provincial Committee wishes to express its own view in a report and furnishes the report to us in time, we shall be glad to give this report full consideration as one of the documents before us, and further that we would, in due course, include such report in appendices which will be printed and presented to Parliament.

"(2) It has been pointed out to us that the necessity of the Commission passing from one Province to another in accordance with a pre-arranged time table might result in placing one Province at a disadvantage as compared with another. A Province which was visited early in our itinerary might suffer because its Committee had conferred with us before certain matters which might emerge at later stages of our tour had become prominent. We think that there is force in this criticism and we shall be glad to arrange after we have been round the Provinces and before we finally leave India to meet representatives from each of the Provincial Committee if they desire it in order to hear from them their final views or confer with them on outstanding matters which seem to require treatment by this means."

The *Pioneer* on the Commission

"Despite the optimistic generalisations of Sir John Simon, *The Pioneer* does not believe that the preliminary visit of the Statutory Commission to India has been a success. It is quite true that sections of the community have greeted their visits to different parts of the country with some enthusiasm, the main result of which has been to mislead the gratified recipients. It is true also that certain bodies of public men have notified their willingness to co-operate with the activities of Sir John Simon and his colleagues. But if these receptions and promises are examined it, will be found that support is sectional and spasmodic and by no means representative of political India. Of course, it may be argued that even if political India were unanimous, in proffering support and co-operation for and with the Simon Commission only a small proportion of the vast public of India would be affected. This, we consider, to be a puerile argument. Any constitution must be worked by the politically-minded members of the society for which the reform or the constitution is to function and any form of government which would venture to function without taking into consideration even the views of an acknowledged minority, is bound to be viewed with distaste, if not with positive hatred. An efficient and alien rule will never be preferred to an autonomous and inefficient one, and this principle must be remembered in all dealings with a country in which it is proposed to examine the incomplete constitution which, at the present moment, it admittedly possesses.

"The two months of the Simon Commission in India have demonstrated that there are two firm convictions in the minds of most politically-minded Indians. The first is that somehow or other, despite the acknowledged honesty of motive inspiring Sir John Simon, the bureaucrats in Delhi and Whitehall will manage so to handle the Commission, the evidence to be brought before it and the report itself, that India will not get a fair deal. The second feeling is one of indignation and anger at what is thought to be the implied insult to Indian nationality in that the appointments to the Commission excluded any Indian. These two dominant feelings are at the back of and inspire all opposition to Sir John Simon and his colleagues. And the problem which, for the sake of true British prestige must be built between the present Commission and its opposition ? It is no use deluding oneself with the belief that opposition will crumble and disappear. That is not the opinion of "The Pioneer." On the contrary, there is ample evidence for the belief that when the Commission returns in the autumn, and nothing is done in the meantime, the opposition will be stronger and more virulent than ever. It is no use adopting what ought to be an obsolete attitude, but which unfortunately is all too common in certain circles, of announcing that what India says does not matter. It is no use uttering fair words, and, like some prominent would-be legislators in London, keeping firm to the belief in their heart of hearts that no Dominion Status with its various implications is possible. If the problem is not solved, India will drift into the same condition as Ireland drifted in the terrible days of the Black and Tans. And whatever people may think no nation can govern or direct the affairs of another group of nations by force alone. Unless Great Britain can live in the future as the purveyor of political ideas superior to those of the rest of the world, her fate will, indeed, be a gloomy one.

"The problem is not insoluble and even at this stage a frank policy, frankly conceived and honestly carried out would, we believe, ensure peace. It is impossible for the

British Parliament to alter the construction of the Statutory Commission. It is not, however, impossible for His Excellency the Viceroy to assert himself on behalf of the many elements of opposition among the people for whom he is responsible. Unless His Excellency is purposely kept in ignorance of the true state of affairs, he must, by now, view with considerable regret the advice that his Government cabled to Whitehall last year to prevent Indians being appointed to the Commission. He must, by now, be looking for some middle way which will preserve the credit of the King-in-Parliament and yet satisfy the desires of the King's Indian Subjects. There is already some vague and nebulous talk- about a parallel commission. Some such solution "The Pioneer" has been examining for some time past, and it considers that it is time to make some definite suggestions of the situation. To begin with, let the Viceroy candidly admit that the situation is not a happy one. Let him state that it is his duty to make provision for peace in his time. What is there then to prevent His Excellency appointing an independent Commission of seven, from names suggested by the Assembly, from a panel, the members of which would be acceptable to and respected by all political parties. It may be urged that unanimity about such a seven is impossible of attainment. To believe this is to take up an utterly pessimistic view of the future of India. This Commission—the Viceroy's Commission—would have to possess equal status with the Simon Commission and similar powers. Every scrap of evidence that would be submitted to and examined by the Simon Commission would have to be submitted to, and examined by the Viceroy's seven. They could sit side by side; they could hear evidence conjointly. If they wished to hold separate sessions—such sessions could be easily arranged. The question of in camera evidence is a matter for arrangement. A joint vote could determine the necessity for hearing evidence in secret, and, if there was a deadlock, the Viceroy could be brought in to decide. Such a Commission's report would be, in the first instance, submitted to the Viceroy, and not only forwarded to the Secretary of State for India, but also broadcasted to the world.

"If such an offer were made by His Excellency, who would dare refuse it ? A Swaraj refusal would be a denial of the validity of any practical political theory and a refusal to believe in ordered government. It would be tantamount to admitting that their case does not bear examination and commitment to paper. It falsifies any previous argument that may have been raised as to the question of a fair deal, because a logical reasoned report from such a body could not but have its influence on the ultimate decision of Imperial Parliament. It would, if accepted, carry with it the co-operation of the Legislative Assembly and the Provincial Councils, and though there are doubtless many Indian politicians who would not be satisfied, there is yet, we believe, a sufficient body of moderate well-intentioned opinion, which would be willing, in such circumstances, to place its evidence before the examining bodies and to give them the benefit of practical experience.

"There will, of course, be those on both sides who will shun any solution. To those on the British side who would raise objections, we have little to say, for theirs must be an attitude on which no amount of logical argument can have any effect. There may be those who would consider such an offer as involving a loss of prestige on the part of Great Britain, but such in truth is not the case. No prestige can be lost when a country does its level best to meet opposition, to mitigate the consequences of an unfortunate mistake, and by generous statesmanship, to consolidate allegiance. Those Indians who would still find it impossible to co-operate are in an equally parlous state. Their country but also gravely endangering their own political future. A Viceroy's Commission constituted from members nominated by the Legislative Assembly, with powers and status equal to the Simon Commission, Would be an offer almost impossible of refusal, and one which, we are firmly convinced, would pave the way to a better understanding and a more healthy set of relationships, between this country and Great Britain.

The evolution of Dominion status must proceed by political reality. Its advocates on both sides have in such an offer on opportunity to justify their words and their beliefs; the Viceroy will write his name on the roll of his country's greatest statemen, and Indian politicians would have the opportunity of proving their worth, their sincerity, and above all their sense of the practical necessities of the present difficult situation.

Lord Olivier on Simon Boycott

In May 1928 Lord Olivier wrote the following in "The Contemporary Review " :—

The situation which developed immediately on the appointment of the Simon Commission, and which still persists, is exceedingly disappointing to all, at any rate in this country, who desire substantial progress towards Indian self-government. In this "Review," in August last, referred to the rumours then current that the Government was intending, at an early date, to appoint the Statutory Commission. I then said :—

"The Swarajist and other Indian Nationalist parties exhibit a certain degree of disinclination that this course should be taken. They distrust the quality and temper of any Commission that may be appointed by a Government which they believe to be unsympathetic to their cause; and they suspect an inclination that the Commission should engage in its survey at a moment when distrust of the future of self-governing institutions for India has been fomented by the continual advertisement of the Hindu-Muslim dissensions."

I had in the same article explained the distrust of many Indian Nationalists in the sincerity of the intentions of the Montagu-Chelmsford Reforms, and I said that if the developments of the next two years should not do more to satisfy Indian feeling as to our sincerity than those Reforms, well-intentioned as they were, had succeeded in doing, there might be worse trouble in India than followed the Rowlatt Acts and Amritsar. The immediate cardinal test of that sincerity in the judgment of all Indian political parties, appeared, I said, to be the willingness of the British Government to invite Indians to propose a concerted scheme of progressive reform before the Statutory Commission should get to work.

The Government decided to open proceedings strictly within the lines indicated in the Act of 1919, and in the first place to appoint a British Parliamentary Commission. This mode of procedure was agreed to by the Labour and Liberal Parties, which consented to the appointment of representatives of each to the Commission, on the understanding that the Indian Legislature should be invited also to appoint a body of representatives to co-operate with the British Commission in their inquiries. The appointment to the Commission was prematurely announced in India before the intention was made known in Parliament here. No explanatory or preparatory statement could therefore be made of the methods in which it was contemplated that its work should proceed. The bald announcement of the intended appointment and membership of the Commission aroused immediate and general indignation among all reformers of all parties and denominations in India. Whether or not that indignation was reasonable or justifiable, it is desirable to understand the grounds of it.

An Affront to India

First, it was taken as an affront to India that no Indians should have been placed upon the Commission. Secondly, quite independently of any opinions as to the open-mindedness and unprejudiced character of the membership, it was felt that a purely British Commission, predominantly informed from the side of Indian officialism, which, it was known, had prepared a mass of material for its guidance, could not possibly be in a position to form unbiased judgments. Thirdly, and, this being a point of national pride, perhaps most strongly, there was the fact that the Indian Reform movement is a Nationalist movement, claiming the right of self-determination, and its spokesmen and representatives were not disposed to plead as suppliants to a British Commission or the British Parliament for just so great an instalment of further self-government as the rulers might think it reasonable to concede to them.

I have mentioned the understanding on which the Labour Party agreed to co-operate in the work of the Simon Commission, and in both Houses of Parliament the character of that understanding was clearly stated. The English Commission and the Indian representative delegates should, we contemplated, sit together and jointly examine and cross-examine all witnesses and consider all documents laid before them. Neither Lord Birkenhead nor Mr. Baldwin made any public promise that so liberal a course would be followed, stating only that it would be entirely open to the Commission to make such arrangements as they pleased. Only on February 6th, in India, did Sir John Simon announce that the Commission would be prepared to follow this course, reserving, however, the right to each national body to sit separately and in private.

The announcement of the Commission was thus launched in untowards circumstances, and a storm of prejudice had been aroused before even the best that could be said for the course intended could be explained. Having regard to all the circumstances, the Labour Party were in accord with the Liberal Party and with the Government that the kind of Commission that was appointed was the only kind suitable to appoint if the Government were to act in strict continuity with the provision of the Act of 1919. Unless that Act were to be altogether ignored and a totally distinct procedure adopted, such as what Indian reformers have repeatedly asked for under the description of a "Round Table Conference" that was the only opening move the Government could suitably make. Of Labour and Liberal Parties it may be said without reservation that they desired the Commission to be appointed in the sincere intention that it should set India on the road to self-government. So far as the action of the Conservative Government was concerned, no question of its good faith could fairly arise on the face of the position. There was nothing in its action to prejudice the cause of progress in Indian reform. There was under the circumstances nothing inherently insulting to India or necessarily wounding to Indian pride in the fact that the Commission was not constituted jointly of Indians and British. There was certainly in the acquiescence of Labour and Liberalism in such an arrangement no shadow of any sentiment in the slightest degree belittling to Indians.

I cannot say how far this first entirely uncalled for feeling of Indians that all British parties had insulted India may have died or be dying away. It appears to friends of India wholly mistaken : it is painful to us to have if imputed, and any such mistaken and erroneous belief must needs weaken the position of any political body that entertain it. We do not wish the position of Indian reformers to be thus weakened, and we are therefore distressed at the feeling of grievance on this account also. It remains of course that Indians may think we ought to recognise that we have insulted them, and the fact that we are too stupid and insensible to see that ourselves only show that all Britons are quite incapable of dealing intelligently without relations with Indians. The pratical fact remains that those relations have to be settled between us and them.

Supposing that the full intentions of the British political parties and the Commission with regard to procedure had been made fully clear from the outset, and that there had been a less universal adoption by Indians of a position from which it is difficult for them now to recede, there would nevertheless remain some causes of dissatisfaction with the procedure and some arguments for the maintenance of their determination to boycott. For the arrangements proposed by Sir John Simon do not in fact go quite so far in the establishment of complete quality and complete publicity for the canvassing of all evidence as Indians consider necessary for an entirely fair handling of the questions in hand. I do not propose here to criticise the validity of those causes of dissatisfaction; it could be of little practical use. I return to the mere statement of the facts of the situation as they now appear to be.

Spirit of Hostile Distrust

Outside of the Mahomedan community, which is divided (the United Moslem League being in favour of co-operation with the Commission, but a minority, led by Mr. Jinnah being solid with all the Hindu political parties for boycott), all Indian political leaders and practically all politicians of the Reform movement are filled with a spirit of hostile distrust towards all British political parties equally. That is highly regrettable, and appears to us to show some limitation of intelligence of realities. This attitude, so far as it arise from the feeling of insult, is distressing not only by injustice but because it excludes us from giving any co-operation and, in so far as it is a positive error, is a source of weakness to the Indian Reform party. There, however, it is.

With regard to the relations between the Moslem co-operators and the Hindu boycotters, and in a minor degree between the Moslem boycott section and the Hindu nationalist parties, the great cause of division is the principle of communal representation. The Muslim majority demand separate representation in the various Legislative Councils and local bodies on the basis of population, a system of separate electorates, a corresponding Moslem share of appointments in the public services.

The conflict between the Muslim community and the Hindu parties with regard to the basis of representations is crucial. Jinnah has endeavoured to establish a compromise with the Hindus for the sake of being able to present a united Reform programme, on the basis of having a common electoral roll, with a reservation of a certain number of seats for Muslims proportional to the number of the local Muslim community. The majority of Muslims stand out absolutely for separate electoral rolls, directly electing their own communal representatives proportional in number to their population. Their reason for adhering to this position as against that of joint electorates and reservation of seats has been explained by a distinguished Muslim as being that "if the majority community desires to send a few ignorant, mean, contemptible and thoroughly un-Muslim candidates as representatives of our community it can easily do it, as our minority votes will be swamped by the majority votes of the other community." It is characteristic of Indian political disputents that they seem always to give the strongest weight to the most extreme hypothesis of contingencies conceivably unfavourable to themselves. At the present moment the prevailing sentiment expressed in the Press and on platforms of the reformist movement is that all British political parties, and the whole British electorate, are now engaged in a conspiracy to diminish their freedom, and have devised the scheme of the Simon Commission as the best means of doing so. We cannot therefore be surprised if Moslems are convinced that any proposal on the part of Hindus as a means of securing their minority rights is also meant as a trap.

Communal Representation

The system of communal representation is a disastrous expedient, bound to be fatal to the satisfactory working of any constitution that embodied. It is an obvious and admitted fact that the existence of the communal electoral system now aggravates and exacerbates communal rivalries and hostilities between Indians whose political interests, in all matters falling within the sphere of the mechanism of Government, are independent of creed. Moreover, the expedient is in itself ineffective. As Sir Tej Bahadur Sapru (himself one of the boycotters) has well put it.

"The Mahomedans may insist on separate electorates—but the insistence on the one or the other representation is not enough. It seems to me that we are bound to arrive at certain conclusions :

(1) that there in need for the adequate political respresentation of the minorities.

(2) that no protection of the minorities can go the length of converting them into a majority : and (3) that in any democratic constitution of a mixed population the minority should, subject to the limits prescribed for the protection of its special interests,

be prepared to accept the decisions of the majority."

Whether, however, the attitude of the Muslims is reasonable or not and whether or not it is possible that any substitute can be found for this expedient to protect minorities (which is what Sir J. Simon's Commission will have to advise), we must accept, as an immediate fact of the situation, that the organised Moslem community will pretty certainly, as a whole, stand out for that principle. Also that they will be found to receive very strong support in their demand from the British in India (as they do from Sir Reginald Cradock) and generally from all those who do not desire the establishment of a satisfactorily working Indian self-government constitution. And I do not think I wrong the Muslim community in believing that they count upon that support. Moreover, whilst I am not prepared to say that their desire to impress this part of their case upon the Simon Commission is more than one of the reason for Muslims disposition to co-operate with it, yet I think that the fact that, on grounds entirely reasonable (as in the general interests of Indian Reform), they are prepared so to co-operate, is an additional cause for regret that the Hindu parties persist in throwing away the advantage to that cause of their co-operation, since one result of their refusal will be to strengthen the probability of the disastrous principle of communal electorates commending itself to British public and Parliamentary judgment. And whether the Hindu Nationalists think it dignified to recognise the fact or not, that is really what those who desire Indian constitutional reform have to deal with.

The basis of co-operation offered in John Simon's letter of February 6th was promptly refused by the leaders of the various Indian parties, principally on the following grounds : (1) Government officials and the Members of the Legislature nominated by the Government were to be allowed to take part along with the elected members in the election of the Indian committees. (2) No provision was made for the election to the Indian committees of persons who were not already members of the Indian legislatures, though this point was left open to the Commissioners in Mr. Baldwin's speech in the House of Commons. (3) The Committee of the Central Indian Legislature was restricted to the consideration of central subjects and treated as a disconnected element during the inquiry in the various Provinces. (4) All Indian members might be excluded entirely from hearing evidence that might be given "in camera." This is regarded by Indians as a fatal stumbling-block to co-operation, especially in view of their experience in connection of the Indian committees in the institution and conduct of subsidiary inquiries—proceedings of investigation other than the joint taking of evidence by the combined committees of the several Legislatures. (5) Indian leaders felt very strongly that the aim of the Commission should be, along with the Indian committees, to endeavour to arrive at an agreed report. This did not appear to be contemplated in the terms of John Simon's letter.

In the debate in the Assembly on the proposal to boycott the Simon Commission, Mr. Jayakar, the leader of the responsive co-operation party declared that the door was still open for negotiations if Indians could co-operate with the Commission on what they considered honourable terms. He insisted that the Indian committees, should have equal status with the Statutory Commission, in which case Indians were still open to consider co-operation. He suggested that it would be easy to explore and find out exactly what they would consider equality by means of negotiations between Sir John Simon and six or seven Indian leaders. Mr. Jinnah also offered to co-operate if Indians could be assured of equality of status and authority. He stressed the point that Indians did not deny the need for an inquiry, nor did they deny the ultimate authority of the British Parliament. They insisted, however, on having an equal share in framing the proposal.

It is impossible to say whether the attitude set forth in the last paragraph can be taken as one in which the whole constellation of Indian reformers would combine.

For although the Labour Part at least have advocated precisely this position, that has been as fiercely denounced as the rest of the British political world as having betrayed the interests of Indian reform and shown themselves unworthy of India's confidence. In hundreds of newspaper articles and speeches, Indian reformers have denounced the Labour Party from Mr. McDonald downwards as Imperialists and reactionaries, seeking only to bind more closely on India the chains of British bureaucracy. It is difficult to speak of that fact without using unconciliatory adjectives about the intelligence and capacity for judgment of realities which it seems to embody. But the attitude has been adopted by men and women whom I myself and many others of my friends and theirs, know too well to be able to think, far less, in a controversy so riddled with prejudice as this is, to say of them anything censorious or uncivil; for we believe that if we could entirely understand, as we cannot, how such delusions and such mistakes can have arisen, we should recognise that there was really, no perversity in the minds of our friends, but only obscuration of the facts of the case. For the present we can only discern the fact that all British opinion, however devoted it has been in the past, and is to-day, to the cause of Indian Nationalism, is just now in disgrace with all sections of Indian Nationalists. I do not believe that it can be—an important for Indians that they should have and should know that they have innumerable supporters and sympathisers in this country.

Equality of Status Conceded

On the 23rd May, the Simon Commission met in London and formally and unanimously resolved that "it is desirable to publish the fact that it is not proposing to make any fresh announcement regarding the procedure already proposed which, it considers, provides suitable basis for co-operation." Notwithstanding this decision, the Committee elected by the Punjab Legislative Council to co-operate with the Commission, consisting of Europeans, Mahomedans and Hindus who had no sympathy with the boycotters, passed unanimously and communicated to Sir John Simon the following resolution :

"The members of this Committee are strongly of opinion that it will be difficult for them adequately and properly to discharge their duties and responsibilities, if any distinction is sought to be made between the members of the Indian Statutory Commission and the members of the Committee in the matter of the examination of witness or access to documentary evidence, and that conclusions based on examination of portions only of the evidence will not command public confidence."

The resolution was backed up by statements on the part of some of the members of the Committee that unless their demand was satisfied, they will not be able to take part in the Committee's work. There were also other indications in the Press suggesting that the house of cards laboriously built up in the Punjab for the accommodation of the Commission by the efforts of Sir Malcolm Hailey and of the officials there, was in danger of an unexpected collapse and there was no doubt that to Sir John Simon this must have looked like the signal of an impending landslide. Apparently, as was indicated in a Simla telegram, through the good offices of the Viceroy, immediate steps were taken to patch up and buttress the situation. The following is the Government communique :—

"His Excellency the viceroy has received from the Secretary of State the following telegram, which has been communicated by the Government of the Punjab to the Committee of the Punjab Legislative Council appointed to co-operate with the Indian Statutory Commission :

"The resolution of the Committee appointed by the Punjab Council to co-operate with the Indian Statutory Commission was duly communicated to the latter body, and has been most carefully considered. It raises a question which also interest the other Indian Committees that may be appointed under the scheme of procedure proposed by the Commission, and I, therefore, think it well to communicate the concession arrived at to you for publication.

"The Commission has decided to draw no distinction between its own members and the members of these

Committees in regard to the matters referred to in the resolution, so that in the matter of examination of witnesses and accessible documents, the Commission will treat each Indian Committee, within whose scope the material in question falls, on equal terms with itself. It considers that the reservation made in Sir John Simon's letter to the Viceroy, of February 6 which in any event would have been put into effect, very rarely, if at all, can be adequately secured by the power which rests with the Chairman to protect any witness and by his discretionary power to exclude the press from the joint sittings, when necessary. I think Your Excellency will share my satisfaction at this decision."

V

The Boycott Procession

The members of the Statutory Commission reached Lahore on the 30th October 1928 in the afternoon by a special train and were received on the platform by the representative of the Governor, by the Chief Secretary on behalf of the Punjab Government and by the hosts of the members of both the bodies. The entire Lahore station area was guarded by the police and barbed wires were used to keep out the crowd. Enthusiastic scenes were witnessed on this day when a procession carrying black flags with the inscription "Simon Go Back" and led by prominent leaders and consisting of about several thousand people, started at about 1 p.m. from the Municipal Gardens outside the Mochi Gate, towards the Railway Station. At the head of the procession were leaders like Lala Lajpat Rai, Pandit Madan Mohan Malaviya, Sardar Mangal Singh, Dr. Alam, Sardul Singh Cavesheer, Lala Dunichand, Lala Bodhraj, Raizada Hansraj, Dr. Gopichand Bhargava, Maulana Zafar Ali, Abdul Qadir Kasuri and other prominent Nationalists including a large number of leaders who had come from the mofussil specially for the occasion.

As the procession proceeded on its way, shouts of "Simon Go Back" rent the air. A large number of citizens joined the procession on the way.

From the Mochi Gate, the procession passed through Brandeth Road and Circular Road via Landa Bazar and halted at the Mulchand Temple Road, a place about 200 yards from the main gate to the railway platform. There the procession was confronted with barbed wires with strong wooden posts barricading the way to the Railway station. On the first row near the barbed wires stood prominent leaders including Lala Lajpat Rai, Maulana Zafar Ali and others. It was alleged that while the procession was perfectly non-violent, some high police officials used their lathis on the first row of the procession, which included Lalaji and other nationalist leaders. It was further alleged that while the police officials were thus using their lathies, one of them struck Lala Lajpat Rai in the chest.

Lala Lajpat Rai's Statement

At a monster public meeting held in the evening of the 30th in the Municipal Gardens outside the Mori Gate in which 15,000 people attended, Lala Lajpat Rai recalled what happened in Lahore in 1921 in connection with the civil disobedience campaign in the days of non-co-operation, how a meeting of the Congress Committee was declared unlawful, and how the volunteers were beaten and how arrests were made. "But to-day" he said, "the campaign against the Commission has been met not by handcuffs, but by lathi blows." Continuing, Lalaji said how at first he was for reasons of his own, disinclined to join the demonstration but when he was informed on his arrival this morning from Etawa, that orders under Section 144 had been promulgated, he at once informed the leaders in charge of the demonstration that he was prepared to go with them wherever they would like him to go. Incidentally Lalaji told the audience that the promise he made to the local Congress leaders that whatever might be his differences with them he would always be with them in times of emergency, he had kept to-day.

Proceeding Lalaji said : "We determined in the morning to carry out our programme without violating any of the conditions laid down in the rules, and we did so. We assembled near the Railway Station, and finding the barbed wire barricades, we made no attempt to cross or rush it. We were absolutely peaceful, and gave no provocation to the police to attack us. But a Police officer, said to be the Superintendent of Police in Lahore, whose name was afterwards given as Scott, began to strike with lathis. He had a knobbed hunter in his hand. He gave me two blows and two of his constables gave me another two. One of these blows was aimed at my heart, and very near my heart I received a stroke which has caused a bruise sufficiently long and broad.

Continuing Lalaji said : "Similar blows were struck at Raizada Hansraj, whose hand was profusely bleeding even there on the spot. Dr. Gopichand received a blow on the head, and the mark on his head was visible. Dr. Alam and Dr. Satyapal received blows on their arms which are still paining, and I can swear, by anything sacred to me, that none of these gentlemen did anything which deserved this cowardly treatment from the police. In the whole procession, consisting of thousands of men, I did not see more than two or three walking sticks of which I had one. Thank God that I kept cool and in spite of the provocation I did not use my stick or else the situation would have become very serious. I am also thankful to the young men in the procession who obeyed my order and sat down and did not retaliate which should have put the European Police officers on the other side to shame. But nothing daunts the arrogance and intoxication born of political power and military strength. Several times I shouted for the name of the officer who had attacked me pointing him out by my finger, but he had not the courage or courtesy to give me his name. Neither did any one else."

Proceeding Lalaji said : "The stray assault on a crowd unarmed, without that crowd having in the least given them any provocation and without declaring that crowd to be illegal or unlawful and without giving any warning to it, is the most cowardly thing that can be done by any man much less by an officer of position. I am on the other hand happy that this Government rules with the help of these cowards because the greater their number the sooner will be the dawn of the day of emancipation."

The Official Version

The official version stated that processions and meetings were never absolutely forbidden and that meetings were never forbidden at all. The only processions forbidden were those which had not had the previous sanction of the Superintendent of Police. Last night, the Superintendent of Police issued orders that he would not interfere with any procession inside the circular road or which proceeded to the station by certain routes indicated to the leaders of the boycott movement in writing in the morning of 30th and they were followed to the letter.

The number of demonstrators that actually came to the station were variously estimated from 600 to 1,000, the latter being the absolute maximum at the railway station. Moveable barbed wire barricades were put across the entrances from the main roads, from the city to the station. The barricade across the road leading from Landa Bazar, which was the road along which the demonstrations came, did not cover the whole width of the road by about four or five feet. At one time, an attempt was made by a part of the crowd to force their way through the gap, and either then or just before, a few stones were thrown at the police holding the barricade. For instance, one European sergeant was hit by a stone in his efforts to prevent breach of the barricade. The police used lathies on those agitators whom they could reach. It is certain that Lala Lajpat Rai's umbrella was broken and it is believed that he and one or two other persons near the barricade were struck by lathies. It is not believed that they received injuries. Apart from that, there was no clash between the police and the agitators at the barriers. the clash which occurred went on perhaps for half-a-minute.

After the Commission left the station, the demonstrators returned to the city and went in procession through the main bazar. The report says the number was about 300. At about 7 o'clock, the procession emerged from Lahori Gate, and showed intention of crossing the circular road into Anarkali. As the Superintendent of Police's orders forbade the crossing of the circular road by any procession they were held up at this point, and informed that if they attempted to disobey the orders, of which they had been made aware, they would be dispersed if necessary by force. They dismissed, and eventually proceeded along the circular road towards the Mori Gate, where a meeting as previously arranged was held.

Lalaji on the Official Version

The following is Lala Lajpat Rai's statement on the official version:

"The official version is full of lies. I challenge its author to bring a suit against me for libel so that I may get an opportunity to expose the doings of the police in a court of justice. The statement published in certain papers that I attempted to enter the prohibited area by crossing the small passage which was not covered by the barrier is a lie. I did nothing of the kind. The more I think of the matter the more I am convinced that the attack on me was deliberate. Again, the statement that there was a shower of bricks and wooden slippers from the rear part of the crowd on the police is another lie, which has been invented to justify the unlawful action of the police. No mention has been made in the official statement of the injury sustained by Raizada Hansraj and others. It is also stated that some members of the crowd returned the blows dealt by the police. There is nothing to beat it. I notice that there is no end to these lies. I repeat my challenge to the officials."

Lahore—1st November 1928

The Simon Joint Free Conference commenced its Lahore sittings on the 1st November in the morning, 21 members being present. Colonel Lane-Fax and Mr. Kikabhai Premchand were absent. The Punjab Committee was fully represented. Sir John Simon announced that it was proposed to hear the evidence of various officials of the Secretariat first and then non-official evidence. Mr. Emerson, Chief Secretary, was called in as the first witness.

Questioned by Sir John Simon he said that he had been in the service for 23 years and had worked in 10 out of 28 districts and in two Indian States.

Sir John Simon asked him what were the functions of Commissioners of divisions.

Emerson explained that a Commissioner was an administrative and appellate officer but not an executive officer.

He explained the important functions he performed and how one part of his work, namely, co-ordinating activities in respect of law and order, had proved most useful during the Akali agitation. A Commissioner's duties in supervising the working of local bodies had almost overtaxed his capacity.

Replying to the Chairman he declared that the responsibility and usefulness of Divisional Commissioners had increased with the Reforms Government and was opposed to their abolition. There was corruption, he said, in all departments of Government and so also in the Irrigation Department. Government considered this an extremely important department.

Examined by Lord Burnham and Captain Sikandar Hayat Khan witness said that Dyarchy in theory would not have worked if the personal factor had not made it a success through the efforts made by members and Ministers to work together in a spirit of give and take.

Chaudhri Chhotu Ram suggested that the Punjab Council played an important part in the success of Dyarchy—Witness agreed.

Raja Narindranath asked whether the selection of Ministers was not made on the ground of their belonging to an agricultural class ?—Mr. Emerson said he had no knowledge of the subject.

Emerson, examined by Sir John Simon, explained the duties of the Commissioner of a division. The officer, he said, kept an eye on criminal work, and if the staff could not cope with it the Commissioner advised the Government to increase the staff. Then again, in the matter of law and order, the Commissioner took action against movements threatening peace. In the days of the Akali movement the Commissioner played an important part in this respect.

The Commissioner was the appellate authority in revenue matters and in respect of local bodies. The Commissioner not only scrutinised their budgets, but had the power of intervention in their affairs. This work had largely increased during recent years, and had overtaxed the capacity for dealing with it.

Finally, Emerson added that, with the removal of the Commissioner, there would be more ground for complaint of centralisation.

John Simon, referring to the Government memorandum, said that it showed that the co-operative movement was very well-organised in the Province. As regards irrigation, this was important as not only they earned water rates, but also the assessment of lands went up where there was irrigation.

Emerson agreed and added that the cannals has a very important bearing on the finances of the Province. The Government waste lands had fetched a good price, with the result that no loans had been found necessary for capital expenditure.

Sir John Simon asked whether the Irrigation Department was free from corruption.

Emerson said the Department was free from corruption. Corruption depended on opportunities and inducements.

Asked by John Simon to describe how dyarchy had worked, Mr. Emerson said that it was realised from the fact that it would be a difficult work. For Dyarchy to be strictly in accordance with the principles which were supposed to underlie it, there must be constant co-operation between the two halves and a tradition had grown up that on important questions there should be joint discussions between the two sides. Members of Government found it useful to consult the Ministers, and the Ministers found it helpful to consult Members.

Dyarchy had thus worked extremely well.

Lord Burnham : Is it then your considered opinion that in spite of theoretical objections the system of Dyarchy has proceed workable and satisfactory in this Province ?—Emerson replied that it was the co-operation between Members of Government and the Ministers who worked the system, which made it possible to work it satisfactorily, and without friction.

Major Atlee asked how far the co-operative movement proved a school for self-government ?—Mr. Emerson said that the Co-operative Department had tried to make the members take an interest in the working of the societies, and he could not say, in the absence of personal experience, how far it had educated the people in self-government.

Captain Sikandar Hayat Khan, Chairman of the Punjab Committee, asked whether any case had occurred in which the Commissioner had turned down the budget of a local board ?—Mr. Emerson replied that he knew of one case in which the budget was sent back for reconsideration.

Captain Sikandar Hayat Khan next pointed out that the Irrigation Department had been in charge of an Indian member ever since the introuction of the Reforms, and wanted to know if any deterioration had taken place in its efficiency.

Mr. Emerson was unable to answer the question.

Captain Sikandar Hayat Khan : You think it was not the system, but the personal factor which made Dyarchy a success ?

Mr. Emerson : Yes, but for it, the scheme might have broken down.

Lord Burnham : Yes, I understood you in the latter sense.

Raja Narindranath asked whether members belonging to the agricultural classes dominated the Ministries and the Ministers were selected from these classes. He also wanted to know whether Lala Harkishan Lal supported the communal policy of Sir Fazli Hussain ?—Mr. Emerson was unable to answer, and Sir John Simon intervening, said that the matter concerned entirely the action of the Governor, and the witness could not be expected to know the motives of the Governor.

Raja Narindranath said he wished to bring on record that he and 26 members of the Council protested in 1922, and he passed on the correspondence on the subject to Sir John Simon for perusal.

Dr. Gokulchand Narang pointed out that the Council had repeatedly asked for the abolition of Divisional Commissionership as it was thought that Commissioners acted as post offices. He wanted to know if any reduction had taken place in the functions of the Commissioners after the Reforms.

Mr. Emerson said, on the other hand, both responsibility and the usefulness of the Commissioners had very much increased under the Reforms.

Dr. Narang asked whether Ministers could initiate any scheme of public utility and earmark funds for that purpose ?

Mr. Emerson replied that neither a Member nor a Minister could earmark any amount till the Council had voted. The Finance Department generally examined the scheme, and if its opinion was not acceptable to the Minister, the latter could take the matter up to the Executive Council; but generally in such cases the Minister and the Finance Member discussed the matter, and in very rare cases the matter went up to the Executive Council.

Dr. Narang asked why the Finance Committee of the Legislative Council was not consulted more often ?—Mr. Emerson replied that their advice was sought on the schemes that had been approved by Government.

Sardar Ujjal Singh pointed out that the Retrenchment Committee had recommended the abolition of three Divisional Commissionership.

Mr. Emerson said that Government did not accept that

recommendation.

Mr. Stead's Evidence

Charles Stead, Inspector-General of Police in the Punjab, examined next by the Conference, declared that all the 22,000 policemen of the Province knew how to bear arms. The force was not affected by communal feeling, and as regards corruption it was probably due to the fact that the men in the force joined it not for the sake of a career, but "for an opportunity." This defect did not apply to the police force only. He was of opinion that compared with the European Investigating Officer, in cases of corruption, the position of the Indian Officer was uncomfortable.

A solemn procession to the banks of the/ Ravi and hoisted the tricolour flag of Indian independence in the presence of a mammoth gathering that dared the biting cold of Lahore. "As the flag showly went up the staff, a thrill of joy shook the vast audience, and imbued them with a new hope and a distant vision of the glorious future of India."

The Nehru constitution got a 'decent burial' on the hands of the Congress at Lahore. Apart from discarding Dominion Status in favour of the goal of complete independence, the Congress also definitely rejected its recommendations about the solution of the communal problem. The resolution adopted by the Congress was as follows : "In view of the lapse of the Nehru Report it is unnecessary to declare the policy of the Congress regarding communal questions, the Congress believing that in independent India communal question can only be solved on strictly national lines. But as the Sikhs in particular, and the Muslims and the other minorities in general, had expressed dissatisfaction over the solution of communal question proposed in the Nehru Report, this Congress assures the Sikhs, the Muslims and other minorities, that no solution thereof in any future constitution will be acceptable to the Congress that does not give full satisfaction to the parties concerned." This resolution put a premium on the intransigence of the communalists by giving them a power of veto on every proposal for communal settlement and rendered a solution of the communal problem wellnigh impossible; for past experience had shown that it was beyond human ingenuity to devise a scheme of communal settlement which would give "full satisfaction to the parties concerned." At the dictate of Gandhi all the left wingers in the Congress, including Subhas Bose and Srinivasa Iyengar, were excluded from the new Working Committee which met on 2 January, 1930. In accordance with the Congress resolution it asked the members of the legislatures to resign. It was also decided that 29th of January should be observed all over India's the *Purna Swaraj* day (day of complete independence). A declaration (prepared by Gandhi) was to be read on that occasion to the people in the villages and towns all over the country, and the assent of the audience was to be taken by show of hands.

The 'declaration' was a long one. It began by emphasizing the inalienable right of the Indians to enjoy freedom, it described in details how "the British Government has ruined India economically , politically, culturally run on.

Ramsay MacDonald to Simon

My dear Simon,

Your letter on behalf of the Statutory Commission raises issues of such importance that I have thought right before answering it to consult the leaders of other parties. I have now been able to ascertain their views, and they have been good enough to concur in the terms of my reply.

His Majesty's Government welcome the intimation that your letter affords of the Statutory Commission's desire to deal in its report with the wider aspects of the subject to which your letter directs attention. It appears to His Majesty's Government, as it does to those behalf of whom you write, that your work would necessarily be rendered more complete if it included a careful examination of the methods by which the future relationship of British India and the Indian States may be adjusted.

His Majesty's Government have given full consideration

to what you have said in you letter concerning the consequential necessity of some revision of the later procedure as at present contemplated, and I am glad to be able to inform you that they concur in the view that you have expressed. His Majesty's Government are, with you, deeply sensible of the importance of thus bringing the whole problem under comprehensive review; and that under conditions which may approach the treatment of the broad question of British-Indian constitutional advance in cooperation with all those who can authoritatively speak for British-Indian political opinion. It seems to them that both these objects can best be achieved by the adoption of procedure that will permit the free representation of all points of view in advance of the stage at which His Majesty's Government will lay any proposals before Parliament, which may be expected later, as you point out, to form the subject of examination by a Joint Parliamentary Committee. When, therefore, you COmmission has submitted its Report and His Majesty's Government have been able, in consultation with the Government of India to consider these matters in the light of all the material then available. They will propose to invite representatives of the Indian States to meet them, separately or together, as circumstances may demand, for the purpose of conference and discussion in regard both to the British-Indian and All-Indian problems.

It will be their earnest hope that by this means it may subsequently prove possible on these grave issues to submit definite proposals to Parliament which may command a wide measure of general assent.

With my best wishes for the success of your further labours.*

Yours very sincerely,

(Sd.) J. Ramsay Macdonald

* Selected from the Report of the Indain Statutory Commission, Vol. I, p.xxiv.

8

Submission of Report and Reaction

In connection with the constitutional problems of India, the Statutory Commission took into consideration the immense area and population of the country; the diversities of race, caste, and creed, the existence of the India states, the predominance in numbers of the rural population; the high percentage of illiteracy and the standing menace of the North-West Frontier Province. At first, it attempted to depict the main constitutional features in British India prior to the reforms and examined the constitutional arrangements devised ten years ago and how far they had proved successful in its functioning. It also described the system of British administration, built up in India on the foundations of the Mughal regime, and indicated the difficulties encountered in drafting new constitutional methods thereon. It weighed the effects—good and bad, of the reforms on the day-to-day working of the government. In the light of these facts, the Commission came to certain general conclusions and gave its detailed recommendations. It stated that the new constitution should, as far as possible contain within its provision for its own development. 'It should not lay down too rigid and uniform a plan, but should allow for natural growth and diversity constitutional progress should be the outcome of practical experience. Where further legislation was required, it should result from the needs of the time, not from the arbitrary demands of a fixed time-table."[1]

Federal Constitution

The Commission made the recommendation that the ultimate constitution of India must be Federal, for it was only in a Federal Constitution that units differing so widely in constitution as the provinces and the states could be brought together while retaining internal autonomy. The alternative method could reduce progress to the pace of the slowest. It did not believe that in matters of federal concern, the states would be always ranged on one side and British India on the other. On the contrary, there were matters in which the interests of particular states and provinces more clearly coincided.[2] The Commission complained that there were a number of administrative areas which had grown up in a haphazard way as a result of conquest, suppression of farmer rules and administrative convenience. Most of them were too popular and extensive, achieving regard to the cultural level and economic conditions of their inhabitants. The Commission made a definite recommendation for reviewing and if possible, resettling the provincial boundaries of India at an early date as possible. Meanwhile, the provinces of India could form the basis on which a Federal structure should be built. Besides the Governors' provinces, there were areas to which the reforms had not yet been applied. These would find their place in the Federation. Thus the scheme, which the Commission recommended, aimed at giving the provincial autonomy and this meant abolition of Dyarchy. It was its intention that in future each province should be as far as possible 'mistress in her own house.' Thus independent life would be given to the provinces which would form the basis of the new Federal structure. While discussing about Dyarchy and the difficulties in its working, the Commission opined that certain portfolios must be in the hands of councilors; and other portfolios must be in the hands of ministers. It was thus hoped to give ministers experience of constitutional responsiblity.[3] It proposed that the rigid division into reserved and transferred subjects should disappear. All alike would be in the common category of provincial subjects. The provincial cabinet should be unitary *i.e.* every member of it should be required and prepared to take responsibility for the whole policy of provincial legislature. But there should be no statutory classification of subjects such as would make it legally impossible for a minister chosen from the elected members to be in charge of any of them. The joint responsibility for all the acts and policies of the cabinet must be accepted by every member.

Powers of the Governor

The Commission discussed the position and powers of the Governor. It opined that he might wish to include in the ministry one or more persons, not elected members of the legislature. Such persons would be experienced officials, but on occasions, it might be found useful to include a non-official, whether Indian or British, not belonging to the legislature. No provincial government and no provincial committee had proposed that the Governor should invariably be bound in reference to all subjects by the advice of his ministry nor did the Central Committee take that view. The attempt to introduce such a practice was thought to be disastrous. The reasons given were the intensity of communal divisions, the general absence of stable parties with assured majorities in the legislature and the lack of experience of the working of a fully responsible system of government. All these factors presented insuperable obstacles.[4] The Commission recommended that the Governor should give such directions in order to preserve the safety and tranquility of the province or in order to prevent serious prejudice to one or more sections of the community as compared with other section. It was made clear that after the general election in the province, the Governor would consider its results and decide from what sources and by what individual selection he would compose his cabinet. He was to consider whether he could draw his advisers solely from one party, or take a wider range. He would be acting, so far as necessary, in consultation with the Governor-General; and the inclusion or exclusion of one or more officials in his cabinet would to some extent be determined by the special needs of his province. The Chief Minister would, of course, be in the special confidence of the Governor and would be able to assist him with advice in selecting other ministers, though the Governor would remain responsible for the actual choice. When the government was fully constituted, it would be for the minister, acting on the principle of joint responsibility, to promote and advance the policies and proposals, which the government resolved to adopt.[5]

Views on Dyarchy

The Commission recommended that provincial Dyarchy should come to an end in the sense that a unitary government should be established, composed of members appointed by the Governor, and that the Statute should be in such form as to make it possible for such a government to include an element drawn from official or other non-elected source. Furthermore, the Commission recommended that the Governor, subject, as in other matters, to the superintendence, direction and control of the Governor-General, should be given statutory powers to declare that a state of affairs had arisen under which the government of the province could be carried on in accordance with the provisions of the Statute, and, thereupon there should vest in the Governor and his cabinet, with the right to appoint any persons to assist him and to delegate powers to them, and the right to nominate any such persons as members of the legislature. The Governor would have further powers to restore rejected demands for grants, and to certify legislation if in his opinion it was essential for any interest in the province. The life of provincial councils, also the subject of recommendation. It was that it would be better to extend the normal statutory life of provincial legislatures to five year.[6] It suggested that unless an increase in the size of the electorate was accompanied by an increase in the number of constituencies, the reality of representation might be still further prejudiced.

Communal Representation

Talking about communal representation, the Commission felt that a particular religious community should be represented in a popular legislature solely by members of its own body, with a guarantee as to how many communal seats there should be, was an undoubted obstacle in the way of the growth of a sense of common citizenship. Communal electorates perpetuated class distinction and stereotype existing relations; and they constituted a very serious hindrance to the development of the self-governing principle. The Commission realized that the Muslim community as a whole was not prepared to give up communal representation. Indeed no provincial government had proposed the abolition of separate electorate for Muslims, although several agreed with the view that they were theoretically objectionable. The Bombay government which went further in this direction and specifically stated that separate communal electorates were not acceptable to it, only advocated their abolition if the consent of both parties could be obtained. In Bengal, the Hindu members of the council dissociated themselves from the views of the rest of the government and recommended joint electorates with reservation of seats. In the Punjab also, the Sikhs and Hindus expressed themselves against the retention of separate communal electorates.[7]

Provincial Committees

Most of the provincial committees did not propose any alteration of the existing proportions in which seats were allocated between Hindus and Muslims: But the Bengal committee would allot seats on the population basis; the Punjab committee would allow weightage to the Hindu and Sikh minorities to such an extent as would not convert the Muslim majority into a minority, and the Bihar and Orissa committee (except the Muslim members) would only set aside Muslim seats, to be filled through the separate electorates, in proportion to the population ratio, though they would allow Muslims also to contest seats in other general electorates.

A majority of the members of the Indian Central Committee took a different view from that of provincial committees, and followed, in the main, the recommendations of the Nehru Report on this question. They proposed that joint electorates should be introduced, with reserved seats for Muslims (excepts in the Punjab and Bengal) allocated either on the population basis or in proportion to voting strength, whichever was the more favourable, and they would give Muslims the right to contest seats in other general electorates. They would apply the same principle to the minority Hindu and Sikh communities in the Punjab. The majority of the Indian

Central Committee did not think that in Bengal either community needed any special protection, and they recommended joint electorates without any reservation of seats.[8]

The European members of the committee recommended that separate electorates should be retained until the minority community was willing to see them abolished. But all the Muslim bodies which appeared before the Commission agreed in demanding the retention of separate electorates and there was general agreement with the view, endorsed at the All-India Muslim conference in January, 1929.

Hindu-Muslim Problems

In the absence of an agreement between Hindus and Muslims, the Commission was unanimous in holding that communal representation for the Muslims of a province must be continued, and that Muslim voters could not be deprived of the special protection until a substantial majority of Muslim representatives in the provincial legislature declare themselves in favour of the change. The Commission was of the opinion that communal feeling might be reduced by making both Hindu and Muslim members relied upon the support of a mixed electorate and that so long as Muslims claimed and received separate electorates in the provinces, it was not possible to deprive the Sikhs of the Punjab of similar treatment.[9] When the Sikhs presented the claims of their community before the Commission at Lahore, they urged an increase to 30 per cent in the proportion of seats reserved for them. So the Commission stated that Sikh representation could not be reduced, thought it was though to be impossible to concede so large a percentage as 30 per cent. If the Sikhs were prepared to exchange separate electorates for the reservation of seats, the Sikh candidates might have the advantage of securing additional seats, over and above those specially reserved for them.

The Question of Representation

Giving its opinion for the representation of non-Brahmans in Madras and Marathas in Bombay, the

Commission stated that the opinion that the non-Brahmans in the Madras Presidency would otherwise be unable to hold their own against the Brahmans, appeared to be groundless. Non-Brahmans were returned in large numbers, and in no single instance at any of the three elections did a non-Brahman secure his seat only because it was 'reserved'. It was clear, therefore, that there was no need to continue to reserve seats for non-Brahmans in the Madras presidency. In the case of the Marathas, the necessity for reservation had not been very clearly either proved or disapproved. The Commission opined that the time had not yet come for the abolition of 'reserved' seats for Marathas.

The Statutory Commission gave venture its feelings about the representation of the depressed classes. The method adopted so far had been that of nomination in accordance with the electoral rules made for each province. Except in the case of Madras, the nomination was intended to secure representation of 'classes which in the opinion of the Governor are depressed classes'—four members were so nominated in the Central Provinces, two in Bombay and in Bihar and Orissa, and one each in Bengal and the United Provinces. There was no depressed class representative in the Legislative Assembly. In Madras, there were ten members who were nominated to represent nine specified communities, which were regarded as depressed. Individuals belonging to the depressed classes were not, of course, debarred from voting in a 'general non-Muhammedan' constituency if they were qualified to be electors, but the minimum property qualification was enjoyed by a very small proportion of them. The Commission was of the opinion that, 'In the long run, the progress of the depressed classes, so far as it could be secured be the, by the exercise of political influence, would depend on their getting a position of sufficient importance for other elements to seek their support and to consider their needs.' Ultimately, it desired to see them maintaining their ground in joint electorates without special protection. It stated that they would make no progress in this direction so long as they get representation solely by nomination, for nomination provided no opportunities for training them in politics.

The Commission stated that its object was to make a beginning which aimed at bringing the depressed classes within the circle of elected representation. In fact, most of the depressed classes associations which appeared before it favoured separate electorate, with seats allocated on the basis of population though one or two wished to retain nomination. Separate electorate was no doubt to be the safest method of securing the return of an adequate number of persons who enjoyed the confidence of the depressed classes; but the Commission was averse from stereotyping the differences between the depressed classes and the remainder of the Hindus by such a step, which, it considered, would reduce a new and serious bar to their ultimate political amalgamation with others. It further stated that in all the eight provinces, there should be some reservation of seats for the depressed classes. These seats would, of course, be reserved in non-Muslim constituencies. If any kind of difficulty would arise, the Commission believed it would only be temporary and to guard against it. It conferred upon the Governor further power provided he was satisfied that it was really the case of authorising persons, whether men or women, who had shown special interest in their welfare, to be amongst the approved candidates, or, alternatively, of nominating them for certain of the reserved seats. The result of this scheme would be that spokesmen of the depressed classes would be returned as elected members in each of the province. On the other hand, representatives would be the choice of non-Muslim electors as a whole, and opportunity would be given for co-operation, while at the same time a strong impetus would be afforded to the more adequate consideration of depressed class problems.

European Representation

As to European representation, the Simon Commission stated that it must continue to be secured by means of separate electorate. In fact, the European representation in the provincial councils arose partly from separate European constituencies, and partly from the choice of Europeans by certain trading organization. It was decided that with the possible exception of a slight increase in

Bombay, the present proportions should be maintained both as regards the ratio of the number of European general constituency seats to Indian general constituency seats, and as regards the ratio of the special commerce and industry and other similar seats, not all of which are Europeans, to the general constituency seats.

As for Anglo-Indians, it recommended that it would prefer to see the choice made by election rather than by nomination. Indeed, in so far as the election was the course adopted, it seemed inevitable that separate electorates must be formed; the numbers of the community were too small to make any other method feasible.

The Christian Community

The Indian Christian community provided another instance where there was a strong desire to be represented by election rather than by nomination, but where the numbers, at any rate in some provinces, made it difficult to suggest a practical means. The Indian Christians had separate electorates in Madras and returned their five members; everywhere else, any representation they had was by nomination. It preferred reservation of seats for Indian Christians to separate electorates. As regards the number of seats to be filled by the existing proportion appeared to be justified in the case of Madras. The single seat allotted elsewhere to Indian Christians might at least be doubled, in view of the increased size of the councils, and a seat added in the Central Provinces, and also in Assam, where there was none.[10]

Recommending about the special representation for the landholders, the Montagu-Chelmsford Report, when making suggestions in paragraph 232 for special electorates, observed: 'Where the great landowners form distinct class in any province, we think that there will be a case for giving them an electorate of their own.' The Commission agreed with the view expressed in this Report that, 'in the circumstances of India, these large landowners represented an element and supplied an influence which ought not be omitted from the provincial councils.'

Regarding the representation of women, the Commission considered it to be highly desirable to facilitate the inclusion of women in the provincial councils.

Extension of Franchise

While giving its recommendations for the extension of franchise, the Commission held that there should be such extension of franchise as was reasonably practicable, and that provision should be made with a view to yet greater extension after a further interval. In this regard, four of the eight provincial governments which had made recommendations unanimously opposed any advance, and the majority of members of the other four governments were of the same view. On the other hand, a substantial advance was advocated by the Punjab Government and by two members in Bengal; and adult suffrage by non-official members in Bombay; both ministers in Assam; and one minister in Bengal. The views of the Provincial Committees were also divided. They left things as they were; of the rest, B.R. Ambedkar alone advocated franchise for all of twenty-one years and over; the Assam committee proposed a vote for each occupied house, or alternatively a vote for everyone of twenty-five years of age or over; the Bengal and United Provinces committees, with the majority of the Punjab committee, recommended a lowering of qualifications which might double or treble the electorate; and the Bombay committee a fifty per cent increase. Three members of the Indian Central Committee were convinced advocates of adult suffrage, and would have it introduced immediately in Bengal of the Indian Central Committee were convinced advocates of adult suffrage, and would have it introduced immediately in Bengal in any case, and that three others thought the present franchise quite wide enough. But there was general agreement among the members of that committee that adult suffrage should be attainable in slightly over thirty years.[10]

New Franchise Committee

The Commission recommended that the new franchise committee or other suitable body under an impartial and experienced Chairman, should be set up with instructions to frame schemes which would enfranchise about ten per cent of the total population. This would make an electorate of about twenty per cent of the adult population. The franchise committee would be directed to consult the provincial governments before determining what modifications in voting qualifications should be made for this purpose, and would be required in drawing up its schemes, to have due regard to the respective claims of rural and urban areas, and to the rights of women as well as men.

While discussing about the question of second chambers in the provinces, the Commission stated that the essential functions of the second chamber would be two; first, the review of Bills and, secondly, endorsing of the Governor's exercise of his special powers. In fact, five of the provincial governments stated that they were opposed to the establishment of second chambers because 'the material from which they could be formed did not exist in the provinces.' The other three provincial governments put forward a different view. The United Province government argued that the conservative elements in the province had distinctive character and would welcome the opportunity of service in separate chamber. The Bombay government held that the need of a revising instrument outweighed both the difficulty of finding the material from which to constitute it and the danger of weakening the lower house in the process. The Bengal government was pronounced unreservedly in favour of a second chamber. Among the provincial committees, all of which had the reports of their governments before them, when they formulated their recommendations, the Madras committee, with one dissentient, had come to the conclusion that the balance of advantage was in favour of a second chamber as likely to prevent antagonism arising between Governor and legislature as a result of frequent resort to the veto. The Assam Committee was in favour of a revisory body, though it proposed to entrust these functions to a council of a rather unusual type. The Indian Central Committee reviewed these opinions, and also noted the verdict of the All-Parties' Conference, which was in favour of single chambers: but its members were divided in their recommendations. Two members would have no second chambers, one would have them in all the province's and six would make an experiment for ten years in the United Provinces alone.

Whatever view may be taken as to the expediency and possibility of establishing second chambers in the provinces, there was a cognate proposal for securing legislative revision on which the Commission agreed. It was also proposed that a small expert body might be constituted to which legislative proposals could be submitted between the report and third reading stage. This body would be required to report on the final drafting of measured and to call attention to any points of conflict with existing legislative or administrative arrangements. It should have no power to deal with matters of principle, but its work might do much to make clear the real effect of proposed legislation and the administrative considerations to which its passage would give rise.

Regarding NWFP

North-West Frontier Province, the Commission stated that responsibility for the administration of this region could not be separated from responsibility for the peace of and control over the tribal area: only thus could the security of the region be effectively maintained. On a review of these considerations, the Commission stated that steps should be taken without delay to frame and carry into effect proposals for the constitutional advance of the NWFP, by setting up suitable representative institutions. In fact, there was much force in the claims put forward by witnesses from the NWFP that the virile inhabitants of this region were not less intelligent than their neighbours, and that their geographical position ought not to deprive them of a share in India's political advance.[11] It also recommended that there should be in the North-West Frontier Province a legislative council consisting of some forty persons with powers of legislation, interpellation and discussion and with the power of imposing certain taxes and voting supplied in respect of those services which were maintained out of provincial revenues; but executive responsibilities should, as at present, rest with the Chief Commissioner.[12] About the composition and powers of the NWFP legislative council, the Commission opined that it should consist of an elected, and the nominated element and it should be composed of representatives of the *Khans* elected from a special constituency, of members elected by municipalities and district boards (which as time goes on will aquire a more representative character as the method of composing them by election becomes more general), and of ex-soldiers.[13] It further recommended that the nominated element would be selected by the Chief Commissioner and would consist partly of officials and partly of non-officials. Due provision was made for the representation of minorities, including Hindus and Sikhs. The Chief Commissioner was to preside over the legislative council. He would have power to appoint a deputy to take his place in the chair when necessary. About the representation of NWFP in the Central Assembly; the Commission recommended that its right to take part in discussing all-India questions should stand on the same footing as that of the Governors' province.

Indeed, these recommendations represented an important advance. For the first time, the NWFP would have its own legislature, containing elected representative, with powers both of taxation and of voting expenditure; the opportunity for putting questions to the provincial administration, and of moving, discussing and carrying resolutions on public matters affecting the province. Moreover, the province, for the first time, was guaranteed full representation in the Central Legislature. Talking of Baluchistan, the Commission opined that British Baluchistan should have some representation in the Central Legislature, and further stated that there was no ground for recommending a change at this stage in the government of the province.

Role of Central Legislature

Giving its comments about the Central Legislature, the Commission recommended that, in place of the existing Legislative Assembly, there should be a new body, called the Federal Assembly. Its members would not be directly elected by constituencies of voters, but would be mainly chosen, in proportions by the provincial councils. A provincial council would select those whom the province would Federal Assembly by the method of proportional representation. Anyone, man or woman, who was on the electoral roll for the province, might stand for election as a member of the Federal Assembly representing that province. The Federal Assembly would have a fixed life of five years. The Commission suggested that a number between 250 and 280 would be suitable. Besides, it recommended the adoption of a population basis for fixing the number of seats to be allotted to each province. It considered that the allocation of one seat per million inhabitants would provide a convenient general principle. In addition to the members representing the Governor's provinces, the minor provinces and the excluded areas, there would be an official element. Members of the Governor-General's Council would be ex-officio members and the Governor-General would have power to nominate not more than twelve other officials.

Problem of Anglo-Indians

The Commission stated that it would be difficult for Anglo-Indians to depend on the votes of members of their own community. Therefore, two seats should be allotted to them in the Federal Assembly by nomination, if they should fail to obtain this number by election. It also stated that NWFP should be represented in the Federal Assembly by four members, three representing the Muslim community and one the Hindu. In the case of British Baluchistan, it did not propose a legislative council, one member should be nominated by the Chief Commissioner after ascertaining the views of the leading persons of the province, in the *Jirga* or otherwise. It further recommended that Coorg should have one member elected by its Legislative Council. The province of Delhi and Ajmer Merwara should also each have one member in the Federal Assembly. The Delhi representative should be elected by the members of the municipal council and district board in a joint session. The Commission was of the opinion that the Council of State had played a useful part in the evolution of representative government in India. There were weighty reasons for the retention of the Council of State as an integral apart of the central government. It contained members of experience and distinction who had made valuable contribution to the discussion of public affairs. No demand for its abolition was brought to the notice of the

Commission. It was, therefore, of the opinion that the Council of State should be retained with its present powers.

In view of the extent to which matters of trade, commerce and finance were central subjects, and occupied the attention of the Central Legislature and the desirability of experience in these subjects being available, the Commission suggested that in each of the cities of Madras, Bombay and Calcutta, one member representing British and one representing Indian commerce should be chosen under rules by the appropriate organizations. The Commission recommended that each Governor's province should be represented in the Council of State by three members. A list of qualifications was drawn up for members. They should be such as to bring to the Council of State the qualifications of distinction, leadership, authority and experience, for instance, distinguished members of the services, ex-judges and ex-ministers, besides these who had gained honour in other walks of life. The Council of State should have a life of seven years. 'The Central Legislature would have power to make laws for all persons, courts, places, and things within British India, for all subjects of His Majesty and servants of the Crown within other parts of India and for all Indian subjects of His Majesty without and beyond as well as within British India.'

While making recommendations about the position of the Governor-General, the Commission opined that the Governor-General must continue to be not only the representative of the King-Emperor in all formal and ceremonial matters, but the actual and active head of the government. In the past, members of the Governor-General's Executive Council were appointed under the advice of the Secretary of State, and in making his recommendations he was, of course, guided by the Governor-General's advice. But under the new plan, the Governor-General would, of course, remain subject to the superintendence and control of the Secretary of State, but apart from this, the choice of his colleagues would rest with him. The Commission recommended that there should rest, in the hands of a provincial Governor, certain limited overriding powers and also emergency power, if the normal provincial constitution should break down, of resuming control over the whole provincial field. Since he was, in wielding them, not constitutionally responsible to the provincial legislature, he must be responsible to some other authority and that authority should ultimately be Parliament. It recommended accordingly that the Governor should be subject to the superintendence, direction and control of the Governor-General and through him, of the Secretary of State, who was, of course, answerable to Parliament.[14]

Talking about powers of central government over provincial governments, the Commission stated that superintendence, direction and control of the Governor-General-in-Council over a provincial government should be exercisable only over a field defined by the following categories:—safeguarding of administration of central subjects, matters which may, in the opinion of the Governor-General, essentially affect the interests of any subject, raising of loans, employment of all-India services in the province; safeguarding of Imperial interests; questions arising between India and the other parts of the Empire and implementing International obligations. While giving its recommendations about educations, the Commission recommended that it would be very valuable to set up an active Central Bureau of Education which would give information and advice to the provincial administrations and would help to make everywhere available the results of experiments and practice in educational method and organization. The central government would continue to be primarily responsible for education in some of the minor administration and would also assume similar responsibility in the excluded areas, but its outlook should be wider than this, in order that the standards of its administration as those parts of British India might benefit by the example of the best that the province could do. It should endeavour to raise the standards in the areas under its own immediate administration. For these purposes, a Central Educational Bureau should be of great utility. The Commission thought that some central coordination would be valuable in respect of the Indian universities, both unitary and affiliated, in order to counteract the tendency towards extreme provincialisation. In the same way, the Commission was convinced that the improvement of public health in India, the increase in the supply of trained nurses and doctors, and the reduction of infant and maternal mortality might be materially promoted if there were a wider central organization staffed by competent officials, both men and women, whose business it should be to coordinate and encourage the work that was so much needed in these directions.

Future of Burma

The future of Burma was also discussed by the Commission. It stated that her political union with India was based neither upon geographical connection nor racial affinity. Burma and India were different countries. Their association was, however, of long standing.[15] In the first place, Burma shared with India a land frontier in the north-east, which, however difficult, had sometimes in the past been traversed by invaders. She was also dependent for much of her properity on Indian labour. India was the largest individual consumer of her produce. A considerable part of the capital and enterprise which had developed her trade was Indian. 'The stage of political and constitutional development which she had now reached has come to her as a part of India, and her reliance upon securing further advance is based upon promises made by British primarily to India. Hence springs that jealous anxiety felt by the politically conscious Burman that Burma's constitutional progress should in no way fall behind that of India.'[16] They thought that Burmese opinion would still be in favour of separation even without the prospect of immediate financial advantage.[17]

The Commission therefore, recommended that separation should be effected forthwith on the practical ground that no advantage seemed likely to accrue from postponement of a decision to a future date. The constitutional difficulties of securing Burma's participation in the central Government of India were not prospective but actual. They would grow with every advance in the Indian constitution and would prejudicially affect not Burma only but India itself. It believed that a decision to postpone separation would be so unpopular in Burma as to endanger the working of any reforms which might be given to her as a province of India. A decision to separate her from India immediately would, on the other hand, it considered, produce an atmosphere in Burma favourable to the satisfactory settlement of many problems to which separation would give ruse.[18]

The Commission showed interest in the future relations of British India with the Indian States. It stated that it would be lawful for the Crown to create by proclamation a Council for greater India for the purpose of consulting on matters of common concern to British India and the Indian States. The Council would consist of, say, thirty members, of which ten representatives would be nominated by the Chamber of Princes; the Viceroy might complete the list by invitation, so as to provide for the representation of those Indian States which did not form part of the chamber. On the side of British India, some of the members would be drawn from the central legislature by the use of the transferable vote; others would be nominated by the Viceroy. The Political Secretary would be a member ex-officio. The council would be presided over by the Viceroy.

Besides the Commission dealt with the necessity for the establishment of provincial Public Service Commission if an efficient and loyal public service was to be maintained. The existing constitutional structure secured to the Governor wide powers to dishcharge the responsibility placed upon him by his instrument of instruction for safeguarding the interests of the services. The establishment of Public Service Commissions in the provinces would have advantages from the point of view of ministers themselves. They should be freed from the technical work of recruitment, which was no part of a minister's duties, and even more important, they should not be exposed to the charge, however ill-founded, of using their position to promote family or communal interests at the expense of the efficiency, or the just administration, of the services.[19]

Protection of Services

'The protection of the services from political influences is an essential condition of the constitutional advances we recommed. With that object, provision should be made in the Government of India Act that, if any provincial council does not pass within a prescribed time an act for the establishment of a Public Service Commission, with a constitution and function approved by the Secretary of State-in-Council, the provincial Government shall be required (1) to conduct its recruitment through the agency of the Central Public Service Commission (2) to submit appeals from members of the provincial and subordinate services to the same body and (3) to accept and apply the same conventions in regard to the Commission's recommendations as are accepted by the Government of India.

Role of Public Survice

'If the provincial Public Service Commissions are to serve effectively the purpose for which we desire to see them established, their members must be completely removed from political influence. In order to secure this no further employment under the Crown in India should be open to them except higher office in the Commission itself or an appointment on the Central Commission. In the second place, they must be appointed by an authority independent of all party interests and they should not be removable from office except by the same authority. The Commission recommended that if it was that the appointing authority should be not the Government but the Governor, and that in making the appointment he should have power to act otherwise than in accordance with the advice of his Ministers. Lastly, the provincial Governments should undertake to observe the same conventions in relation to the findings fo the Commission as were observed by the Government of India in its dealings with the Central Commission. It would be open to the provincial Government to require the Commission, to select candidates with particular qualifications or from a particular community; but the Commission should be strong enough and independent enough to secure that the standards of qualifications for the public service were not lowered thereby.'

The Commission further examined the bonafides of the Secretary of States' Council. The Joint Select Committee in recommending the retention of the Secretary of State's Council in 1919 took the view that it would be absolutely necessary, at any rate from some time to come, that the Secretary of State should be advised by persons of Indian experience. "If no such Council existed, the Secretary of State would have to form an informal one if not a formal one." The arguments that weighed with it still held good. There would rest upon the Secretary of State a heavy responsibility, for he would still be answerable to Parliament for fundamentally important matters administered by the Government of India. The Commission thought this responsibility to be a real one and in its view it was essential that there should be a body of experts to whom the Secretary of State could have recourse for advice and information. It stated that the advisory council which it recommended should not be as large as the present council. It attached great importance to securing that the members appointed from India, whether they were officials or non-officials should have full knowledge of the country. The Government of India Act permitted the appointment of a member who had left India five years before. The practice had been to appoint the members within a few months of their leaving India. It recommended that the interval between leaving India and appointment was five years, but the Secretary of State might for reasons of public advantage reappoint for a further term of five years. It further recommended that no members appointed on account of his Indian experience should be eligible for reappointment.

In the end, the Commission stated that 'Our object throughout has been to bring to the notice of the British Parliament and the British people such information as we are able to supply about the general conditions of the problem which now awaits solution,together with our considered poposals. We hope, at the same time, that our Indian fellow-subjects, after doing us the courtesy of studying the Report as a whole (for isolated sentences may give to any reader a wrong impression), will find that what we have put forward has been wrritten in a spirit of genuine sympathy. 'Success can only be achieved by sustained goodwill and cooperation, both between the great religious committees of India which have so constantly been in conflict, and between India and British. For the future of India depends on the collaboration of East and West, and each has much to learn from the other. 'We have grown to understand something of the ideals which are inspiring the Indian national movement, and no man who has taken part in working the representative institutions of Britain can fail to sympathise with the desire of others to secure for their own land a similar development. But a constitution is something more than a genealisational, it has to present a constructive scheme. We submit our Report in the hope that it may furnish materials and suggest a plan by means of which Indian constitutional reconstruction may be peacefully and surely promoted.'[20]

When we turn to the central legislature, the proposals of the report were still more inadequate. The retention of the nominated official members was universally condemned by Indian nationalists and there was also vehement criticism in Parliament on the ground that it would not sufficiently express the idea of the unity of India, which was behind all nationalist agitation and which nationalists regarded as the fervent hope of bringing order out of the existing chaos.

Besides the legislature proposed by the Simon Commission was neither democratic nor responsible. The upper non-representative body, with a majority of members was either officially nominated or represented special interests. The Commission whilst re-constituting the council on a federal basis, recommended that the proportion between the elected and non-elected members should remain unchanged, twenty-seven of the fixty members were to be appointed by the Viceroy and of these, twenty might be officials; the provinces were to have three representatives each, appointed by provincial second chambers, where such were created, or by the councils. Besides, the commercial classes of Madras, Bombay and

Calcutta were to have six representatives—three appointed by the Indian business community and three by the British. The Commission thus proposed that the class from which the members of the senate were drawn should be more restricted than it was. They should, for example, consist of distinguished members of the services, ex-judges and ex-ministers beside those who had gained honour in other walks of life. It was apparent that a senate of this character would entirely fail to reflect the living forces in India of the time. Indeed, the retired civil servants, judges and ministers would perpetuate the spirit of the old regime. The report said that there would be no further need of a fresh Commission every ten years, for according to the proposed constitution, it would have the power of natural growth until it acquired complete self-government. But the Commissioners had given no indication as to when India could attain that goal. This was one of the greatest drawbacks in the recommendations of the Commission.

Moderate nationalists, of course, tended to concentrate on the reforms recommended in the central government and were practically unanimous in pronouncing them inadequate. Others—as for example, certain Europeans—suggested that, irrespective of the question whether the changes would satisfy nationalist sentiments, the form of government proposed would have distinctly cumbrous and difficult to work. There was, to some extent, gratification amongst a few sections of Indian political thought at the prospect of provincial autonomy, but leaders of the minority communities were, generally speaking, of the opinion that neither in the provinces nor in the centre was proper provision made for safeguarding their special interests. The Muslims, for example, raised objection to quite a number of the proposals, and the Sikhs complained particularly that the percentage of seats allotted to them in the central legislature was insufficient. In this connection, the Maharaja of Patiala led a Sikh deputation to the Viceroy and in the course of his address expressed disappointment at the recommendations. Besides, there was serious dissatisfaction amongst certain sectional groups, mostly the landlords, who were much disturbed by the proposals made with regard to the taxation of agricultural incomes and the abolition of their separate franchise: The Commission by abolishing the special representation of the landlords throughout the country had left them no alternative but to identify themselves with the people.

Lord Irwin had taken four months' leave and had gone to England at the end of June, 1929, to devise some means whereby the constitutional question might be clarified and a greater degree of cooperation obtained from all sections of Indian political opinion before Parliament was asked to pronounce upon whatever scheme of reforms might be laid before it as a result of statutory enquiry. The Simon Commission had not yet submitted its report, when on May 13, the Viceroy made a statement announcing that the Round Table Conference would be held on October 20. He emphasised that 'neither my Government nor His Majestys' Government will be deflected by these unhappy events from our firm determination to abide by the policy I was privileged to announce on behalf of His Majesty's Government on November 1 last.' He also gave an assurance that the Report would not be the necessary and inevitable basis of the future reforms and declared, 'It is the belief of His Majesty's Government that by way of the Conference, it should be possible to reach solutions and all parties and interests in them can honourably accept an agreement at which the Conference is able to arrive, will form the basis of the proposals which His Majesty's Government will later submit to Parliament.' This announcement was soon after followed by a full dress debate in the two Houses of Parliament at Westminster, wherein some members of the Liberal and Conservative parties fell foul of the scheme, though some of the speeches showed that they had no objection to the ultimate goal of India being Dominion Status. Winston Churchill was pessimist in seeing India attain Dominion Status. In a speech at Waltham Abbey he declared, 'No responsible person supposed for a moment that the forthcoming Round Table Conference can produce Dominions Status for India or that Dominion Status is likely to be obtained within the life time of any one now living.'

In the case of the Indian States, the Commissioners were for the maintenance of the *status quo*. To them, the princes in the States were everything and the subject nothing and it had not occurred to them that the states' subjects were also likely to have ambitions and desires for the betterment of their condition. Besides, the Commissioners made no effort to present the case for a federal Constitution in a Favourable light. While protesting that they were preparing the country for an all-India federation, they suggested the setting up of a council composed of representatives of British India and Indian States to serve as a permanent machinery of consultation and they talked of the creation of a tradition in the working of that council. The words quoted here either misrepresented the intentions of the Commissioners or they indicated a desire on their part to relegate the question of the Federal Union to the Greek Kalends.

But keen disappointment was expressed in India at the recommendations of the Simon Commission, which were condemned by all shades of Indian opinion. They were characterized as 'reactionary, short-sighted and petty-minded recommendations' which instead of easing the political situation, were going to aggravate it. At places processions were taken out to 'mourn' the Simon Commission's report and resolutions were passed in which regret and indignation were expressed over it. Thus virulent criticism continued unabated and the Congress leaders had made a united front with Madan Mohan Malaviya, Veer Savarkar, Aney and others who thought that it was in total disregard of all national interest. Their watchward was 'intensive propaganda' against the findings of the Commission. As a result of this, the nationalists succeeded like an avalanche. They made no secret of their mind in saying that they mistrusted the findings of the Simon Commission. Thus there was tremendous amount of anti-British feeling in the country. If the people committed excesses, though very rare, the government were not behind-hand in doing likewise. Harshness and severity provoked indignation in the whole country.

Even the Viceroy, Lord Irwin, was quite clear in his mind

that the Simon report stood no chance of public acceptance in India and it would thus prolong the political dead-lock. John Simon in a broadcast speech on 'The Problem of India' on June 18, 1930, outlined the difficulties that confronted Britain's task in India. He said that the desire to advance towards self-government which was so deeply felt and fervently expressed by the spokesmen of political India, was but a reflection of the belief held by Englishmen in virtue of the responsible institutions as had developed in the course of history of the British Empire. He admitted that the special circumstances of India had to be understood. He also opined that the growth of a belief in self-government among Indians was an achievement brought about by the power of the idea which Britain had spread throughout the world.[21]

Severe Criticism

The recommendations of the Simon Commission met with severe criticism by the Indian leaders. Motilal Nehru stated that the report stood boycotted as far as the Congress was concerned, and they were not going to pay the slightest attention to what the Commission recommended or did not recommend. 'We must be masters in our house, but we are ready to agree to reasonable terms for the period of transfer of power from a British administration in India to a responsible Indian Government. We must meet the British people to discuss these terms as nation to nation and on an equal footing.'[22] Jinnah had no doubt in his mind that the recommendations would not be acceptable either to Hindus or Muslims and certainly not to the Indian nationalists. He never expected that the Simon Commission would go far enough to satisfy the Indian national aspirations.[23]

The most cogent arguments in criticism were put forward by C.F. Andrews who opined that the Commissioners had done painstaking work, but they had failed to meet Indian public opinion on its most sensitive side. 'The main reason for this lies on their not clearly appreaciating what the National Movement had already accomplished under his leadership and has brought about a new India which is seeking by its own inner urge to find self-expression.'[24] Besides, while speaking on 24, June

1930, at a meeting under the auspices of the Union of Democratic Control, he stated; 'Being ruled from abroad has so weakened India's moral fibre that the hope of gradual improvement is precarious. Britain must, therefore seek to hand over responsibility as quickly as possible and make such a definite transfer of authority that India may be indisputable the mistress in her own house. Gradual constitutional change is now impossible.'[25]

The Muslims did not conceal their appreciation of one or two recommendations contained in the Simon report, they on the whcle, considered the report to be retrograde and reactionary. The views of the Muslims were expressed in unambigous and unmistakable language in the resolution passed on the 5th July, 1930, by the Executive Board of the All-India Muslim Conference held at Simla.

All–India Muslim Conference

'In the opinion of the Executive Board of the All-India Muslim Conference, the report of the Simon Commission, as a whole, is unacceptable to other Mussalmans of India because it falls short of their demands formulated by the All-India Muslim Conference in Delhi on 1st January 1920, and because it is retrograde and reactionary. 'Provincial autonomy should be real and should not be whittled down by the unlimited overriding powers of the Governors. All the ministers should be elected non-official.'

'Muslims must be guaranteed a clear majority in Bengal and the Punjab. While Simon Commission has maintained such a Hindu majority in six provinces, they have deprived the Muslims of Bengal and the Punjab of their majority in the only two existing provinces, viz. Bengal and the Punjab.

'The Board is emphatically of opinion that Sindh should be separated from Bombay without further delay and constituted into an autonomous province.

'The Board is emphatically of opinion that North-West Frontier Province should have the same measure of reforms as the other provinces of India.

'The Board is emphatically of opinion that Baluchistan should be guaranteed full provincial autonomy, possessing the same powers as are enjoyed by other provinces of India.

'The Simon Commission has not made adequate provision for the representation of Muslims in the public services of the country or the cabinets of the Governments of the various provincial and the Federal Governments. In Board's opinion it is essential to the stability and success of any constitution that the Muslim community should be guaranteed adequate and effective representation in the cabinets and the public sevices of the country. A provision to this effect must be embodied in the Constitution.'[26]

Criticism of Assembly Members

In the Legislative Assembly of India, prominent members irrespective of caste and religion levelled criticism against the recommendations of the Simon Commission. Mian Mohammed Shah Nawaz maintained that no constitution framed by any Commission or by the British government would be of much value, if it did not have behind it, the goodwill of those who would be willing to make it function. Judged by this test, he had no hesitation in saying that the recommendations and suggestions in Vol. II of the report were inadequate, disappointing and unsatisfactory. It was not a complete provincial autonomy in which the powers of the ministers would be unfettered. The powers of the Governor were still very wide. In fact, all the powers were centralized in him. He could select his ministers who would hold office during his pleasure. He opined that the official element should be eliminated because a ministry which had one or two officials would not be working well. The timorous and subservient ministers, as some of them no doubt might be, would do what the official ministers would tell them to do. In fact, an official minister who could not be removed and could be reappointed would always defy the wishes of the legislature. He stated that the franchise in the North-West Frontier Province should be widened, in fact, it should be as wide as in other provinces. He wished to grant a full-fledged constitution for the frontier people. He said, 'It is a demand of the Mussalmans, the Hindus and the Christians, all alike. It is an all-India demand. It is the demand of the Congress. It is a demand of the Muslim League. It is the demand of the All-Parties Muslim Conference. There is no reason why constitutional reforms should not be given to this province.'[27]

There was so much agitative mood about the report in the central assembly that a member cried out, 'Burn it.' Gaya Prasad Singh said, 'Perform its funeral ceremony.' Dr. Ziauddin called it an 'unimaginative, uninspiring the unsympathetic.'[28] M.R. Jayakar, another prominent member of the central assembly, was critical of the findings of the Simon Commission. He opined: 'The Commissioners were reporters. I think I am right in describing Sir John Simon and his party as 'reporters and the duty of reporters is faithfully to report things as they exist at the date of their report. He and his friends forget their most primary duty, for the omission of which they strangely take credit for themselves, that they wrote this Report without taking note of recent conditions; the great intensity of feeling that has appeared in India during the last three or four months.

'As regards the Report itself, I think we are justified in saying that this is a worthless document, unlookable at as one of Hon'ble friends said here.'[29]

The Assessment

Thus the recommendations of the Simon Commission had fallen short of the demand of the people at large, who, irrespective of political parties or religions, had voiced for a common political solution for India. All those factors had aroused and intensified the consciousness of the people. The masses, saturated with an agitational psychology, were drawn into active politics. They clearly realized the fact that freedom would not come as a voluntary gift from 'our rulers', but that it would have to be won.

References

1. Report of the Indian Statutory Commission, Vol. II, p. 5.
2. *Ibid.*
3. 'It must be realised that the charge involved is very great and far reaching. Henceforward, in the provincial sphere, all branches of the administration may pass into the hands of Indian ministers. We should not have felt justified in recommending such an advance without at the same time providing for broadening the basis of representation. Unless

there were a considerable measure of enfranchisement, it is clear to us that there would be a danger that important element in the population might fail to use the voice in the affairs of the province to which they are entitled.' *Ibid*, p. 17.

4. 'In the other hand, the constitutional development at which we are aiming, and the growth of a sense of responsibility, would be unnecessarily hampered if the Governor had absolutely unlimited powers of overriding his Ministry.' *Ibid*, p. 36.
5. *Ibid*, pp. 39-40.
6. In the past, its life was for three years and the Governor could extend it by a year.
7. *Ibid*, p. 57. As regards the allocation of seats between Hindus and Muhammedans, provincial governments either did not propose to interfere with the *status quo* or only suggested minor modifications. The Bengal government formed an exception. Its memorandum, with two dissentients (one European and one Hindu) proposed that the representation of Muslims should be on the basis of their population ratio. The Sikh minister in the Punjab considered that, if communal representation was retained, it should be on the basis of voting strength.

   In fact all the provincial committees (except the Burma Committee, which was not concerned) recommended either unanimously or by a majority the retention of separate electorates for Muhammedans.
8. *Ibid*, p. 58.
9. This was recognised in the Montagu-Chelmsford Report.
10. *Ibid*, h pp. 90-91.
11. 'The proposals which we are going to make endeavour to meet these claims as far as they can be met, but it is not possible to change the plain facts of the situation. The inherent right of a man to smoke a cigarette must necessarily be curtailed if he lives in a powder magazine.' *ibid*, p. 103.
12. *Ibid*, p. 103.
13. These recommendations were in conformity with the view of the majority of the Bray Committee.
14. *Ibid*, p. 119.
15. The Commission opined, 'The central power of intervening in case of absolute necessity through the Governor in the internal administration of the province, for purpose which may in some instances concern solely that province and not the rest of India, should not, we think, rest in the Governor-General-in-Council.' *ibid*, p. 150.
16. *Ibid*, p. 182.

17. *Ibid*, p. 184.
18. *Ibid*, pp. 187-88.
19. The Bihar Orissa Committee recommended that the Governor-General should be the appointing authority, p. 296.
20. *Ibid*, pp. 315-16.
21. *See* John Simon's speech in *Times of India*, June 20, 1930.
22. *See* Pandit Motilal's statement in *Times of India*, June 25, 1930.
23. *See* M.A. Jinnah's statement in *Times of India*, June 25, 1930.
24. *See* C.F. Andrews' statement in *Times of India*, June 26, 1930.
25. *Ibid*.
26. Debates, Legislative Assembly, July, 1930, Vol. IV, pp. 131-32.
27. *Ibid*, pp. 47ff.
28. *Ibid*.
29. Debates, Legislative Assembly, July 1930, Vol. IV, pp. 165 ff.

9

Conclusion

The Report of the Simon Commission met with critical remarks at the hands of all sections of politicians in our country. The Congressmen, Liberals, Muslims, Parsees, Sikhs, representatives of the landowning classes and the commercial community—all alike condemned it as disappointing, unsatisfactory and reactionary. When for years past, the whole country had been agitating for Dominion Status, it was surprising that John Simon and his colleagues did not even mention the words and they even did not seem to contemplate it for India even at a distant future. They, indeed, had failed to appreciate the full significance of the nation's demand for self-government. Motilal Nehru vehemently condemned it by saying. 'To read the Report is a crime, to purchase a copy a greater crime. The Simon Commission was a farce, but the Report is an even greater farce.'

Criticism Regarding Central Government

The recommendations with regard to the central government were worse still. The introduction of indirect elections for the central legislature, the apparent failure to provide for any responsibility on the part of the central legislature, the removal of the entire subject of defence from the purview of the legislature, the failure to provide for Indianisation of the army at any reasonable pace, the retention of the India Council, maintenance of the Secretary of State's control and the retention of communal electorates were some of the most unsatisfactory features of the report. Under the Commission's proposals, the central legislature would be slightly enlarged, the representatives of the people who might go into it, might make speeches and criticise government measures to their heart's content, but they would have no power to dismiss the executive council or ministry and replace it by their own nominees. The direct elections proposed would reduce even the quality of that criticism. Thus there was no advance whatsoever in the central government. Until that was done, there was going to be no peace in the country.

Wedgewood and other 'frank critics' pointed out that the Simon report tried to undo all that Montagu had achieved. Even those who were bitterly opposed to the composition of the Simon Commission and had participated in its boycott, had some hope that it would at least recommend provincial autonomy and responsibility in the central government except with regard to the army and foreign relations. Their expectations turned out to be false. The Commission's recommendations for the provinces fell short of those recommended by some local governments such as Madras. Thus, the provincial autonomy suggested by the Commission was nothing but a camouflage. It was merely in name. There were still to be non-votable items and the Governor was to have power of restoring grants and certification of bills. The provincial cabinet was to have one or two officials from the civil service. Similarly, law and order were transferred, but C.I.D. was under the Governor. Kikabhai Premchand criticised the report and said, 'The so-called provincial autonomy recommended by the Commission is a misnomer and a camouflage as all the portfolios are not held, by the ministers or elected members.'

No Reference of Dominion Status

The second volume of the Simon report made no reference to events in India in 1929 and 1930. Even the important statement made by the Viceroy on October 31, with the consent of the British cabinet, was not mentioned. The expression 'Dominion Status' did not appear in its pages. On the other hand, the goal of British policy was stated in these word: 'India, as a whole, not merely British India, will take her place among the constituent States of the Commonwealth of Nations united under the Crown.' But whether this place would be one of equality with the constituent states was left in doubt. Besides, the Indian report was not reviewed and it was quietly ignored for obvious reasons. In the case of the Indian States, the members of Commission were for the maintenance of the *status quo.* To them, the princes in the States were everything and the subjects nothing, and it had not occurred to them that the states subjects were also likely to have ambitions and desires for the betterment of their conditions.

Unhappy Minorities

The report disillusioned the minorities. It was unfair to the Sikhs who would only have two per cent representation in the Assembly. St. Nihal Singh said, 'Sir John Simon has laid an addled egg. Some Muslim separatists may relish its flavour, but it will nauseate most Indians.' The Maharaja of Mahmudabad called it, 'Absurd and fit only to be consigned to the waste paper basket...I do not think, it is worthwhile wasting time on its perusal. The recommendations are characteristically unsympathetic and hopelessly prejudiced and utterly impracticable.'

Towards Independence

The significant political currents moved over the placid surface of India. It was evident that the new constitution must be such as would take full account of these new forces. The Lahore resolution of the Congress in 1929 had unequivocably shown the trend of thinking of the Indian leaders who were to participate in the Civil Disobedience Movement in the following years. At this point of time the Congress was not in a mood to agree to any proposal of the British government which was short of complete independence. 'India must sever the British connection and attain *purna swaraj.'* This pledge had been renewed thereafter year after year, with due solemnity and equal fervour by Congressmen till 1947. The most sensational development occurred when, on January 26, 1930, Independence Day was celebrated all over India, and towns and villages vied with each other in showing their enthusiastic adherence to independence. Much talk was in the air in connection with the Round Table Conference.

But Congress, under the stewardship of Mahatma Gandhi, understood the hollowness of the outcome of the arguments, suggestions and conclusions of the proposed conference launching. In this regard, he wrote to the Viceroy before the Civil Disobedience Movement.

Demands of the Congress

The Civil Disobedience campaign was carried on without any slackening of pace, with even greater vigour than before. The course of the Civil Disobedience Movement in a few months and exhibited with sufficient plainness the strength of the nationalist forces and also their limitations. The working committee of the Congress met in the middle of May and after reviewing the situation in the country reiterated its abiding faith in the Civil Disobedience Movement and resolved to carry on the struggle during the incarceration of Gandhi with redoubled vigour.

In fact Gandhi was quite clear in his mind that the Congress could not accept the position, unless Dominion Status was guaranteed and certain other preliminaries gone through. His movement had extraordinary effects and developed a new and extensive feeling of self-reliance among Indians and it had compelled the British authorities to face the situation in a new way. It became evident that the agitation had its roots in the sentiments of the Indian people in every province. India wanted the substance of independence—the power to control her purse, her army, her foreign relations and her government. Any kind of reconciliation was 'pitifully bogged down on the dark, muddy road of compromise.' Indians had the feeling that the British were betraying their interests on account of their non-acceptance of democratic guarantees. This did not smoothe matters and showed dangerous symptoms. The signs of discontent and defiance were motivated by a desire of independence. Thus, from India's point of view, one happy, indeed the favourable result, of the appointment of the Statutory Commission was the immediate drawing close together of members of all communities—irrespective of caste, colour and creed—in India, in a united protest against the Commission.

Appendix I

Simon to Ramsay MacDonald

My dear Prime Minister,

The Indian Statutory Commission has now entered upon the final stages of its work and hopes to be able to present its Report early next year. Before proceeding further however, we desire to address you with an enquiry and a suggestion.

As our investigation has proceeded, we have become more and more impressed, in considering the direction which the future constitutional development of India is likely to take, with the importance of bearing in mind the relations which may develop between British India and the Indian States. We are not at present in the position to forecast the Report which we shall hope in due course to present to Parliament. It is, however, already evident to us that, whatever may be the scheme which Parliament will ultimately approve for the future constitution and governance of British India, it is essential that the methods by which the future relationship between these two constituent parts of Greater India may be adjusted, should be fully examined.

We have carefully considered the Report of the Butler Committee but the terms of reference to that body did not cover the whole ground to be surveyed so far as these relations were concerned. Our own recommendations, if we were to exclude from our purview the wider problem which we have indicated, would, we feel, be unduly restricted, and we therefore wish, before going further, to ascertain whether we should have the approval of His Majesty's Government in giving this possibly extended interpretation to our own terms of reference. It is not our purpose to seek to explore the field already traversed by the Butler Committee; but it seems clear that we can not afford to ignore the reactions of the presence of the States on the problem we are studying in British India, or the possible repercussions on the former of any recommendations we might frame regarding the latter. At certain points an inevitable contact takes place.

We venture to point out that if the Report we are preparing and the proposals to be subsequently framed by the Government take this wider range it would appear necessary, because of the need of consulting the States, for the Government to revise the scheme of procedure to be followed after these proposals are made known. It seems to us that what would be required would be setting up of some sort of conference after the Reports of the Statutory Commission and the Indian Central Committee have been made, considered and published and their work has been completed, and that in this conference His Majesty's Government would meet both representatives of British India and representatives of the States (not necessarily always together) for the purpose of seeking the greatest possible measure of agreement for the final proposals which it would later be the duty of His Majesty's Government to submit to Parliament. The procedure by Joint Parliamentary Committee conferring with delegations from the Indian Legislature and other bodies, which was previously contemplated and is referred to in my letter to the Viceroy of February 6th, 1928, would still be appropriate for the examination of the Bill when it is subsequently placed before Parliament, but would, we think, obviously have to be preceded by some such conference as we have indicated.

We realise that it is not for the Statutory Commission to devise this subsequent procedure in details, for our task will be discharged when we have report. But we feel that it is desirable to obtain an assurance from His Majesty' Government that we shall not in their view be travelling beyond the terms of reference approved by Parliament if we pursue what seems to us an integral element in our investigation. We have also thought it right to make plain to His Majesty's Government the consequence that such an

assurance from His Majesty's Government is likely ultimately to involve, in order that the future course of procedure may be so shaped as to provide means for consulting with the Indian States and to promote the full cooperation of all parties and interests in the solution of the Indian problem as a whole.*

Your very sincerely,

(Sd.) John Simon

* Selected from the Report of the Indian Statutory Commission, Vol. I, pp. xxii-xxiii.

Chronology

1927

8 **November.** The Viceroy's announcement of the Reforms Commission.

10 **November.** Congress president appealed for complete boycott of Statutory Commission.

15 **November.** The House of Lords passed the second reading of the Indian Statutory Commission Bill; Labour party assured its cooperation.

16 **November.** All-parties' Conference at Bombay under C. Setalvad protested against the exclusion of Indians from the Statutory Commission and urged its boycott oll over India.

17 **November.** The House of Lords passed the third reading of the Indian Statutory Commission Bill.

19 **November.** Independent Labour party at a meeting in London passed resolution strongly protesting against the exclusion of Indians from the Commission.

20 **November.** Motilal Nehru, asked Lansbury, the Labour leader, to withdraw labour members from the Commission.

23 **November.** The Statutory Commission Bill passed the third reading in the House of Commons and the Royal assent given.

24 **November.** Personnel of the Indian Statutory Commission announced. Birkenhead's statement in the House of Lords approved.

25 **November.** The European Association at its annual meeting at Calcutta opined that the Parliamentary Com-

mission was likely to do more service to India than a mixed Commission.

30 November. At a meeting of Muslims at Kanpur, Hasrat Mohani urged the settlement of the Muslim claim as a condition precedent to boycott of the Commission.

1 December. Mrs. Annie Besant inaugurated the Boycott Committee.

2 December. Women meeting at Bombay under Mrs. Sarojini Naidu urged boycott of the Commission.

7 December. A Manifesto issued by prominent Muslims of Lahore urged Muslims not to boycott the Commission, the doing of which will bring shame and sorrow to them.

11 December. All-Parties meeting at Allahabad under the presidentship of Madan Mohan Malaviya to boycott the Simon Commission.

26 December. Dr. M.A. Ansari at Congress session in Madras in 1927 said, 'It is an insult to the elected representatives of our people, and consequently to the entire Indian nation.

1928

5 January. Public meeting in Madras under Kaleswar Rao. He urged the need for concerted action against Simon Commission.

12 January. The executive committee of the Bombay Indian Merchants' Chamber endorsed the resolution passed by the Industrial Congress urging all commerical bodies to boycott the Simon Commission.

17 January. The All-Parties' Boycott Conference held at Banares under the presidentship of Dr. M.A. Ansari, decided to boycott the Statutory Commission and to observe *hartal* throughout India on 3 February. Meeting of 6,000 persons of all classes held at Banares under the presidentship of Bhagwan Das. Leaders appealed to the audience to observe *hartal* on 3 February.

18 January. The campaign to prepare the ground for organising *hartal* on 3 February started in Bombay,

Poona, Calcutta and other places.

20 January. In the C.P. Council, Biyani's motion for the boycott of the Commission carried after heated debate.

24 January. In the Madras Council, the Swarajist's motion for the boycott of Simon Commission carried after heated debate.

2 February. Viceroy's inaugural address in opening the Central Legislature.

3 February. All-India *hartal* observed as a mark of protest against the Simon Commission. Bombay were deserted appearance when the Commission landed there. It was greeted with black flags and slogans of 'Simon, go back.' Meeting of 50,000 persons in Bombay resolved to boycott the Commission in any shape or stage. In Madras, the boycott demonstrations were marked by disorderly scenes in different parts of the city necessitating police to open fire. *Hartal* at Lahore, Calcutta, Allahabad, Patna and several other cities and towns.

4 February. Arrival of the Simon Commission in Delhi. John Simon, in an interview, told the representative of the Associated Press that he had received three hundred telegrams of welcome.

7 February. John Simon's statement on the 'Joint Conference' scheme issued in Delhi.

16 February. Debate on the appointment of Simon Commission in the Central Assembly. Lala Lajpat Rai levelled trenchant criticism. His censure motion was carried.

19 February. Simon Commission arrived in Calcutta. Public meeting held in the Shradhananda Park against it.

22 February. The Congress Working Committee in Delhi issued instructions to the Boycott Committee to observe *hartal* on 26th on the arrival of the Simon Commission.

25 February. Special session of the All-India Depressed Classes Conference in Delhi under M.C. Rajah passed resolution advocating cooperation with the Simon Commission.

1 March. Campaign for the boycott of British goods commenced in Calcutta.

3 March. Ladies in a meeting in Calcutta took solemn vow to boycott British goods.

13 March. In the Central Assembly, Motilal Nehru's motion refusing the Simon Commission's demand carried: his boycott decision reaffirmed.

18 March. Bombay Provincial Nationalist Non-Brahmin Conference held at Nasik under the presidentship of M. Manekji. Simon Commission denounced.

22 March. The Madras District Congress Committee inaugurated campaign of boycott of British goods as an answer to the Simon Commission.

31 March. Departure of Simon Commission from Bombay after completing preliminary visit to India.

9 April. The Assam Council elected a committee to cooperate with the Simon Commission, Congress members abstaining.

1 July. Eighth Session of the Surma Valley Conference at Sylhet urged the boycott of the Simon Commission and supported the Bardoli Satyagraha movement.

15 August. Opening day of the autumn session of the C.P. Council. Governor gave them the choice of electing a committee to cooperate with the Simon Commission or refuse to do it.

29 August. All-Parties' Conference at Lucknow. Jawaharlal Nehru whose ideal was complete independence dissociated himself with the resolution of Dominion Status.

11 October. Second landing of the Simon Commission at Bombay; left for Poona the same day.

12 October. Arrival of the Simon Commission at Poona. Complete *hartal* in the city; hostile demonstration; 'Simon, go back,' from a crowd of 10,000 persons under the leadership of K.F. Nariman and N.C. Kelkar.

13 October. The Delhi Provincial Political Conference at Meerut under the presidentship of Jawaharlal Nehru.

15 October. First public sitting of the Simon Commission at Poona.

C.W.A. Turner, Chief Secretary, Bombay Government, examined.

18 October. Birkenhead resigned from the Secretaryship of India and Viscount Peel appointed his successor.

30 October. Simon Commission arrived at Lahore. Police assault on Lala Lajpat Rai and other leaders of the boycott procession near the Railway Station.

3 November. The AICC meeting held in Delhi under the presidentship of Dr. M.A.Ansari.

17 November. Passing away of Lala Lajpat Rai.

29 November. Lala Lajpat Rai Day observed throughout India and glowing tributes were paid to him at public meetings. Police *lathi* charged on boycott processionists at Lucknow on the eve of arrival of Simon Commission. Jawaharlal Nehru and Govind Ballabh Pant received *lathi* blows of the Police.

30 November. A number of students were hurt in a clash at Lucknow where they had gathered with black flags to 'welcome' John Simon and the members of the Commission.

16 December. J.P. Saunders shot dead at Lahore while leaving the office.

21 December. Arrival of Motilal Nehru, the president-elect of the Congress, at Calcutta. A salute of 101 rockets was fired. A huge procession throughout the prominent streets and bazars of the city.

1929

10 January. Muhammed Yakub declared that many Muslims including himself were in favour of joint electorates.

11 January. Mahatma Gandhi exhorted students of Gujarat Vidyapith to strive for deliverance of the country from her miseries.

12 January. The members of Simon Commission and the Central Committee arrived at Calcutta. Huge boycott demonstrations by the citizens.

28 January. Opening day of winter session of Legislative Assembly. Viceroy's speech reviewing the political situation in India.

29 January. Motilal Nehru's comment on the Viceroy's Assembly speech. 'The door of negotiation is not closed.

3 February. Students Day celebrations in Bengal with meeting and processions.

18 February. Arrival of Simon Commission at Madras. Black-flag demonstration.

4 March. Mahatma Gandhi arrested at Calcutta for setting fire to a collection of foreign cloth in disobedience of an order under Calcutta Police Act.

14 March. Arrival of Simon Commission at Nagpur. A large number of demonstrators numbering 3,000 shouted, 'Simon go back' and waved black flags.

17 March. Khadi Day celebrated in Delhi, Calcutta, Madras and other places.

30 March. Subhash Chandra Bose appealed for boycott of foreign cloth.

2 April. The annual conference of the Independent Labour party held in London condemned the repressive policy of Government of India and pledged itself to work for bringing about recognition of the right of India to self-determination.

10 April. J.M. Sen Gupta elected unopposed the Mayor of Calcutta.

26 April. Arrival of Simon Commission in London. One hundred and fifty Indians who held a boycott procession were roughly handled and had their flags and emblems taken away by police.

3 May. Dr. Satyapal, a leading Congress leader in Punjab, arrested under section 124-A.

20 June. The Viceroy's speech at the Chelmsford Club, Simla on the Dominion Status issue.

28 June. Disclosure made by Sankaran Nair to a Free

Press representative in London on the status and work of the Central Committee of Simon Commission.

5 **July.** Meeting of Congress Working Committee in Delhi. It was resolved that all Congress members of the legislatures should resign their seats.

8 **July.** At the Jessore District Conference, Subhash Chandra Bose, the President, warned that the repression resorted to by the government since the appointment of Simon Commission was directed against most peaceful and legitimate political movement of the people.

22 **July.** Mrs. Sarojini Naidu gave impressions of tour to Europe and America. She observed, 'Gandhiji is a great influence right throughout the world.'

27 **July.** Meeting of All-India Muslim Nationalist Party at Allahabad under the presidentship of Maulana Abul Kalam Azad.

29 **July.** A meeting of Bombay Congress Muslim Party held under the Presidentship of S.A. Brelvi.

30 **July.** Report of Punjab Simon Committee issued.

2 **August.** The Madras Simon Committee Report issued. It recommended grant of full responsible government and a declaration by British government of full Dominion Status within the British Empire and within a definite period.

3 **August.** The Bengal Simon Committee report recommended complete provincial autonomy.

5 **August.** The Burma Simon Committee Report recommended the immediate separation of Burma from the rest of British India.

12 **August.** Congress workers walked out in a body from the Madras Council when the Simon Committee Report was presented.

5 **September.** The U.P. Simon Committee Report recommended complete provincial autonomy, special powers for the Governor and Muslim rights based on Lucknow Pact.

13 **September.** Death of Jatindranath Das at Lahore after a prolonged hunger-strike of 64 days as a protest against

the treatment meted out to political prisoners in jails.

17 September. The Report of the Bihar and Orissa Simon Committee issued.

18 September. Debate on the Punjab Simon Report.

28 September. Jawaharlal Nehru elected President for the Lahore Congress at a meeting of All-India Congress Committee at Lucknow.

1 October. Labour party conference at Brighton. Speech of Fenner Brockway about political situation in India.

19 October. Conference of Punjab Students held at Lahore under the Presidentship of Subhash Chandra Bose.

22 October. Lahore Conspiracy Case. Allegations of ill-treatment against police, made by prisoners, before the magistrate.

31 October. The Viceroy's historic announcement on the Round Table Conference to settle Indian political problems to be convened after the Simon Commission had submitted its report.

1 November. Political leaders' conference at Delhi following Viceroy's announcement.

5 November. Viceregal announcement discussed in the House of Lords.

7 November. Debate on Viceroy's announcement in the House of Common; hollowness of announcement exposed.

24 November. Gandhi, during his tour of U.P., asked the students, at Etawah, to be like Chinese students, courageous, pure and strong.

29 November. C.P. Youth Conference held at Nagpur under the Presidentship of Subhas Chandra Bose.

23 December. Report of the Central Simon Committee issued. Attempt to blow up the special train in which the Viceroy, Lord Irwin was returning to Delhi from his south Indian tour, near Nizamuddin Station, about six miles from Delhi railway station.

27. December. Meeting of All-India Congress Committee at Lahore.

29 December. The forty-fourth session of Indian National Congress under the Presidentship of Jawaharlal Nehru was held at Lahore. He advocated complete independence.

1930

3 January. Motilal Nehru appealed to Congress members of the legislatures to tender their resignations.

23 January. Subhas Chandra Bose charged with sedition and sentenced to one year imprisonment.

26 January. The Independence Day celebrations all over India.

30 January. Gandhi's eleven-point demand addressed to Viceroy.

9 February. Students' Day celebration in Calcutta.

4 March. Gandhi's ultimatum to Viceroy served.

12 March Gandhi's historic march to Dandi, commenced from Sabarmati Ashram, Ahmedabad.

13 March. J.M. Sen Gupta arrested.

28 March. Motilal Nehru gifts his house, 'Anand Bhavan' to the nation.

18 April. The Chittagong armoury raid.

30 April. C.Rajagopalachari arrested under the Salt Act.

12 May. The Viceroy announced the Round Table Conference.

21 May. Raids on Dharsana salt works.

1 June. The Wadala salt raid.

7 June. Release of Simon Commission's Report.

Bibliography

Primary Sources

Home Department

Political Branch 1927-30

Available in National Archives of India

Available in Sapru House Library, New Delhi

Debates: Legislative Assembly, 1927-30

Debates: House of Commons, 1927-30

Debates: House of Lords, 1927-30

Papers of Lord Halifax, Governor-General of India (1926-1931).

Available on microfilm in Nehru Memorial Library, New Delhi

Lord Irwin's correspondence with His Majesty the King Emperor, May 1926 to April 1931.

Lord Irwin's correspondence with the Secretary of State for India, April 1926 to April 1931.

Telegraphic correspondence of Lord Irwin with the Secretary of State for India, April 1926 to April 1931.

Telegraphic correspondence of Lord Irwin with the Secretary of State for India (Confidential), January 1927 to April 1929.

Lord Irwin's correspondence with persons in England and abroad (Confidential), April 1926 to December 1929.

Correspondence of Lord Irwin with persons in England and

abroad, January 1930 to April 1931.

Correspondence of Lord Irwin with persons in India, April 1926 to April 1931.

Correspondence of Lord Irwin with Viscount Halifax, April 1926 to April 1931.

Lord Irwin's correspondence while in England, June 1929 to October 1929.

Correspondence of Lord Irwin with the Secretary of State for India on the Statutory Commission (Confidential), June 1928 to April 1929.

Extracts from letters and telegrams from Secretary of State to Viceroy and from Viceroy to Secretary of State, June 1926 to April 1929.

Correspondence of Lord Irwin with Sir John Simon on the Statutory Commission (Confidential), November 1927 to March 1929. (East India Constitutional reforms).

Report of the Indian Central Committee, 1928-29.

Government of India's despatch on proposals for Constitutional reforms.

Indian Round Table Conference (Proceeding), 12 November 1930 to 19 January 1931.

Lord Irwin's Legislative Assembly decisions, April 1926 to April 1931.

Lord Irwin's Order-in-Council (Confidential), April 1926 to April 1931.

Oral Evidence, Memoranda and Reports—Published and Unpublished

Indian Statutory Commission, Oral Evidence, Assam, Vols. I and II.

Indian Statutory Commission, Oral Evidence, Bengal, Vols. I and II.

Indian Statutory Commission, Oral Evidence, Bihar and Orissa, Vols. I and II.

Indian Statutory Commission, Oral Evidence, Bombay, Vols. I, II and III.

Indian Statutory Commission, Oral Evidence, Burma, Vols. I and II.

Indian Statutory Commission, Oral Evidence, Central Provinces.

Indian Statutory Commission, Oral Evidence, Delhi, Vols. I and II.

Oral Evidence before the Indian Statutory Commission in London.

Indian Statutory Commission, Oral Evidence, North-West Frontier Province.

Indian Statutory Commission, Oral Evidence, Madras, Vols. I and II.

Indian Statutory Commission, Oral Evidence, Punjab, Vols. I and II.

Indian Statutory Commission, Oral Evidence, Sind.

Indian Statutory Commission, Oral Evidence, United Province, Vols. I and II.

Memoranda prepared for the use of the Indian Statutory Commission, by the Government of the Punjab, Lahore, 1928.

Memoranda submitted to the Indian Statutory Commission by the Government of Burma.

Memoranda submitted to the Indian Statutory Commission by the Government of India, Vols. I and II, Calcutta, 1930.

Memoranda prepared by the Government of Bombay for submission to the Indian Statutory Commission, Bombay, 1928.

India Office Memoranda submitted to the Indian Statutory Commission.

Informal Conference at Delhi with the Provincial Committees, Indian Statutory Commission.

Proceedings of the informal meetings of the Executive Council to consider the recommendations of the Indian Statutory Commission.

Representation of the Muslims of U.P. to the Indian Statutory Commission, July, 1928.

Report of the Indian Statutory Commission, Vols. I and II, Calcutta, 1930.

Report of the committee appointed by the U.P. Legislative Council to cooperate with the Indian Statutory Commission, Allahabad, 1929.

Report of Indian Central Committee.

Summary of items expressed to the Joint Conference, Indian Statutory Conference by Members and Ministers in Provinces.

Summary of evidence given to the Joint Conference of the Indian Statutory Commission by Members of the Governor-General's Executive Council on the main constitutional issues.

Views of the Local Governments on the Recommendations of the Indian Statutory Commission, Calcutta, 1930.

Newspapers and Periodicals

Amrita Bazar patrika

Bengal Past and Present

The Bombay Chronicle

The Hindu

The Indian Review,

Indo-British Review,

Journal of Indian History

The Modern Review

The Pioneer

Proceedings of Indian History Congress

The Quarterly Review of Historical Studies

The Statesman

The Times of India

The Tribune

Published Works

Andrews, C.F., *How India Can Be Free,* Madras, 1921.

—,*India and the Simon* Report, London, 1937.

Besant, Annie, *India: Bond or Free,* Adyar, 1939.

Bipan Chandra, *Rise and Growth of Economic Nationalism in India, New Delhi, 1966.*

Birkenhead, The Earl of, *Frederick Edwin, Earl of Birkenhead, The First Phase and Last Phase,* London, 1965.

Bolitho, Hector, *Jinnah, Creator of Pakistan,* London, 1954.

Brockway, A.F., *India and its Government,* Madras, 1921.

—,*The Indian Crisis,* London, 1930.

Brown, Judith M., *Gandhi's Rise to Power: Indian Politics, 1915-22,* London, 1972.

Cadogan, Edward, *The India We Saw,* London, 1933.

Caveeshar, S.S., *India's Fight for Freedom,* Lahore, 1936.

Chintamani, C.Y., *Indian Politics Since the Mutiny,* Allahabad, 1937.

Coatman, J., *India. 1927, 1928, 1929. and 1931,* London, 1932.

Coupland, R., *The Goals of British Rule in India,* London, 1948.

Das, C.R., *India for Indians,* Madras, 1921.

Fischer, Louis, *The Life of Mahatma Gandhi,* London, 1962.

Gandhi, M.K., *Speeches and Writings of Mahatma Gandhi,* Madras, 1933.

Gopal, S., *Viceroyalty of Lord Irwin,* London, 1957.

—,*Jawaharlal Nehru: A Biography,* vols. I London, 1975.

—,*Selected Works of Jawaharlal Nehru,* Vols. II, III, IV, and V,

New Delhi, 1972-73.

Gour, H.S., *The Future Constitution of India,* Nagpur, 1930.

Griffiths, P.J., *The British Impact on India,* London, 1957.

Halifax, the Earl of, *Fullness of Days,* London, 1969.

Irwin, Lord, *Indian Problems,* London, 1932.

Iyer, C.S. Ranga, *India in the Crucible,* London, 1928.

Joshi, Vijaya Chandra, *Lala Lajpat Rai: Writings and Speeches,*Vols. I and II, Delhi, 1966.

Keith, A.B., *A Constitutional History of India,* Allahabad, 1961.

Keith, Midddlemas and John Barnes, *Stanley Baldwin: A Biography,* London, 1969.

Kidwai, M.H., *Swaraj and How to obtain it,* Lucknow, 1945.

Liberal A., *The Commission and After,* Bombay, 1928.

Lovett, V., *A History of the Nationalist Movement in India,* London, 1921.

Majumdar, R.C., *History of the Freedom Movement in India,* Vol. III, Calcutta, 1963.

Mehrotra, S.R., *India and the Commonwealth, 1885-1925,* London, 1965.

Mitra, H.N., *and N.N. The Indian Annual Register, 1925-30.*

Mody, H.P., *The Political Future of India,* London, 1908.

Munshi, K.M., *Indian Constitutional Documents,* Vol. I, Bombay, 1967.

Nehru, Jawaharlal, *An Autobiography,* New Delhi, 1962.

Pal, B.C., *The Spirit of Indian Nationalism,* London, 1910.

Pole, D.G., *India in Transition,* London, 1932.

Rai, Lajpat, *The Political Future of India,* New York, 1919.

Sapru, Tej Bahadur, *The Indian Constitution,* Madras, 1926.

Setalvad, C.H., Recollections and Reflections, Bombay, 1946.

Shafi, M., *Some Important Indian Problems,* Lahore, 1930.

Singh G.N., *Landmarks in Indian Constitutional and National Development,* Vol. I, Bombay, 1946.

Sitaramayya, Pattabhi B., *The History of the Indian National Congress,* Vol. I, Bombay, 1946.

Speeches by Lord Irwin, Vols. I and II, Simla, 1931.

Tara Chand, *History of Freedom Movement in India,* Vol. II, New Delhi, 1973.

Thompson, Edward, *The Ronstruction of India,* London, 1930.

Index